No. 838.

THE AMERICAN Weekly Mercury.

From Tuefday January 13, to Tuefday January 20, 1735,6.

GENEALOGICAL ABSTRACTS
from the
AMERICAN WEEKLY MERCURY

1719 - 1746

Compiled by

KENNETH SCOTT

CLEARFIELD

Reprinted for
Clearfield Company, Inc. by
Genealogical Publishing Co., Inc.
Baltimore, Maryland
1991, 1995, 1998, 2019

Library of Congress Cataloging in Publication Data

Scott, Kenneth, comp.
Abstracts from American weekly mercury, 1719-1746.
    1. United States—Genealogy. 2. Pennsylvania—Genealogy. 3. American weekly mercury. I. American weekly mercury. II. Title.
CS61.S36   929'.1   73-17031
ISBN 0-8063-0597-5

Num. 1097

THE AMERICAN
WEEKLY MERCURY.

From Thursday *January* 1, to Thursday *January* 8. 1740-1.

An Extract of a Letter from the Hague, dated the 18th of October.

EVER since the States General caused their Answer to the Declaration of the French Court to be deliver'd to the Marquis de Fe-
That he would however inform the King, his Maſter, with their High Mightineſſes Intention; but that for his Part, he very much queſtion'd whether the Court of France had really conceiv'd any Thoughts of repairing the Fortifications of that Port, becauſe his moſt Chriſtian Majeſty was not ſo

in the Conference wmer they had with him a few Days ago, gave him to understand in clear and exprefs Terms, that the Republick having been inform'd that the Court of France had given Orders for, and that People were actually employ'd in repairing the Fortifications of Dunkirk, their High Mightineffes could not reconcile a Defign of this Nature with the Declaration which his moft Chriftian Majefty had very lately caufed to be made here, namely, that he had no other View of fending his Squadrons of Obfervation into America, tham to fupport Spain in her Poffeffions there, purfuant to the Treaty of Utrecht, feeing the Reeftablifhment of the Fortifications of the Port of Dunkirk would be rendering one of the moft effential Articles of that fame Treaty of no effect; and that it was not to be fuppos'd that his moft Chriftian Majefty, at a Time when he was juftifying the Steps he had taken in favour of Spain, from the Obligation he was under of maintaining certain Conditions in the Treaty of Utrecht, would, at the fame time, make an Infringement of others of 'em: Their High Mightineffes could not therefore avoid, in Cafe his moft Chriftian Majefty thought ferioufly of putting Dunkirk into its former Condition, making upon this Occafion Reprefentation to that Monarch. The Marquis de Fenelon anfwer'd the Deputies of their High Mightineffes, that he perceiv'd very plainly, that from the Solicitation of the Court of Great Britain, which was very loud in its Complaints of what was doing at Dunkirk, the Republick had determin'd to make Reprefentations to his Court upon this Subject:

M...bers of the Regency have nad certain Intelligence, that befides the Foot which is already in that Place, fome Cavalry is fpeedily expected there: that three or four Batteries are actually erected; that fome Chaloupes are arming; that the Duke of Boufflers and the Marquis de Givry, with a great Number of Workmen, are bufily employ'd; and that the Englifh who live there, have been order'd to retire from the Town in a very fhort and fix'd Time under Pretence of its having been difcover'd that they defign'd to fet fire to it. Tho' France pretends to juftify thofe Meafures, her Arguments are fo weak and ridiculous, that People are furpriz'd that is fo hardy as to make ufe of them.

Extract of a Letter from the Hague.

The Marquis de Fenelon, Ambaffador from France, continues to exhort the States General to make a Common Caufe with his Court for maintaining the Treaty of Utrecht, in regard to the Poffeffions of his Catholick Majefty in America; and for this Purpofe, that their High Mightineffes would join a Squadron with thofe of his moft Chriftian Majefty, in order to prevent the Commerce in the Weft-Indies from being interrupted by any Power whatfoever. The Deputies of their High Mightineffes manifefted their Surprize at the Propofition of this Ambaffador, and told him, that it was not by the Englifh that their Merchants who traffic to the Weft-Indies had in the leaft fuffer'd, but that it was from the continual Vexations and injurious Treatment they had met with from the Spaniards, that they had only Caufe to complain of; and that their High Mightineffes

INTRODUCTION

On 22 December 1719 appeared the American Weekly Mercury, first newspaper published in Pennsylvania and the third in British North America. Andrew Bradford and John Copson were the publishers but on the issue of 25 May 1721 Copson's name disappeared and with the number of 13 December 1739 the imprint became Andrew and William Bradford, while with the copy of 6 November 1740 Andrew Bradford alone is given as publisher. Andrew died on 24 November 1742 and one issue was omitted, for which his widow, Cornelia, apologized to the readers in the number of 2 December 1742, which she printed. On 1 March 1743 Isaiah Warner was editor and publisher, together with Cornelia Bradford. The issue of 18 October 1744 names Cornelia Bradford alone as publisher and from then, up to 22 May 1746, when what was probably the last issue appeared, she remained sole publisher.

Andrew Bradford, the son of William Bradford (1663-1752) and Elizabeth Sowle (daughter of Andrew Sowle, chief London Quaker printer), was born in 1686 in America, where his parents came in 1685. At the age of seven he went to New York City with his father, who had been appointed official printer for the Province of New York. In 1712 Andrew, who had learned his trade from his father, removed to Philadelphia. There in 1714 he printed the Laws of the Province of Pennsylvania, later was appointed official printer of the Province and began, as has been stated, in 1719 publication of the American Weekly Mercury. From 1728 to 1738 he was Postmaster of Philadelphia and for many years was a vestryman of Christ Church in that city. His first wife was named Dorcas and his second wife was Cornelia Smith, of New York City. He adopted as his son William Bradford, son of his brother William.

In the beginning his newspaper was primarily concerned with shipping news, and what genealogical material is found in the earlier issues comes chiefly from advertisements of runaway indentured servants or Negro or Indian slaves. After a few years, however, items from the various colonies, along with news from Europe, became much more diverse.

Advertisements about runaway white servants, who chiefly came from England, Ireland, Scotland and Wales, frequently gave not only place of origin but also age and trade of the runaway, along with residence and status of the master. And the same holds true of apprentices and Negro and Indian slaves.

Colonial jails were notoriously insecure, so that presentments of the prisons by grand juries were extremely common. Hence jail-breaks were recorded with frequency in the press, as were escapes by prisoners from the custody of sheriffs, their deputies or constables. Descriptions of an escapee usually mentioned his age and trade, as was almost without exception the case when rewards were offered for the apprehension of deserters from the army or from ships.

i

Births were rarely noted but marriages were occasionally reported, mostly of persons of distinction or those concerning whom something was considered out of the ordinary, as when a bachelor of 85 married a widow of 45.

Deaths, on the other hand, were very frequently noted, especially of governors, judges, customs collectors, other government officials, clergymen, eminent merchants and Indian sachems. The age of the deceased, as a rule, was noted, sometimes with a brief sketch of his career, mention of his place of birth, ancestry or relatives.

Advanced age or numerous descendants were concerned items of interest, as in the case of Deborah Towner, who died in her 104th year, leaving 253 descendants; John Houghton, who had 134 descendants when he died at the age of 87, or Mary Hazard, aged 100, who left 205 descendants.

Deaths, by execution, suicide, drowning, lightning, fire, bursting cannon, falling trees, oversetting of vehicles, exposure to excessive heat or cold, frequently found their way into the news paper and yielded much information about the deceased. If a plasterer drank a gallon of "Cyder Royal" and expired within a few hours, if a man was crushed to death by the cogs of a grist mill or if a child expired as a result of the bite of a rattlesnake, the event was newsworthy, as it would be today.

"Elopements" of wives often were advertised with name and residence of the abandoned husband, occasionally with mention of a lover who disappeared with the runaway.

Insertions requesting settlement of accounts yield the names of widows, widowers, executors or administrators, and sales of real estate afford knowledge of the residence, wealth and status of the deceased.

Advertisements seeking knowledge of missing heirs or relatives not infrequently reveal when persons came to America, where they came from and sometimes where they first lived in the New World.

In short, an early newspaper such as the American Weekly Mercury is a valuable source of information for genealogical research and the index of some 3400 persons should prove helpful. At the same time, it is entertaining, at the least, to read that David Brintnall, who died in 1732 at the age of 77, was the first man to have a brick house in Philadelphia; that when Benjamin Brown died at Salem, Massachusetts, in 1737, a brother and heir found a silver hoard of 1053 ounces of silver, including about 6,000 New England shillings; that the Indian sachem Ninnicraft in 1723 left an estate of £30,000 in trust for his sons.

The news in the Mercury is by no means limited to Pennsylvania. Many items are concerned with persons in Delaware and New Jersey (provinces which had no newspapers in the period 1719-1746), Maryland, Virginia, South Carolina, New York, and New England.

The author wishes to express his appreciation to Mrs. F. Spencer Roach and to Dr. Kenn Stryker-Rodda for their assistance.

Kenneth Scott

Johney, Mulatto slave, age c. 22, coachman - runaway from Phillip
     Ludwell, of Green-Spring, Va. (12/29)

1720

FARE, Thomas (alias Thomas Price), Welshman, age c. 21 - run-
     away from the forge at Monataunoy, Phila. Co. (3/1)

MINNEMAN, William, Scotchman, age c. 25, butcher by trade - run-
     away from Capt. Joseph Mackintosh (3/8)

BAILY, Thomas, born in Yorkshire, servant - runaway from Jacob
     Rice, of Unabanna, Rapahanock in Virginia (3/17)

PENHOOK, Samuel, North-countryman, servant, sailor, age c. 21 -
     same as above

SMITH, William, of Charlestown, Mass. - sentenced to death at
     Boston (3/17)

TRAVIS, Hannah (commonly called "Dancing Hannah") - same as
     above

SIMMONS, John, servant, age c. 21 - runaway from Samuel Driver,
     of Manta Creek, Gloucester Co., N.J. (4/14)

COULTON, Henry, printer, late servant of Mr. Bradford, of Phila. -
     broke out of Salem Goal (4/21)

JOHNSON, Reyner (alias John Lee), servant, bookbinder, late ser-
     vant of Mr. Bradford, of Phila. - same as above

MACCABEE (or MAKEE), John, servant, age c. 18 - runaway from
     James Patterson, Indian-trader at Pexton on Susquehanna
     River (4/21)

Toby, Indian slave, age c. 23 - runaway from Andrew Radford at
     Amboy Ferry (4/21)

HOWELL, Nicholas, Welsh servant - runaway from Cornelius Wil-
     liams, of Appaquimena in New-Castle Co. (5/5)

AYRES, Absalom, age c. 18, bricklayer by trade - runaway from
     Thomas Sapinton, of South River in Maryland (5/12)

ROBERTS, Thomas, servant, age c. 30 - runaway from Samuel Lewis,
     of Harford, Chester Co. (5/26)

WEBB, Richard, late of Chester Co., dec'd - plantation there to
     be sold by the executrix, Elizabeth Webb (6/20)

RICHARDSON, Anna, servant, age c. 40 - runaway from David Straham, of New Jersey; if she is captured, notice to be given
to Samuel Kirk, of Brandy Wine Ferry (6/23)

BINGHAM, James, dec'd - his widow and executrix will sell the
house where Davis Evans now lives, at the Sign of the Crown
in High St., Phila.; she lives next door to the Sign of
the White Horse in High St. (6/30)

HOPKINS, Alexander, age 25 - broke out of the Goal of Cecil Co.
in Maryland; reward for his capture offered by James Van
Bebber, High Sheriff of Cecil Co. (7/7)

FENTON, John, servant, age c. 22 - runaway from John Hyatt, of
Phila. (7/7)

PASTOW, Richard, servant - runaway from Col. Ludwell at Green
Spring and Thomas Ravencroft in James City Co., Virginia (7/14

COULTON, Marmaduke, servant - runaway from Griffith Jones, High
Sheriff of Kent Co. upon Delaware (7/14)

TAYLOR, Alexander, Irish servant, joiner by trade - runaway from
Col. Ludwell at Green Spring and Thomas Ravencroft in James
City Co., Virginia (7/14)

WALKER, Thomas, servant, blacksmith by trade - same as above

DOUGLASS, Archabald, Scotch servant, age c. 25 - runaway from
James Pemberton, of Queen Ann Co., Maryland ; if runaway
is captured, notice to be given to Israel Pemberton of
Phila. (7/21)

GRIGG, James, Scotch servant, age c. 23, tailor by trade - same
as above

WILLSON, William, Scotch servant, age c. 26 - same as above

ROBINSON, John, Scotch servant, age c. 24 -runaway from
Samuel Peirson, of Queen Ann's Co., Maryland (8/4)

HARDMAN, Thomas, servant, age c. 40 - runaway from Benjamin
Denhall, of Concord, Chester Co. (8/11)

MOLSON, Richard, Mulatto slave, age c. 40 - runaway from Richard
Tilghman, of Queen Ann's Co., Maryland; he left with two
white persons, Garrett Choise and Jane his wife, servants
to neighbors of Mr. Tilghman (8/11)

BROWN, Henry, age 30 - escaped from custody at Salem in West
Jersey, having stolen £200 from house of Benjamin Holm,
of Salem (9/8)

ASHWOOD, John, servant, cooper by trade - runaway from Dr.
William Lock, of Ann Arundel Co., Maryland (9/15)

CORMELE, Benjamin, servant, gardener by trade - same as above

GAUGH, William, servant, joiner by trade - same as above

FOX, William, servant, smith by trade - same as above

FIEZ, Thomas, servant - same as above

JONES, Thomas, servant, age c. 21 - runaway from Israel Pemberton's plantation in Bucks Co. (9/22)

COWLEY, John, English servant, age c. 17 - runaway from Edward
Farmer, of Whitemarsh (10/6)

SKELTON, Richard, servant, age c. 18 - runaway from Peter Dicks,
of Upper Providence, Chester Co. (10/13)

HUNT, Edward, of Phila., whitesmith - sentenced in Phila. to be
executed for counterfeiting; Martha his wife was fined and
imprisoned for passing counterfeit coin (10/20)

PEECOCK, John, servant, age c. 17 - runaway from John Williams,
tailor (10/27)

PIKE, John, West-countryman, servant, age c. 22, husbandman -
runaway from John Brome, of Calvert Co., Maryland (11/17)

HUSON, Ann - sentenced to be executed in Phila. Saturday next
for robbing the Widow Green (11/17)

BARNS, Thomas, convict servant from Oxfordshire, age c. 23,
farmer - runaway from James Carroll, of Maryland (11/17)

CORBETT, John, servant, age c. 23 - runaway from Alexander Falconer, of the Freshes of Petuxon (11/17)

GOATLY, Henry, Scotch-Irish convict servant, age c. 18 - runaway from James Carroll, of Maryland (11/17)

LERNER, Edmund, convict servant from Oxfordshire, age c. 23,
carpenter by trade - same as above

WILLCOX, Hugh, age 30 - runaway from Joseph Hawley, of Frankford; one Grace Mac-Ward, who passes as his wife, and a
girl aged 1 month are with him (12/1)

COLLINGS, Nicholas, servant, shoemaker by trade - runaway about
2 years ago from Abel Van Burkeloo, of Cecil Co., Md. (12/13)

4

MERVIN, Samuel, servant, plasterer by trade - runaway from
Notley Rozer, Esq., of Prince George's Co., Md. [12/20]

1721

HUFF, Samuel, servant, age c. 18 - runaway from Shadrach Wakley, of New-Town, Bucks Co. [1/3]

Bedford (or Ducko), Negro slave, age 16 or 17 - runaway from
Austin Paris, of Phila., founder [1/31]

WEYMAN, Richard, servant, age c. 22 - runaway from Robert Wills,
of Phila., innholder [2/14]

HEATHCOTE, Caleb, Esq., Surveyor General of H.M.'s Customs for
the Eastern District of North America, Judge of the Court
of Admiralty for New York, New Jersey and Connecticut and
Member of H.M.'s Council for New York, brother of Sir Gilbert Heathcote of London - died Feb. 28 in New York - New
York dispatch of March 6 [3/16]

HOWELL, Nicholas, servant, age c. 25 - runaway from Thomas Jones,
of Phila. [3/30]

MAC-NEMAR, Francis, Irish servant, age c. 24 - runaway from
William Noble, of Warminster, Bucks Co. [3/30]

MAC-WARD, Miles, Irish servant, age c. 20 - runaway from Edward
Brooks, of Phila., butcher [3/30]

RENOLDS, John, servant, age c. 22, sailor - runaway from Abel
Pearson, of Derby, Chester Co. [3/30]

SWAIM, James, servant, shoemaker by trade - runaway from John
Wheldon, of Phila. [4/13]

LASEY, John (alias THORNTON), servant, age c. 21 - runaway from
William Ward, of Sexifras River, Cecil Co., Maryland [4/13]

GRAY, Jeffery, age c. 50, who formerly lived in New England but
for many years has used Cheseapeek Bay as a merchant - broke
out of Goal of Baltimore Co., Maryland [4/27]

VARNILL, William, servant, age c. 25 - runaway from Philip Taylor,
of Chester Co. [4/27]

WOOD, Joseph, who served his time with Samuel Hadley, of Whitely
Creek in New-Castle Co. - runaway from Morris Carter on
Chester River, Maryland, to whom he is bound servant by
order of court [5/4]

VRESSHER, John Mattuse, Dutchman, age c. 28, late a privateer
belonging to Capt. Jennings - is sought because he lately
murdered William Bostick, of New York, butcher [5/4]

NICHOLAS, Charles, servant, joiner by trade - runaway from
   Lewis Debny, of Williamsburgh, Virginia (5/18)

LEMMONS, Francis, Scotch servant, transported rebel - runaway from Ranier Vanhist, of Salem, New Jersey (5/18)

HUDDY, Martha, widow, dec'd - accounts with estate to be settled with Mrs. Margaret Newman, in Second St., Phila., administratrix (5/18)

HAND, James, young Irish servant - runaway, together with Eleaner Trayner, from Thomas Waughop, of St. Mary's Co., Maryland (5/18)

DAVIS, Edmund, late of Phila., pewterer, dec'd - his moulds
   and tools for sale by Owen Roberts and Thomas Tresse, executors (5/25)

TRESSE, Hugh, dec'd - his land fronting River Schoolkill for
   sale by Mary, his widow, or Thomas Tresse in Phila. (5/25)

SHAUGHNESAY, Thomas, Irish servant, age c. 20 - runaway from
   Thomas Marle, of Bristol Twp., Phila. Co. (6/8)

MACWARD, Miles, Irish servant, age c. 20 - runaway, in company
   of Patrick Boyd and Thomas Shauny, from Edward Brooks, of
   Phila, butcher (6/8)

NEWBERRY, William, servant, age c. 20 - runaway from Thomas
   Rutter at the ironworks in Phila. Co.; reward will be paid
   for his capture by the master or by John Rutter, of Phila.,
   smith (6/8)

LEICESTER, Thomas, servant, age c. 21 - runaway from William
   Chancellor in Phila. (6/15)

ANDERSON, John, servant, age c. 20 - cooper by trade - runaway
   from Major Doudall, of Cecil Co., Maryland; reward will be
   paid if servant is btought to Dr. Ryley in New-Castle (6/22)

JONES, Thomas, servant, age c. 22 - runaway from John Orton, of
   Phila., gunsmith (6/22)

ALLEN, Richard, young servant, shoemaker by trade - runaway from
   Henry Rothwell, of Phila., cordwainer (7/6)

MIDDLETON, Richard, servant, shoemaker by trade - same as above

WILLIAMS, William, servant, age c. 30 - runaway from Tobias
   Leech, of Phila. Co. (7/13)

SMITH, John, servant, from Yorkshire, carpenter by trade - runaway from Widow Elizabeth Brooke, of Prince George's Co., Maryland (8/10)

WILLIAMS, John, Scotch servant, tinker by trade - runaway from Evan Powel, of Phila. (8/10)

PIPER, Henry, chief mate, a Cumberland man, coming from near Whitehaven, age c. 25 or 26 - forced away by pirates out of the ship Sizargh, Matthew Piper master, from Dublin (9/7)

FEARON, James, carpenter, age c. 25 or 26, a Cumberland man, from near Whitehaven - same as above

GILEAD, Matthew, mariner, age c. 25 or 26, a Cumberland man, from near Whitehaven - same as above

LAMPERY, Richard, age c. 28, a passenger - same as above

MACKALL, Nathaniel, Mulatto slave, age c. 15 - runaway from John Kirke, of Cambridge, Dorchester Co. (9/21)

Cesar, a slave, said to be a Bumbar Negro, age c. 25 - same as above

TROUGHER, Joseph, blacksmith, who came to North America about 8 years ago - is to come or to send word to Josiah Rolph, merchant at Boston (9/21)

HAMILTON, Col. John, Postmaster-General of North America - married last week to Mrs. Elizabeth De Peyster - New York dispatch of Sept. 25 (9/28)

Pompey, an Indian, age c. 30 - runaway from Thomas Hill, of Salem (9/28)

EVANS, Rev. Evan, who had been a minister in Phila. for 20 years and then removed to Maryland - on a visit to Phila. was taken with an apoplectic fit and died there Oct. 11 (10/21)

HALLIWELL, Mr., late of New-Castle - two houses, one in possession of the Rev. Mr. Ross and the other of Mr. Read, to be sold at auction (11/2)

PYLE, Joseph, of Chester Co., three small children of - burned to death on Nov. 18 when the house burned to the ground (11/23)

PALMER, John, age c. 29, servant - runaway from Joseph Jones, near Phila. (11/23); he broke out of Goal of Phila. on Feb. 15, 1722 (2/20/1722)

PERRY, Micajah - his death reported by Capt. Simmons, commander of a brigantine (1/16)

OUGHTOPAY, Daniel, age c. 24, Dutch servant of Dr. Johnston,
of Amboy - broke out of Phila. Goal (2/20)

MALLARY, Ebenezer, a New England man, age c. 24 - same as
above

FLEMMING, John, Irish servant, age c. 18, belonging to Mr.
Miranda, of Phila., merchant - same as above

DULANY, Matthew, Irishman - same as above

CORBET, John, Shropshireman, who once taught school at Joseph
Collings's in the Jerseys, runaway servant from Alexander
Faulkner, of Maryland - same as above

DAVIS, James, age c. 26, servant for 3½ years to Henry Badcock,
of Phila., brewer, then hired out to George Campion, of
Phila., brewer - refused to put false brand on barrels of
beer for George Campion and Samuel Bond (husband of Campion's
daughter, Honsey Bond) (2/27)

PAWLEY, George, dec'd - his large shallop at a wharf near John
Jones's in Phila. to be sold by Thomas Prior in Water St.,
Phila. (2/27)

HARDING, Samuel, servant, cooper by trade - runaway from Gabriel
Stelle, of Shrewsbury in the Jerseys (3/22)

LEE, John, servant - runaway from Daniel Martin, living at Abraham Pride's in Phila. (3/22)

PARKER, William, servant, age c. 23 - runaway from Mr. Fitzgerald, Mr. Genings and Mr. Chamberlin in Hanover, Virginia (4/19)

PAGE, Adam, age c. 40, sawyer by trade - same as above

GRIFFINS, Joseph, servant, age c. 27 - same as above

LACY, Samuel, born in Northamptonshire, who came to America
about 20 years ago with Charles French, who lives at Anco-
cus Creek in Burlington Co., West Jersey - will hear something to his advantage if he will come to Henry Flower,
Postmaster in Phila. (4/19)

BURNET, Mrs., wife of the Governor of New York - gave birth to
a son at New York on April 21 (4/26)

MOORE, Eleanor and GARRETSON, Elizabeth - sentenced to death
by court in New-Castle Co. upon Delaware for murder of the
bastard child of Eleanor Moore - New-Castle dispatch of
April 24 (4/26); they were executed May 9 (5/17)

OVER, Thomas, of City of Gloucester, who in 1715 came from Bristol to New York in ship of Capt. Totterdel and is said to
be married and living in Pennsylvania or the Jerseys - is
to come to Obadiah Hunt in New York City, who will inform
him of an estate he has inherited; his sister, who came to
America with him, has been left a legacy (5/9)

DAVIS, John, of Phila., lately dec'd - accounts with estate to
be settled with his widow in Second St. (5/9)

GARLAND, Sylvester, dec'd - two plantations at head of Apequi-
nimanck Creek in New-Castle Co. for sale; apply to Ebenezer
Empson, Esq., near Brandy-wine Ferry in New-Castle Co, or
to the Rev. James Anderson in New York City (5/17)

THOMAS, Edmund, age c. 25, carter and husbandman, English servant of Col. Spotswood - runaway from Germanna, Virginia
(5/31)

REDWOOD, Henry, English servant, who speaks West-country dialect,
age c. 30, sawyer by trade - same as above

MacDonnald, George, age c. 22, tailor by trade, servant of Col.
Spotswood - same as above

GAAR, Solomon, West-countryman, age c. 30, miller by trade but
wagoner upon occasion, servant of Col. Spotswood - same as
above

COLE, John, age c. 30 - wheelwright by trade, who speaks West-
country dialect, servant of Col. Spotswood - same as above

WALDRON, Capt., commander of the man-of-war Greyhound - killed
by Spaniards at Cuba in cabin of his ship - Boston dispatch of May 28 (6/7)

GOMEZ, Jacob, a Jew - murdered by Spaniards in cabin of the man-
of-war Greyhound in Cuba - Boston dispatch of May 28 (6/7)

EARLE, John, servant, age c. 20 - runaway from John Sutton, of
Frankford (6/14)

HARRIS, Richard, carpenter, age c. 30 - runaway from Robert Tunbroll, in Phila. (6/14)

READS, Peter, servant, age c. 21, tailor by trade - runaway
from John Sutton, of Frankford (6/14)

HILLYARD, Benjamin, servant, age c. 25, blacksmith - runaway
from William Hunt, of Bucks Co.; he took with him one Quam,
age c. 22, Negro slave of Samuel Blake (6/21)

TUFFO, Henry, Swedish servant, born in New-Castle Co. - runaway
from William Cox, at head of North East, Maryland (6/21)

MAKANULTIE, Dennis, servant, age c. 19 - runaway from the Rev.
Daniel Magill, A.M., at head of Elk River, Maryland (6/28)

HAMLIN, Michael, Irish servant, age 24 - runaway from Zechariah
Hutchins, of Phila., butcher (6/28)

FOULKS, John, Welshman, joiner and cabinetmaker by trade, age
c. 28 - runaway from the Ironworks near Susquehannah in
Maryland; reward for his capture offered by Stephen Onion
(6/28)

GUMLY, Nathan, apprentice, age between 14 and 15 - runaway from
James Armitage, smith, near the Welch Tract (7/12)

WILLSON, James, servant, age c. 25 - runaway from William Webb,
Kennet Twp., Chester Co. (7/12)

Lawrence, Mulatto slave, age c. 29 - runaway from Benjamin Cottman, of Somerset Co., Maryland (8/2)

LAWS, Samuel, servant, dyer by trade - runaway from Obadiah Prichard, at head of Bush River, Baltimore Co., Maryland (8/2)

GIBBS, James, servant, age c. 26 - runaway from Obadiah Prichard, at head of Bush River, Baltimore Co., carpenter (8/2)

EATON, Moses - killed by Indian; his body taken to Brunswick,
where his brother lives - Boston dispatch of July 23 (8/2)

Amaro, Negro slave, age c. 45 - escaped from the sloop Benjamin,
Samuel Burrows master, from Jamaica, as she lay at Marcus
Hook (8/16)

STANBURY, Nathan, late of Phila., dec'd - real estate in Phila.
to be sold (8/16)

BATTIN, William, age 17 (son of William Battin, of White-Parish,
Wiltshire, England) in speech before he was hanged at Chester on Aug. 15 he told of stealing a whip from Henry Whites,
a cane from his uncle, John Battin, and a fork from Lawrence
Tuck; he was sent to Pennsylvania and sold to John Hannam,
of Concord, Chester Co., who sold him to Joseph Pyle, of
Bethel, Chester Co.; William Battin burned down Mr. Pyle's

house and thus caused the death of Mr. Pyle's three children, Robert (age c. 6), Joseph (age c. 4) and Ralph (age c. 2); his confession was taken down in prison by William Davies, of Chester, schoolmaster, in the presence of Thomas Griffing and John Hughes (8/23)

HARDING, Samuel, servant, cooper by trade - runaway from Gabriel Still, of Shrewsbury, Monmouth Co., East New Jersey, merchant (8/23)

WILLIAMS, John, servant, age 21 - runaway from Edward Hardman, of Shrewsbury, East New Jersey (8/23)

WHEELER, Robert, dec'd - real estate in Burlington to be sold by Mrs. Rebeccah Wheeler, executrix (9/6)

MILNER, Nathaniel, merchant, dec'd - tract of land in Shrewsbury, Monmouth Co., lately in tenure of dec'd, for sale (9/13)

ROLFE, Thomas, middle-aged man - runaway from Ambrose Barcroft, of Solebury, near Buckingham Meeting-house, Bucks Co. (9/20)

CONNAR, William, age c. 24 - broke out of Monmouth Goal in East New Jersey (9/27)

EMANS, John, age c. 30 - same as above

MACKANDRES, Edmund, age c. 30 - same as above

REDMAN, Joseph, late of Phila., merchant, dec'd - accounts with estate to be settled with his widow, Sarah, the executrix, and with John Richardson, of Christeen, merchant, at the home of Mr. Read in New-Castle (9/27 and 10/25)

Jack, Negro, a carpenter - runaway from James Heath at the head of Sassafrax in Maryland (9/27)

VARNILL, William, servant, age c. 23 - runaway from Philip Taylor, David Danis, Richard Bavenson and Thomas Marshall, of Chester Co. (10/4)

BEAUMONT, William, servant, age 24 - same as above

CHAPMAN, John, servant - same as above

COOKE, Edward, servant - same as above

CEADLES, Joseph, servant, age c. 30, who speaks West-country dialect - runaway from John Copson, of Phila. (10/18)

BINGLY, Thomas, servant - runaway from Daniel Darborow, of Phila.
   (11/1)

FRANSH, Manuel, Negro slave, who formerly belonged to John Raymond, of Fairfield in New England - runaway from William
   Yard, of Trenton, West Jersey (11/15)

Dick, Indian slave - runaway from Ezekiel Balding, of Hempstead
   on Long Island (11/23)

KEES, Andrew, Irish servant, age c. 25 - runaway from William
   Hays, of Phila., shipwright (12/18)

RIVES, David, age c. 20, farmer by occupation, who speaks West-
   country dialect - runaway from William Hunt, at the Falls
   Ferry in Bucks Co. (12/18)

1723

M'CURDY, James, servant, age c. 22, who came from Ireland on
   ship that was cast away Dec. 9 at Manisquan - runaway from
   Samuel Dennis, Jr., of Shrewsbury, Monmouth Co., N.J. (1/1)

DICKINSON, Jonathan, late of Phila., merchant, dec'd - accounts
   with estate to be settled at house of James Logan (1/1)

CARLETON, Edward, late of Phila., merchant, dec'd - accounts
   with estate to be settled with John Harrison, living in
   Second St., or Benjamin Paschal at lower end of High St.
   (1/8)

DREWRY, David - hanged Jan. 4 at Gloucester, West Jersey, for
   larceny (1/15)

LISLE, Maurice, dec'd - accounts with estate to be settled with
   Mary Lisle, widow and administratrix of the dec'd, at Mr.
   Henry Badcock's (1/15)

ROGERS, Mr., of Ipswich - his corpse found in Black Rock Creek -
   Boston dispatch of Jan. 21 (2/11)

Ninnicraft, the Great Sachem, age c. 50 - died about a fortnight
   ago at Westerly, leaving an estate worth about £30,000 in
   trust with Col. Wanton, of Rhode Island, Capt. Scranton, of
   Westerly, and Major Fry, of Greenwich; he left two sons -
   Boston dispatch of Jan. 21 (2/11)

BORNE, George, mariner, who had a wife and two children in England - executed Feb. 1 in New York for felony and burglary -
   New York dispatch of Feb. 4 (2/11)

ADAMS, Rev. Mr. - drowned Feb. 23 or 24 when passing in a boat
   from Weockacomica to Annapolis (3/28)

DESKELE, Mr. - same as above

MACANOULLY, Denith, servant, age c. 18 - runaway from the Rev.
Daniel Magil, of London-Tract, New-Castle Co. (3/28)

PRICKET, William - escaped from Chester Goal (3/28)

STOCKBRIDGE, Samuel - accidentally killed when going from Arrow-
sick near the Amerescoggin - Boston dispatch of March 11
(3/28)

STOTTE, Mr., the Collector - drowned Feb. 23 or 24 when passing
in a boat from Weockacomica to Annapolis (3/28

WOOTEN, Richard, servant, house-carpenter by trade - runaway
from Messers William Chapman and Richard Hill, both of Lon-
don-Town, Maryland (4/11)

BECKETT, Joseph, servant, bricklayer by trade - same as above

LINCH, Cornelius, Irish servant, shoemaker by trade, age c. 20 -
runaway from Garet Scank, of Middletown, East New Jersey (4/25

Tom, Negro slave, age c. 16 - runaway from Hugh Hughs and Henry
Munday, of Phila. (4/25)

Kent, Negro slave, age c. 16 - same as above

Cloe, Negro slave, age c. 16 - same as above

LOWDON, Hugh, dec'd - his dwelling in High St., Phila., for sale
(5/2)

COOMBES, Thomas, servant from Somersetshire, weaver by trade,
age c. 22 - runaway from Joseph Townshend and Thomas Hayward, of Chester, Pa. (5/16)

GIBSON, Benjamin, chaplain to the English forces engaged against
the Indians to the eastward in Mass. - lately died - Boston
dispatch of April 1 (5/16)

JONES, Edmund, servant from Shropshire, weaver by trade, age c.
26 - runaway from Joseph Townshend and Thomas Hayward of
Chester (5/16)

ROBINSON, James, servant - runaway from George Shead, of Phila.,
periwig-maker (5/23)

SKELTON, Richard, servant, age c. 23 - runaway from William
Cooke, of Concord, Chester Co. (5/30)

BEALEY, John, servant, age c. 19 or 20 - runaway from Robert
   Harris and William Hunt, at the Falls, Bucks Co. (6/6)

REEVES, David, servant, age c. 19 or 20 - same as above

BROWN, Charles, servant, age c. 19 or 20, baker by trade -
   runaway from Samuel Bonham, of Trent Town in West Jersey (6/6)

Quam, Negro slave, age c. 19 or 20 - runaway from Samuel Beaks,
   of the Falls, Bucks Co. (6/6)

Tom, Negro slave, age c. 30, formerly belonging to Capt. Palmer -
   runaway from Joseph Coleman, in the Great Valley (6/20)

EME, William, servant - runaway from Richard Hughs, of Calo, at
   the head of Brandy-Wine (6/20)

MEREDITH, William, age c. 21, joiner by trade - deserted from
   the ship Richard and Mary at Phila.; reward for his capture will be paid by Samuel Dicker in Phila. (6/27)

WILLSON, John, age 23, born in New London Co. - imprisoned in
   H.M.'s Goal in Rhode Island for piracy (7/4)

WALTERS, John, quartermaster, age 35, born in Devonshire - same
   as above

TOMKINS, John, age 23, born in Gloucestershire - same as above

STUEFIELD, William, age 40, born in Lancaster, England - same
   as above

SOWOD, Joseph, age 28, born in Westminster City - same as above

RICE, Owen, age 27, born in South Wales - same as above

REEVE, Thomas, age 30, born Rutland Co. - same as above

READ, William, age 35, born Londonderry, Ireland - same as above

POWELL, Thomas, age 21, gunner, born in Wethersfield, Conn. -
   same as above

MUNDON, Stephen, age 29, born in London - same as above

LINNECER, Thomas, age 21, born in Lancashire - same as above

LAWSON, Edward, age 20, born Isle of Man - same as above

LAUGHTON, Francis, age 39, born in New York - same as above

LACEY/LACY, Abraham, age 21, born in Devonshire - same as above

KEWES, Peter, age 32, born at Exeter in Devon - same as above

JONES, William age 18, born in London - same as above

JONES, Thomas, age 17, born at Flur in Wales - same as above

HUGGET, Thomas, age 24, born in London - same as above

FITZGERALD, John, age 21, born in Co. of Limerick - same as above

EATON, Edward, age 38, born at Wreaxham, Wales - same as above

CHURCH, Charles, age 21, born in Margaret Parish, Westminster - same as above

BROWN, John, age 29, born in Co. of Derham, England - same as above

BROWN, John, age 17, born at Liverpool in Lancashire - same as above

BRINKLEY, James, age 28, born in Suffolk, England - same as above

BLADES, William, age 28, born in Rhode Island - same as above

BARNES, Henry, age 22, born in Barbados - same as above

SULLEVAND, James, Irish servant, age c. 25 - runaway from Thomas Moor, of Calne, Chester Co., yeoman [7/11]

JORDAN, Dominicus - shot and killed by Indians to the Eastward, near North Yarmouth - Boston dispatch of July 8 [7/18]

HARNUS, Morris, Palatine servant, age c. 40 - runaway from Philip Davis, of New-Munster, on the branches of Elk River [7/18]

CLIFF, John, servant, age c. 19 or 20 - runaway from Nathan Watson, of Borough of Bristol, Bucks Co. [7/18]

AYMET, John, servant, West-country man, age c. 22 - same as above

BRIGHT, John - on July 12 sentenced to death for piracy [7/24]

GERLACH, John Ierich, Palatine servant, age c. 30 - runaway from Robert Alexander, of Phila., merchant [7/24]

HARRIS, Capt. Charles - on July 12 sentenced to death in Rhode Island for piracy [7/24]

HAZELL, Thomas - same as above

HYDE/HIDE, Daniel, age 23, born Eastern Shore of Virginia - same as above

KURES, Peter, middle-aged Palatine servant - runaway from Robert Alexander, of Phila., merchant (7/24)

SMITH, William, middle-aged Palatine servant - same as above

LEBBY, Joseph - July 12 sentenced to death for piracy (7/24)

Jack, Madagascar Negro slave - runaway from Gabriel Stelle, of Shrewsbury (8/8)

NEALE, Jacob, a Marylander, age c. 30 - supposed forced away from the sloop Farley by pirates near Nantucket Island (8/8)

CALDER, Thomas, Scotchman, age c. 30, master of the sloop Farley, belonging to James Harris, of Maryland - same as above

CARR, Peter, Englishman, mate of the sloop Farley - same as above

HILLIARD, Benjamin, servant, blacksmith, age c. 25 - runaway from Major Richard Alderburgh, of Arch St., Phila. (8/15)

WELLERD, Mr., minister in Rutland - murdered Aug. 14 by Indians - Boston dispatch of Aug. 19 (8/29)

STEVENS, Joseph, of Rutland, two sons of - same as above

M'CURDEY, James, servant, age c. 21 - runaway from John Keyll, on Cristeen Creek in New-Castle Co. (8/29)

MUMFORT, Tom, an Indian, age 22, born at Marthas Vineyard - in H.M.'s Goal in Rhode Island as a pirate (9/5)

SWEETSER, Jos., forced, age 24, born at Boston - same as above

KENCARD/HINCHARD, John, doctor, age 22, born near Edenb., North Britain - same as above

TOMSON, James, servant, age c. 20 - runaway from William Whitret, of Appoquinamonk in New -Castle Co. (9/5)

DREW, John - murdered about 5 weeks ago by Indians at Canso - Portsmouth dispatch of Aug. 23 (9/5)

WATKINS, Capt. John - same as above

QUITTAMOG, John, Indian living in Nipmug country, near Woodstock, age 112 - entertained Monday last at Judge Sewall's and on Tuesday at Judge Dudley's - Boston dispatch of Sept. 2 (9/19)

YATES, Jasper, Esq., dec'd - real estate in Chester Co. for sale
    (9/19)

CHAMBERLAIN, Richard, servant, tailor by trade - runaway from
    Sir William Keith (9/19)

JUERY, James, servant, age c. 30, fuller by trade - runaway from
    Jonathan Hanson, of Baltimore Co., Maryland (9/19)

HARMSON, Henry, a German, age c. 23, watchmaker by trade - run-
    away from brigantine Caesar, Robert Abbott commander (9/26)

ASHETON, William, Esq., Councellor-at-Law, 2nd Judge of the Court
    of Vice Admiralty for Pennsylvania, Member of the Governor's
    Council - died Monday last in his 33rd year (9/26)

MACKNISH, Rev. George, late of Jamaica, Long Island, dec'd - ac-
    counts with estate to be settled with Joseph Smith, Jr., of
    Jamaica, or John Nicolls, of New York City, administrators
    (10/17)

FORLONG, Peter - runaway from the ship Gambol, Joseph Ruddock
    commander (10/24)

Nan, Negro slave, age c. 32 - runaway from William Chancellor, of
    Phila. (10/31)

COLEBY, Ensign - lately killed to Eastward by Indians - Boston
    dispatch of Oct. 14 (10/31)

SOMPER, Joseph, servant, age c. 27 - runaway from Nicholas Os-
    burn, of North East, Cecil Co., Maryland (11/7)

MAY, Charles, servant, age c. 30 - runaway from William Hugh, of
    White-Clay Creek Hundred, New-Castle Co. (11/14)

MAC DANIEL, Robert, servant, doctor or mountebank - runaway from
    Thomas Hynson and Daniel Pearce, of Kent Co., Maryland (11/14)

ARNETT, Alexander, Scotch servant, cooper by trade - same as above

COGSHALL, Mr. - killed Nov. to Eastward by Indians (11/28)

TOMSON, Neal, a Highlander - runaway from the ship Joseph, John
    Bennet master, now at Phila. (12/5)

Robin, Negro slave, age c. 21 - runaway from John Joyce at the
    head of the Eastern Branch of Potowmack River in Maryland
    (12/17)

VANABLE, Joseph, servant, blacksmith, age c. 29, who formerly be-
    longed to Hugh Lowdon - runaway from Nathaniel Caruthers,
    near New-Castle (12/31)

1724

PARLOUR, Thomas, English servant, gardener and husbandman - run-
away from Frances Elrington's plantation in Somerset Co.,
N.J.; reward offered if servant is brought to Mrs. Elizabeth
Elrington at the plantation, Andrew Johnson at Amboy or
George Willocks in Phila. [1/7]

BURROWS, Edward, English servant, carpenter by trade, age c. 35 -
same as above

POTTER, William, servant, age c. 25, who pretends to be a blacksmith - runaway from William Baldwin at Namans Creek Mill
[1/21]

BRADLEY, John, from Shropshire, servant, age c. 25, who pretends
to be a bricklayer and to know the glass-trade - runaway from
Edward Weston, of Phila. [1/21]

BARROW, George, age c. 30, commander of the sloop Content - deposes about events of a voyage from New England to Barbados
[1/28]

JACKSON, John, passenger on sloop Content, age c. 30 - deposes
about capture of the sloop by pirates [1/28]

SINTON, William, a Quaker, age c. 23 - escaped from County Goal
of New-Castle, to which he had been committed for counterfeiting; reward for his capture offered by Rowland Fitz
Gerald, sheriff [1/28]

FORRESTER, William, of Richmond Co., Virginia, surgeon - murdered
by Thomas Glascock, of Richmond Co., planter, age c. 50; said
Glascock's son, Gregory, is aged c. 22 [2/4]

JONES, John, age c. 18 - escaped from Phila. Goal, to which he
had been committed for counterfeiting [2/4]

DICKINSON, Jonathan, dec'd - real estate to be sold by Isaac Norris and George Claypole, executors [3/3]

Franck, Negro slave, age c. 40 - runaway from Joseph Coleman,
of Whitland Twp., in the Great Valley, Chester Co. [3/12]

SCHUYLER, Hon. Peter, late President of New York - died at Albany on Feb. 18 - New York dispatch of March 9 [3/12]

CARTER, William, Esq., late Comptroller of H.M.'s Customs at New
York - died March 5 at a very advanced age - New York dispatch of March 9 [3/12]

HUGH, Owen, of East-Town, Chester Co. - will not pay debts contracted in future by his wife Ann, who has eloped [3/12]

MACABOY, Francis, Irishman - on March 19 sentenced to death at
a court held at Dover, Kent Co. on Delaware, for having
killed his servant lad (3/26)

JACOBS, Caleb, late of Phila., dec'd - accounts with estate to
be settled with Edward Roberts, John Knight and John Cadwalader, executors (4/2)

SMITH, John, servant, house-carpenter by trade - runaway from
Patrick Creagh, painter, and William Rogers, both of Annapolis, Maryland (4/9)

ROGERS, Morgan, servant, house-carpenter by trade - same as above

ROBINSON, Thomas, Irish servant - same as above

ROBESON, John, Scotch servant, age c. 26 - runaway from Stephen
Warne, of Perth Amboy, East New Jersey (4/9)

BICKLEY, May, Esq., of New York City, eminent lawyer - died in
New York City on April 2 - New York dispatch of April 6 (4/9)

LEA, Roger, servant - runaway from Thomas Paschall, of Blockley
Twp., near Phila., and John Marshall, of Derby (4/30)

OWEN, James, servant - same as above

TRESSE, Hugh, late of Phila., dec'd - his plantation, about 6
miles from Phila., adjoining Andrew Robinson's land and
the River Schuylkill, to be sold by Charles Read and Thomas
Tresse (4/30)

VAUGHEN, Valentine, servant, age c. 26 - runaway from George
Bostock, of Chester Co. (4/30)

Scipio, Negro slave, age c. 24, glazier, spoon-maker and tinker -
runaway from Philip Reynolds, living in Nansemond at James
River in Virginia (5/7)

Harry, Negro slave, coachman - runaway from Col. Diggs at York
River (5/7)

SWINDALL, Jonathan, servant, age c. 28 - runaway from John Wood,
of Phila., mariner (5/7)

PHILLIPS, the pirate - killed April 28 by Andrew Harradine (the
master of a sloop belonging to Cape Ann), Edward Cheeseman
and others - Boston dispatch of May 4 (5/14)

BURRELL, boatswain of the pirate ship commanded by Phillips -
same as above

CARR, James, Irish servant - runaway from George Cutts, of Phila.,
tallow-chandler (5/21)

MOUNTAIN, Philip, late of Phila., dec'd - accounts with estate
to be settled with John Danby, distiller, next door to the
Sign of the Tun, in Water St., Phila. (5/21)

POLLATTO, John Baptist, born in France, servant, barber by trade -
runaway from George Sheed, periwig-maker, of Phila. (5/21)

THORNTON, William, servant, husbandman, age c. 30 - runaway from
Philemon Lloyd, Esq., of Maryland (6/4)

KERSEY, John, servant, carpenter by trade, age between 40 and 50 -
same as above

ELLIS, Robert, Welsh servant, age c. 24 - runaway from John Cratho, of Phila. Co. (6/11)

EDGO, John, servant, age c. 20 - runaway from Samuel Powel, near
Germantown (6/11)

ARCHER, John Rose, quartermaster of the pirate sloop commanded
by Phillips - executed Tuesday last at Charlestown Ferry
in Massachusetts - Boston dispatch of June 8 (6/18)

WHITE, William, one of crew of pirate ship commanded by Phillips -
same as above

HIGGONS, Alexander, Irish servant, age c. 19 - runaway from
George Dunbar and Major Nathaniel Sheffield, of Newport,
Rhode Island (6/18)

LAHUR, Peter, servant, age c. 26 - same as above

CASE, Robert, age c. 19 - same as above

WILD, Henry, servant, blacksmith by trade - runaway from Patrick
Creagh, of Annapolis, Maryland (6/18)

STED, Joshua, servant, age c. 17 - runaway from John Throckmorton, Esq., of Shrewsbury, Monmouth Co., New Jersey (6/18)

LOFTUS, Lefon, dec'd - accounts with estate to be settled with
his widow, who is executrix (6/25)

THOMAS, John, servant, age c. 23 - runaway from David Marpole,
of Abington Twp., Phila. Co. (6/25)

FRANCIS, Isaac, an Indian - killed May 1 by hostile Indians at
St. George's River - Boston dispatch of June 29 (7/9)

Ephraim, an Indian - same as above

WINSLOW, Capt. Josiah - same as above

WALKER, John - same as above

SIMPSON, Samuel, an Indian - same as above

SHERRIN, David, an Indian - same as above

RANSON, Joshua - same as above

MOSES, Titus, an Indian - same as above

MANASSIS, Amos, an Indian - same as above

LEE, John - same as above

HARVEY, Nathaniel, Sr. - same as above

DENNIS, John - same as above

BRIGGS, Ezra - same as above

ALLEN, John - same as above

HERRING, Benjamin, servant, age c. 20 - runaway from John Annis,
    commander of the ship London Hope (7/9)

CLARK, Robert, age between 40 and 50, servant - same as above

BRUSTALL, Richard, servant - same as above; ship was lying at
    Dickinson's Wharf in Phila.

ANNIS, Capt. John, commander of the ship London Hope, out of
    Phila. - died July 14 in Phila. of a fever (7/16)

BOON, Richard, servant, age 18 - runaway from Alexander Morgan,
    of Pensawkin Creek, Gloucester Co., West New Jersey (7/16)

Caesar, Negro slave, age c. 10 - same as above

WALL, Richard, a smith or candlestick-maker, of Birmingham in
    Warwickshire, who has been absent 5 years from his wife
    Ann and last wrote her four years ago when he was servant
    to Thomas Billinger, of Eversham Twp., New Surrey, Pa. -
    his wife Ann, who lives at Macclesfield in Cheshire, Eng.,
    has news for him, since a relative lately died and left
    him a considerable legacy; he left a child in England (7/23)

NORTON, Ruth, who came about 27 years ago from Ireland as a
gentlewoman's servant and is supposed since to have married Thomas Brown, mariner, will learn something to her
advantage by going to George Brown, clerk to John Moore,
of Phila., Esq. (7/23)

ASHETON, William, Esq., lately dec'd - his household goods for
sale by his widow in Second St., Phila., who plans to leave
for Barbados (7/30)

TRESSE, Hugh, late of Phila., dec'd - his plantation, about 6
miles from Phila., to be sold at the house of Andrew Robison (8/5)

DUNGANNON, Peter, servant, a Moscovite - runaway from William
Levis, of Kennet, Chester Co.; reward for his capture will
be paid by William Levis or Samuel Levis, of Springfield
(8/5)

BURROUGH, William, mariner, a married man, age c. 27 - on April
30 was forced into pirate ship, commanded by one Spriggs,
from on board the pink Sea Nymph, of Topsham (8/13)

BUTLER, John, mariner, age c. 22 - same as above

HANCOCK, Stephen, age c. 34 - same as above

ROSE, Aquila, dec'd - lease of the ferry at the end of High St.
over the Schuylkill to be sold by the executors (8/13)

MOORE, Simon, servant - runaway from Walter Nevil, of Queen
Ann's Co., Maryland (8/20)

MACDEWELL, Sergeant - shot and killed by Indians on July 4 -
Boston dispatch of Aug. 3 (8/20)

DADE, Joseph, late of Phila.,dec'd -his house in Second St.,
near the Market Place, for sale (8/27)

TURNER, Francis, servant, age c. 21, carpenter and sawyer by
trade - runaway from John Cassell, upon Schuylkill; reward
for his capture will be paid by his master or by Arnold Cassell in Phila. (8/27)

RALLE, M., a Jesuit - killed Aug. 12 by the English at Norridge-
wock - Boston dispatch of Aug. 31 (9/17)

BOMARZEEN, Col., Indian chief - same as above

CARABSERT, Capt., Indian chief - same as above

JOB, Capt., Indian chief - same as above

MOGG, Capt., Indian chief - same as above

WISSEMEMET, Capt. (son-in-law of Bomarzeen), Indian chief - same
as above

Tom, a Maligasco Negro slave - runaway from plantation of Cornelius Van Horne on Rariton River (9/24)

WELLS, Joseph, servant, age c. 22 - runaway from Abraham Porter,
of Porters Field, Co. and Twp. of Gloucester (10/1)

SMITH, Clodius, servant, age c. 35 - same as above

SALTONSTALL, Gurdon, Esq., Governor of Connecticut - died there
Sept. 20 (10/15)

BURROWS, Edward, servant, age c. 35, house-carpenter - runaway
from Benjamin Vining, near Salem; reward offered if said
servant is captured and brought to his master or to Abraham Vining in Phila. (10/29)

BELL, Henry, servant, age c. 18 - runaway from Sir William Keith,
Governor of Pennsylvania (11/19)

WILLIAMS, Jonathan, servant, age c. 18 (formerly servant to William Baldwin, of Namans Creek, miller) - runaway from Thomas
Hill, of Salem, West Jersey (12/3)

YEILDS, Mr., of Island of Jamaica - married Thursday last in
Phila. to the daughter of Sir William Keith (12/15)

CALCORD, Peter, age c. 18, who was captured by Indians May 16
last at Kingstown in New Hampshire - escaped Nov. 7 and
made his way to Wells and then back to New Hampshire (12/22)

TRENT, William, Esq., Chief Judge of New Jersey - died of apo-
plexy on Dec. 25 at his house in Trent Town (12/29)

MASTERSON, Hugh, Irish servant - runaway from Lawrence Reynolds,
of Phila., currier (12/29)

JONES, Edward, servant, age c. 35, who has been in the army and
claims to be a drummer - runaway from Benjamin Davis, of
Indian Town, Salem Co., near Cohansie (12/29)

COATS (or COUTS?), William, from Devonshire, servant, age c. 23,
husbandman - runaway from John Moore, of Phila., Esq.
(12/29)

1725

LASLEY, George, servant, age c. 19 - runaway from Richard Dobson,
    at the head of Elk River (1/9)

COURTS, William, servant; age c. 23, from Devonshire - runaway
    from John Moore, of Phila., Esq. (1/9)

BROWN, Capt. John, Sr., a son of - drowned Nov. 25 when Bristol
    Ferry overset - Rhode Island dispatch of Dec. 4 (1/12)

CRANSTON, Col. John, eldest son of - same as above

PEREY, Elisha, servant, age c. 18 or 19 - runaway from Ralph
    Pile, of Concord (1/12)

SQUIBB, Robert, dec'd - Thomas Byerly, Esq., is invested with
    two whole Proprietaries in the Western Division of New Jer-
    sey in right of Squibb (1/26)

BARBER, Peter, English servant, age c. 22 - runaway from Thomas
    Parke, of Kent Co. (2/2)

BURK, Richard, Irish servant - same as above

SYMMONDS, Capt. - murdered in South Carolina by a sect called
    Sabbatharians (2/9)

OULDISWORTH, Stephen, servant, who pretends to be a clock-maker
    by trade - runaway from James Sykes and John Curtis, of the
    City of New Castle (2/9)

BARRY, Mathias, servant, age c. 25 - same as above

WILLIAMS, Thomas - murdered by John Murray, who on Feb. 10 was
    tried in Phila. and found guilty (2/16)

HIDE, William, servant, born in England - runaway from George
    Rescarrick, of Middlesex Co., N.J. (2/23)

MILLER, John, servant - same as above

SCHOWTHRIP, Thomas, Yorkshireman, carpenter by trade - runaway
    from George Rescarrick, who lives at Cambray Brook, Middle-
    sex Co., N.J. (2/23 and 5/27)

PAINTER, Nicholas, dec'd - land in Maryland lately belonging to
    the dec'd to be sold by Reynolds Courier, in Chesnut St.,
    Phila. (2/23)

HAYES, John, Irish servant, age c. 22 - runaway from James
    Morris, sawyer, in Phila. (3/25)

GIBBON, William, Esq., Member of H.M.'s Council for South Carolina - died March 4 in South Carolina; his heir is his sister (wife of Capt. Caywood, of South Carolina), who has
only one daughter (4/8)

PETERS, Thomas - real estate belonging to his estate in Phila.
for sale; apply to Rese Peters at Abington or Thomas Peters
in Chesnut St., Phila., executors (4/8)

HIGGINS, Timothy, servant, age c. 22 - runaway from Edward Thompson, of Edgmont, Chester Co. (4/29)

LLOYD, John (only son of John Lloyd, Esq., Deputy Postmaster-
General of North America) - died April 29 as result of a
fall from his horse between Anatomy and Cambridge on April
27; he was buried May 2 from the house of Andrew Feneuil -
Boston dispatch of May 3 (5/13)

LOVEWELL, Capt. - mortally wounded by Pigwocket Indians on May 8 -
Boston dispatch of May 17 (6/3)

ROBINS, Ensign - same as above

PAINTER, Nicholas, Esq., dec'd, and CORNWALLIS, Hon. Thomas,
dec'd - great tracts of land for sale by William Cornwallis,
of Mulberry St., Phila.; land was purchased from Dame Penelope Cornwallis and Henry Bray (6/3)

Jack, a Malagasco Negro, age c. 40 - runaway from Gabriel Stelle,
of Shrewsbury, Monmouth Co., N.J. (6/3)

Rachel, Negro slave, age c. 40 - runaway from Samuel Carpenter,
Sr. (6/24)

Jack, Negro slave, age c. 50 - same as above

WESTRON, John, servant, age c. 45, born in Morchet, Devonshire,
who came over in the ship Stanhope - runaway from John Nay-
lor, of Bucks Co. (6/24)

PROUSE, James, servant, age c. 16, sail-maker by trade - runaway
from William Chancellor, of Phila. (6/24)

HARRIS, Robert, servant, age c. 30 - runaway from Joseph Goulding,
of Middletown in Freehold (7/1)

DAVIS, Lewis, servant, bricklayer by trade - runaway from John
Gibbin, of York Town, Pa. (7/8)

PARNEL, James, attorney-at-law, who came in the ship Hanover
    from London this spring - accidentally drowned at Phila.
    on June 7 when washing himself in the river (7/8)

PEARSE, William, servant, age c. 25, carpenter by trade - runaway
    from Man Page, of Gloucester Co., Va. (7/8)

SMITH, William, servant, age c. 30 - same as above

WEST, Robert, age c. 20, bricklayer by trade - same as above

Marra, Carolina Indian female slave, age c. 40 - runaway from
    William Bissell, of Phila., blacksmith, and John Coats, of
    Phila., brick-maker (7/15)

Peter, Carolina Indian slave, age c. 26 - same as above

TAYLER, William, late of New York City, brazier, dec'd - accounts
    with estate to be settled with the executors, Joseph Leddel,
    pewterer, and Thomas Grant, ironmonger (7/22)

STEVENS, George, bricklayer by trade, passenger or servant - de-
    serted from ship Stanhope, William Bragginton commander, at
    Phila. (7/22)

RESE, Edward, sailor - same as above

HOPKINS, Nicholas, sailor - same as above

AQUITTIMAUG, John - died July 21 near Woodstock, age c. 114 -
    Boston dispatch (7/22)

CAPER, Rev. Joseph, pastor of church at Topsfield, Mass. - died
    there June 30 - Boston dispatch of July 10 (7/22)

BYNG, Mrs. Thomas - beaten Thursday last by her husband, felt-
    maker by trade and a soldier in the garrison in New York
    City, so that she died at once - New York dispatch of July
    19 (7/22)

MOORE, Capt., master of a sloop - drowned when his sloop overset -
    New York dispatch of July 26 (7/29)

DOUBLE, John, servant, age c. 24 - runaway from George Carter,
    living near the forks of Brandewine, Bradford Twp., Ches-
    ter Co. (8/26)

SMITH (alias SPURLING), James, age c. 40, utterer of counterfeit
    gold bars - broke out of goal of Dorcester Co., Maryland;
    reward for his capture offered by Charles Ungle, High Sheriff
    of that county (8/26)

TURNER, Francis, servant, age c. 23 - runaway from Mr. Ham Overthrow, sawyer, living up Coopers Creek [8/26]

ALLEN, William, eminent merchant of Phila. - died there Aug. 31
[9/2]

WESTWOOD, Elijah, servant - runaway from John Swinyard, of Baltimore Co. [9/23]

BURNS, Thomas, servant, thought to be an Irishman - same as above

ROGERS, George, servant, age c. 30, nailer by trade - runaway
from Lawrence Reynolds, of Phila. [9/23]

BILLET, William, age c. 24, cooper by trade - escaped from the
prison yard in Phila. [9/30]

DAWSITT, Philip, servant, age c. 18 - runaway from Samuel Smith,
of Burlington [11/4]

REYNES, Daniel, servant, age c. 18 - runaway from Ennion William,
of Bristol, Bucks Co. [11/4]

ROBERTS, Owen, High Sheriff of Phila. Co. - died in Phila. on
Tuesday last [12/21]

Will, Negro slave belonging to Thomas Lawrence and formerly to
Jacob Weldon, blacksmith, near Christeen, New-Castle Co. -
runaway from the sloop Betty, Capt. Scollard master, at Lads
Cove [12/28]

1726

POLLARD, Mrs. Anne - died Monday last in Boston in her 105th
year - Boston dispatch of Dec. 11 [1/4]

TALBOT, Robert, late of Burlington, dec'd - accounts with estate
to be settled with his widow, Mrs. Katherine Talbot [1/4]

BASS, Jeremiah, Esq., late of Burlington, dec'd - accounts with
estate to be settled with Fenwick Lyell, of Middletown, Monmouth Co., or with the widow and executrix in Burlington [1/4

CARVER, Robert Mullard, formerly of Phila. - drowned last week
in New York City [1/4]

COOPER, James and Mary his wife (administratrix of John Burrows) -
Edward Mullen, Jr., Joseph Smith and Thomas Morrill were
sentenced at court in Phila. for forging an obligation with
intent to recover money for James and Mary Cooper [1/11]

BACON, Butts, Esq., Collector of Customs for New Hampshire - died last Monday - Boston dispatch of Dec. 16, 1725 (1/18)

SMART, James, apprentice, age c. 18 or 19 - runaway from Henry Enocks, of Bensalem Twp., Bucks Co., blacksmith (1/25)

ROBERTS, Owen, dec'd - plantation in Merion Twp., about a mile from Andrew Robinson's mill, for sale; apply to Ann Roberts, executrix, at John Roberts's, near the Market Place in Phila. (2/15)

THOMPSON, Thomas, servant - runaway from Zachariah Hutchins in Phila. (2/15)

TIDMAN, Thomas, servant, age 23 - runaway from John Hutton, of Phila. (3/8)

DAVIS, Thomas, servant, age c. 19 - runaway from Jeremiah Effreth (3/8)

JONES, Edward, convict Welsh servant, age c. 30, glazier and plumber by trade - runaway from Patrick Creagh, of Baltimore Co., on Patapsco River, Md. (3/17)

ENSWORTH, James, a young man - runaway from the ship John Gally, John Ball master (3/24)

NEWELL, Joseph - same as above

WHITE, Capt. - drowned Sunday last when going up the river in a boat (Phila. item) (3/24)

KNIGHT, Joseph, servant, age c. 28 - runaway from Robert Shephard, of Phila., carter (4/28)

RIDMAN, Thomas, servant, age 23 - runaway from John Hutton, of Phila., cordwainer (4/28)

HYNES, John, Irish servant, age c. 20, skinner by trade, lately brought into New-Castle by Mr. Paterson, merchant, from Dublin - runaway from Edmond Farrel, of Phila., tanner (5/12)

BICKLEY, Abraham, late of Burlington, dec'd - accounts with estate to be settled with the executors, William Hudson, George Fishwater, James Stell, all of Phila., and Samuel Bickley (son of Abraham), of Burlington (5/12)

CLARE, Peter, Irish servant, age c. 24, tanner by trade, lately brought into New-Castle by Mr. Paterson, merchant, from Dublin - runaway from Edmond Farrel, of Phila., tanner (5/12)

COLLET, Robert, age c. 20 - deserted from the ship Betty, Samuel
   Manthorpe master, at Phila. (5/12)

THWAIRS, James, age c. 15 - same as above

WILLSON, Edward, age c. 20 - same as above

WILLSON, John, Irish servant, age c. 20, butcher by trade, lately
   brought into New-Castle by Mr. Paterson, merchant, from Dublin - runaway from Lawrence Reynolds, of Phila., currier
   (5/12)

HALL, Archibald, Scotchman, age c. 28 - deserted from the ship
   Betty, Timothy Williamson master (5/19)

HALL, John, Scotchman, age c. 28 - same as above

TICHUM, Richard, servant, born at Malbrough in Wiltshire, age c.
   18 or 20, baker by trade - runaway from Joseph Buckly, of
   Phila., merchant (5/26)

EDWARDS, Evan, servant, age c. 17 or 18, saddle-tree-maker by
   trade - runaway from Benjamin Rhodes, of Phila., bricklayer (5/26)

JACKSON, John, indented servant, born in England, age c. 28 or 30 -
   runaway from John Crosby, of Ridley, Chester Co. (6/2)

BANNET, William, Irish servant, who formerly belonged to Mr. Hunter, of Chester Co., tanner - runaway from William Moore,
   of the Great Swamps, Richland Twp., Bucks Co. (6/30)

CORKER, William, late of Phila., dec'd - accounts with estate to
   be settled with his son and executor, William Corker, of
   Phila. (7/14)

CHILD, Cephas, of Wright Town, Bucks Co., six children of - burned to death in conflagration of their house on July 17
   (7/21)

RILEY, James, servant, age c. 25 - runaway from Thomas Ashton,
   of Phila., shipwright (8/11)

COOPER, William, servant, shoemaker by trade - runaway from
   Frederick Engle, of Chester Co. (8/18)

DRYSDALE, Major, Governor of Virginia - died July 17 (8/18)

MULLOWNY, Patrick, servant - runaway from Mr. Taylor, of Baltimore Co., Maryland (8/18)

TOMLINSON, Thomas, servant, East-Indian , age 22 or 23 - runaway
from John Sewers, of Phila. (8/18)

PARLER (alias SARTIN), Sarah - runaway, in company of one Ri-
chard Sartin, who served his time at the ironworks at French
Creek in Pennsylvania, from Dr. John Browne, in York Road,
West New Jersey (9/1)

LEWIS, John, servant, age c. 25 - runaway from Richard Wright, of
Burlington (9/1)

EDWARDS, John, Welsh servant, age c. 21 - same as above

BASS, Mrs. Elizabeth, of Burlington - collection of books (doubt-
less those of her dec'd husband) offered for sale by her (9/1)

DAY, William, servant from the west of England, age 21 or 22 -
runaway from Samuel Atkinson, of Burlington Co., West New
Jersey (9/8)

BROMLEY, John, servant - runaway from James Wood, boat-builder
(9/15)

EVANS, John, apprentice - runaway from John Sherburn, of Phila.,
joiner (9/15)

SPRING, John, servant, age 25 or 26, joiner by trade - same as
above

PRICHARD, John, servant, age c. 24, watchmaker by trade - runaway
from John Throckmorton, of Shrewsbury, East New Jersey (9/15)

Jack, Negro slave, age c. 40 - runaway from Gabriel Stelle, of
Shrewsbury, Monmouth Co., N.J. (9/15)

_____, Philip, servant, age 23 or 24 - runaway from William
Hays, of Phila., shipwright (9/15)

CAPER, William, servant, age c. 26 - runaway from John Campbe'l,
of Cecil Co., Maryland (9/29)

MOOR, Richard, Irish servant - runaway from Sapins Harison,
living near Duck Creek, New-Castle Co. (10/6)

WATMORE, James, servant - runaway from Richard Moore, of Maryland (10/13)

MARKHAM, Mrs. Joanna (widow of Capt. William Markham, formerly
Lt.- Governor of Pennsylvania) - died Tuesday last in New
York City - New York dispatch of Oct. 10 (10/13)

JENNINGS, John, servant, age c. 45 - runaway from ship Constantine, Edward Foy commander (10/20)

GAMMON, Philip, sailor, age c. 24 - same as above

FORTUNE, William, sailor, age c. 24 - same as above

SCOBELL, Henry, late of Phila., dec'd - accounts with estate to
be settled with Charles Read, Esq., and Benjamin Paschall,
of Phila. (10/20)

ARMIT, Thomas, late of Phila., dec'd, cooper - real estate in
Front St. offered for sale by his widow, Elizabeth Armit, and Thomas Sober, merchant (10/20)

ASKEW, John, of London, merchant, a considerable trader to Phila.
died Aug. 9 in London (10/27)

WOOD, Catherine (wife of Joseph Wood, of Phila., carpenter) -
has taken her daughter and left her husband and removed
from the province, so that her husband will not pay debts
contracted by her in the future (11/3)

MACCOLESTER, Alexander, apprentice lad - runaway from John Brocken
bury, of Phila., sadler (11/3)

TURCY, Henry, Swedish servant, age c. 29 - runaway from John
Worral and Henry Grubb, both of Edgment, Chester Co. (11/10)

KENTON, Henry, English servant, age c. 22, butcher by trade -
same as above

BONO, Joseph, dec'd - plantation late in his possession, near
Bristol, Bucks Co., to be sold by William Fishbourn, of
Phila. (12/1)

CROUOFRS, James, Irish servant, belonging to the ironworks, age
c. 22 - runaway from Charles Read (12/1)

HENDRICKS, Mr., age c. 60, passenger - runaway from the ship
Apphia, George Smith commander (12/13)

1727

PETERS, Thomas, dec'd - accounts with estate to be settled with
Rice Peters, of Abington, or Thomas Peters, of Phila., executors (1/31)

HIRST, Samuel, young man of Boston, nephew of Judge Sewell - on
or about Jan. 14 suddenly dropped dead upon the Long Wharf
in Boston - Boston dispatch of Jan. 16 (2/7)

LEWIS, Thomas, of Boston, publisher of the Boston Gazette -
    died Jan. 14 in Boston of an apoplectic fit in his 32nd
    year - Boston dispatch of Jan. 16 (2/7)

LONGSTREAT, Theophilus, of Shrewsbury, Monmouth Co., East Jersey,
    age c. 60 - on Dec. 31, 1726, with one shot killed six out
    of seven swans flying over a meadow (2/21)

PEARSON, Henry, sailor, age c. 35 - runaway from ship Shadwell,
    John Jones master (2/28)

HILL, Hannah (wife of Richard Hill, Esq.) - died Saturday last
    in Phila. (2/28)

MAC NAYLE, John, servant, age c. 20 - runaway from Richard Barry
    and Nathaniel Gubb, both of Willistown, Chester Co. (3/7)

MULHOLLAND, Arthur, servant, under age of 20 - same as above

LEECH, Toby, dec'd - accounts with estate to be settled with
    the executors, Thomas Leech and Isaac Leech, in Phila. (3/16)

MUGGLEWAY, Charles, Irish servant - runaway from Martha Rawle,
    widow of Franck Rawle, near Phila. (3/23)

MORE (alias BROWN), Thomas, supposed to be a servant - jailed
    in Phila. (3/30)

MILLS, Samuel, of Jamaica, Long Island, yeoman - died there March
    10, aged 95; he lived 68 years with one wife, who is still
    alive, by whom he had 16 children; he has left 9 children,
    80 grandchildren and 54 great-grandchildren - Jamaica dis-
    patch of March 10 (3/30)

BOWEL, William, late of Phila., dec'd - accounts with estate to
    be settled with his widow, Elizabeth Bowel, of Phila. (3/30)

BOND, Samuel, servant, age c. 22 - runaway from John Bryant, of
    Phila., baker (4/13)

COLLINS, John, servant - runaway from William Bantoft, of Phila.,
    baker (4/13)

ELFORD, John, servant, age c. 22 - runaway from Charles West, of
    Phila., ship-carpenter (4/13)

PARK, Nicholas, servant - runaway from Thomas Pryer, of Phila.,
    baker (4/13)

RUDYARD, John, late of Perth Amboy, gentleman, dec'd - plantation
    in Perth Amboy for sale by John Barclay, one of the execu-
    tors (4/13)

James, Negro slave, age c. 24 - is in custody of William Nichols, Esq., High Sheriff of Monmouth Co. (4/13)

COLLINS, Thomas, servant - runaway from John Justus, at the head of North East, Cecil Co., Maryland (5/4)

CYPHERS, Elizabeth [alias Elizabeth Willson], servant, age c. 23, whose mother has sent her something from Bristol - runaway from Samuel Holt, of Phila. (5/4)

RAWLE, Francis, dec'd - his plantation, 2½ miles from Phila., for sale by his widow, Martha Rawle, or by William Rawle in Phila. (5/11)

MURRY, Timothy, servant, age 40 - runaway from John Macdaniel, of New-Castle Co., near Christeen (5/18)

Will, Negro slave, age c. 26 - runaway from James Leonard, of Somerset, N.J. (5/25)

WILLSON, John, late of Phila., merchant, dec'd - accounts with estate to be settled with the executors, Joseph Buckly and John Dickinson, merchant, in Phila. (5/25)

THOMPSON, John, servant, age c. 20 - runaway from William Bantoff, of Phila., baker (5/25)

HILLTON, Andrew, servant - same as above

ASHETON, Robert, Esq., Recorder of Phila., Prothonotary of the Court of Common Pleas of Phila. Co., Member of the Governor's Council - died suddenly Monday last at the council table in Phila. in his 58th year; he was born at Salford, Lancaster Co., Great Britain (6/1)

BISSET, David, late of Phila., post-rider, dec'd - accounts with estate to be settled with the executors, Thomas Boore and Margaret Bisset (6/1)

HUMPHRY, John, servant, age c. 17 - runaway from Stephen Jackson, near Schuylkill Ferry (6/1)

PRAT, John, servant, age c. 22, tailor by trade - runaway from Stephen Onion at the Principio Ironworks, Cecil Co. Md. (6/1)

WEST, James, late of Phila., apothecary, dec'd - accounts with estate to be settled with Joshua Johnson, tin-plate-worker in Phila., administrator (6/8)

SEAMORE, Thomas, servant - runaway from George Bowels, of Phila., blacksmith (6/15)

PRAT, Richard, servant, age c. 18 - runaway from Joseph Jackson,
of London Grove, Chester Co. (6/15)

BLANCHET, John, servant, age c. 24, who speaks broad West-country -
runaway from Widow Aemy Sheppard, of Phila. (6/15)

Philip, Negro slave, last belonging to Everard Bolton, dec'd, in
Southampton, Bucks Co. - runaway from Margaret Bolton, of
Abington Twp., Phila. Co.; reward will be paid for capture
of the slave by Margaret Bolton or by Richard Clayton, of
Southampton, Bucks Co. (6/29)

Wequalla, an Indian king - sentenced to death June 23 at Perth
Amboy for murder of John Leonard, of Perth Amboy (6/29); exe-
cuted Friday last at Perth Amboy; Perth Amboy dispatch of
July 4 (7/6)

MORRIS, James, late of Phila., sawer, dec'd - accounts with estate to be settled with Edward Price, executor (7/13)

HUMPHREY, John, servant, age c. 18 - runaway from Stephen Jackson at Schuylkill (7/13)

BULLOCK, Thomas, late of Phila., dec'd - accounts with estate
to be settled with the widow, who is administratrix (7/20)

GARLAND, Sylvester, dec'd - two of his plantations (formerly belonging to Capt. Haily) at head of Apoquilick Creek in New-
Castle Co. for sale; apply to James Anderson, minister, late
of New York but now of Donnigall, Chester Co. (8/3)

GATAN, Nicholas, dec'd - accounts with estate to be settled with
the executrix, his widow, who desires to let his house about
a mile from Phila. (8/10)

GIBBENS, David, servant - runaway from Edward Smout, of Chester
(8/17)

BROWN, Hugh, Irish servant, age c. 35 - runaway from John Knowles,
of Phila. (8/17)

COOK, Gregory, servant - runaway from Ruth Hoskins, of Chester
(8/17)

DAVIS, William, servant, age c. 28 - runaway from George Farinton,
of Phila. (8/17)

MURPHY, Margaret, servant - runaway from John Bryan, Sr., living
near New-Castle (8/17)

GRIFFE, Thomas, Welsh servant, age c. 40 - runaway from Alexander
Lockart, of Trenton, Hunterdon Co., N.J. (8/31)

CROSSET, Thomas, apprentice, age c. 20 - runaway from George
House, of Phila., shoemaker (8/31)

WRIGHT, Thomas (alias Thomas Smith), weaver by trade, who says
he was born in Maryland and has lived on Long Island and
in New England - suspected of stealing a horse (9/7)

OWEN, Evan, late of Phila., dec'd - his widow, Mary Owen, will
sell 700 acres of land (9/14)

MATTOCKS, Edward, from Herefordshire, servant, smith by trade -
runaway from William Cox and John Copson, of North-East,
Maryland (9/14)

FERRY, William, servant, age c. 19 - runaway from Lawrence
Smyth, of Monmouth Co., N.J. (9/21)

FLETCHER, Robert, dec'd - accounts with estate to be settled
with his widow or with his son, Thomas Fletcher (9/21)

WORLEY, Henry, of Chester Mills, dec'd - accounts with estate
to be settled with Evan Morgan, of Phila., administrator
(9/21)

CHARADON, Clement, servant, age c. 18 - runaway from William
Hudson, Jr. (9/28)

JONES, James, late of Lower Merion, gentleman, dec'd - accounts
with estate to be settled with his widow and with Joseph
Jones, his son, administrators (10/5)

JOHNSON, John, servant - runaway from Benjamin Fairman, living
near Phila. (10/5)

DEMPSY, Vallentine, servant, age c. 18, rope-maker by trade,
lately imported with Capt. King from Ireland - runaway
from John Goure at New-Castle (10/12)

HULL, John, of Newton, Conn. -arrested and committed to Fairfield
Goal for murder of his three-months-old son - Boston dispatch
of Sept. 28 (10/12)

JONES, John, servant, age c. 20 - runaway from James Steward, of
Phila., tailor (10/16)

MAN, John, servant, age c. 18, tailor by trade - runaway from
Alexander Frame, of Phila., tailor (10/16)

SITCH, John, servant, age c. 24 - runaway from Robert Miller, in
Caln (10/19)

WILLIAMS, William, Welsh servant, age 21 - runaway from Samuel
Jones, of Cadbury, Chester Co. [10/19]

BURNET, Mrs. Mary [wife of Governor William Burnet, of New York] -
died Saturday last in New York City - New York dispatch of
Nov. 6 [11/9]

PECKFORD, Richard, servant, stone-cutter by trade - runaway from
Anthony Wilkinson, of Phila., carver [11/9]

Will, Negro slave - runaway from Charles West, shipwright [11/23]

PATTISON, Sarah [now wife of James Nisbitt, of Perth Amboy, tai-
lor] - has eloped from her husband [11/23]

RYLEY, Dennis, late of Acrington, Lancashire, England, but now of
the Twp. of New-Hanover, Burlington Co., West New Jersey -
seeks news of his uncle, John Cunliff, said to reside in or
near Christeen, New-Castle Co. upon Delaware [11/30]

TALBOT, Rev. John, formerly minister at Burlington - died there
on Nov. 29 [11/30]

WATKINS, Thomas, servant, age c. 40 - runaway from George King,
of Phila., mast-maker [11/30]

1728

MARSHALL, John [son of Alexander Marshall, of Over-Stowey, near
Taunton, Somerset Co.], who has been absent a considerable
time at sea or beyond the seas - reward offered for information about him [1/2]

KANN, Conrad, and his wife Mariana, Palatines, who arrived in
Phila. on Oct. 30 from London in the ship John Galley, John
Ball master - have run away to escape paying for their
passage [1/16]

DERRYMAN, Mary, who at Tollard-Royal on Sept. 29, 1727, wrote a
letter directed to her son, Arthur Oliver, at Phila. - her
son is asked to claim the letter [2/6]

TOWNSEND, Grace - died Friday last in Phila. in her 58th year
[2/6]

STAPLER, Stephen, late dec'd - his plantation will be sold at
auction in Nottingham, Chester Co. [2/13]

Peter, Negro slave, born in this country, age c. 30 - runaway
from Isaac Norris [3/14]

GARRETT, Amos, noted merchant of Annapolis, Md. - died there on
March 8 [3/21]

RYLEY, Dr. Patrick - real estate in New-Castle for sale by Margaret Ryley, widow and executrix of said Patrick (3/21)

OWEN, Evan, dec'd - two tracts of land near Mauahatony Ironworks,
Phila. Co., and the sixteenth part of ironworks in New- Castle Co. for sale by Mary Owen, of Phila., widow of Evan (4/4)

BULL, Sarah (widow of Richard Bull) - offers for sale house and
land at Gloucester that were conveyed to her by Nathaniel
Tylee, dec'd (4/4)

HORSMAN, Mary, indented servant of Samuel Ferguson, of New-Castle, who was sold to him by John Copson, of North -East,
Cecil Co., Maryland - runaway from her master (4/4)

EDMONDS, Deborah - has eloped from her husband, Roger Edmonds,
of Phila. (4/4)

Peter, Negro slave, born in this country, age c. 30 - runaway
from Isaac Norris (4/4)

SNAGGS, Richard, servant, age c. 26 - runaway from the ironworks
on French Creek, Chester Co.; reward for his capture offered
by William Branson and Samuel Nott (4/11)

CONALLY, William, Irish servant, age c. 25, weaver by trade -
runaway from Joseph Forman, of Freehold, N.J. (4/11)

EMMIT, Capt., master of a schooner belonging to Rhode Island -
died April 7 when schooner was wrecked on breakers near
Point Judith (4/25)

HENRY, John, servant, who lately belonged to Isaac Watson, near
Trents Town - runaway from Joseph Brittain, of Croswicks,
West New Jersey (4/25)

ROGERS, John, of Phila., potter - absconded, taking with him
Limos, a "Malagascow" Negro, age c. 18, who belongs to
Solomon Goard, of Phila. (5/9)

HILL, John, servant, brazier by trade - runaway from John Hyart,
of Phila.; he is thought to be in the company of two sailors
who have absconded from a brigantine lately from Madera;
they are a man from Yorkshire named Thomas Wittaker, age
c. 30, and James Letcher, an Irishman, age c. 21 (5/23)

WILSON, Thomas, servant, butcher by trade - runaway from William
Bareford, of Phila. (6/6)

RYAN, Thomas, Irish servant - runaway from Thomas Wilcox, of
Concord, Chester Co. (6/6)

CLASSON, Nicholas, servant, age c. 21, printer by trade, who formerly lived with William Parks, of Annapolis, printer -
runaway from Andrew Bradford, of Phila. [6/13]

NICHOLS, Joshua, servant, born in London, stocking-weaver by trade -
runaway from Archibald Craige, of Freehold, East New Jersey
[6/13]

MAYNARD, John, Irish servant - runaway from Samuel Peele, William
Chapman and Richard Hill, of London Town, Maryland [6/27]

WILLIAMS, George, English servant, a young man, who pretends to
be a gardener - same as above

PICKFORD, Richard, servant, age c. 23, stone-cutter by trade -
runaway from Anthony Wilkerson [6/28]

KENEDY, Patrick, servant, age c. 21 - runaway from Thomas Bonde
[6/27]

WINTER, Robert and WINTER, Walter, Welshmen, brothers - executed
July 3 at Chester for murder of three Indians [7/4]

BRODERICK, Darby, Irish servant - runaway from Samuel Wright, of
New-Hanover, N.J. [7/4]

BACKER, _____, Irish servant, age c. 25 - runaway from ship
Waring [7/4]

SMITH, William, servant, age c. 23 or 24, shoemaker by trade -
runaway from Richard Landon, of Town of Chester [7/4]

SMITH, William, servant, age c. 23 or 24, shoemaker by trade,
who served his time in Dublin to a clog-maker - runaway
from Duncan Dummond, of New-Castle Co., merchant [7/11]

CONOR, Lawrence, Irish servant, age c. 26 - runaway from William
Reed, of Great Egg Harbour [7/18]

BURN, Roger, Irish servant, age c. 27 - runaway from John Pas-
more, of Kennet, Chester Co. [7/18]

CAREY, Roger, servant, age between 30 and 40, weaver and comber
by trade - runaway from Charles Crosby, of Muddle Town,
Chester Co. [7/18]

GIBBS, James, servant - runaway from Thomas Yeatman, near Ellis
Lewis Mill, New-Castle Co. [8/8]

Dick, Negro slave, age c. 35 - runaway from Christopher Tomson, of Phila. [8/8]

MORFFEE, William, servant, stay-maker by trade - runaway from William Harrison, of New Hannover, Burlington Co., N.J. [8/8]

CARVER, James, age c. 40, millwright by trade - broke out of Burlington Co. Goal [8/15]

BRIGHTWELL,John, age c. 28, tailor and stay-maker - same as above

PURNEL, James, servant, age c. 30 - runaway from Samuel Worthington, of Manor of Moorland, Phila. Co. [8/15]

BOWEN, Richard, young servant - same as above

HERNE, Launcelot, servant, age c. 24, nailor by trade - runaway from Samuel Bowls, of Phila., blacksmith [8/22]

M'COY, Neal, Scotch servant, age c. 24, joiner by trade - runaway from John Sherburn, of Phila. [8/22]

CHENEY, Thomas, Welsh servant, age c. 21 - runaway from Stephen Onion, of the Principio Ironworks, Cecil Co., Maryland [8/22]

GIBEONS, David, Irish servant, age c. 25 - same as above

WENTWORTH, Benjamin - drowned some days ago when he fell from a bridge into the Cocheco River in New Hampshire - Boston dispatch of Aug. 5 [8/29]

BRANDRIFF, Timothy, servant, born at Cape May, age 23, weaver by trade - runaway from John Rutter, at the Ironworks at Manatawney [8/29]

DENHAM, Thomas, dec'd - accounts with estate to be settled with Clement Plumfield, of Phila., by order of Richard Martin, executor [9/5]

MACK CELLICK, Peter, Irish servant, age c. 20 - runaway from Henry Pugh, of Merion, Phila. Co. [9/5]

HODGES, Joseph, servant, age c. 19 - runaway from Joseph Taylor, Jr., of Kennet Twp., Chester Co. [9/12]

JONES, Morgan, Welsh servant, age c. 30 - runaway from Thomas Boels, of Freehold, Monmouth Co. [9/26]

RENALDS, Robert, late of Phila., merchant, dec'd - accounts with estate to be settled with Ralph Asheton and Andrew Bradford, executors [9/26]

DICKINSON, Jonathan, dec'd - real estate in Chester Co. for sale
at house of Ruth Hoskin in Borough of Chester (10/3)

WHITE, Edward, servant, shoemaker by trade - runaway from John
Wheldon, of Phila., cordwainer (10/3)

WEST, Robert, servant, age c. 19 - runaway from Capt. John Manlester, of Somerset Co., Maryland (10/17)

SHADICK, Edward, English servant, age c. 32, who has been about
17 years in America - runaway from James Reid, of Freehold,
taking with him a horse belonging to Adam Crosby, of Freehold (11/21)

RICHARDSON, Joshua, late of Phila., dec'd - accounts with estate
to be settled with Richard Preston and George House, executors (11/21)

NEWMAN, George, Irish servant, age c. 30, shoemaker - runaway
from John Bayley, cordwainer (11/21)

BRAZIL, Michael, Irish servant, age c. 30, shoemaker - same as
above

BELL, John, servant, age c. 40, bricklayer - runaway from John
Austin, of Kent Co., Maryland, gunsmith (11/28)

WILSON, Samuel, servant, age 26 - same as above

CALLSEY, William, servant, born in Ireland, age c. 20 - runaway
from William M'Dowell, of White Clay Creek, New-Castle Co.
(11/28)

CONRON, Edward, Irish servant, age c. 21, who pretends to be a
barber surgeon - runaway from the ship Borden, William Herbert commander (12/5)

RAWLINSON, Mary, servant, who has changed her name to Sarah Wood -
runaway from Andrew Cornish, of Conescogoe, Chester Co.
(12/18)

1729

LOWE, Nicholas, Esq., Member of Council, Agent and Receiver of
Revenues in Maryland - died last week at his house in St.
Mary's Co., Maryland - Annapolis dispatch of Dec. 3 (1/14)

HALL, Aquila, of Baltimore Co. - reported to have been shot and
killed on Dec. 25 by one of his Negroes who had run away
(1/14)

WILSON, Mr., a carpenter - about a month ago fell from the roof
of a house he was building in Annapolis and died - Annapolis dispatch of Dec. 31 [1/14]

SUTTON, Josias, of Cecil Co., Maryland - died about a month ago
when gravel caved in on him - Annapolis dispatch of Dec. 31 -
[1/14]

BUTLER, John, servant, age c. 20 - runaway from the brigantine
Thomas and Sarah, William Mason commander [1/28]

TERNAN (or TEENAN ?), Thody, Irish servant, tailor by trade,
age c. 36 - runaway from William Farmer Terbury, of Phila.
[2/11]

PIDGEON, Joseph, dec'd - his plantation on the Delaware River,
about 3 miles below the falls, for sale by Mrs. Anne Pidgeon
[2/11]; accounts with estate to be settled with the widow
[who is executrix] or with Thomas Biles [6/5]

HARRIS, John, servant, age c. 19 - runaway from Humphrey Day, of
Gloucester Co., West New Jersey [2/25]

STURGUS, Joseph, of Phila., servant, saddletree-maker - runaway
from Caleb Ransted, of Phila., turner [2/25]

BULLIN, James, dec'd - accounts with estate to be settled with
Richard Crukshank, of New-Castle upon Delaware, administrator [3/27]

COOK, Richard, servant, born in Staffordshire, brick-mason by
trade - runaway from Mrs. Aves French and William Battell
[3/27]

DUNCAN, Bridget, Irish servant - same as above

LOWRY, Thomas, Irish servant, age c. 23, shoemaker by trade -
runaway from Samuel Warne, of Middle-Town, Monmouth Co.,
New Jersey [3/17]

WILLIAMS, Joseph, a Mulatto, age c. 24 - runaway, together with
a white woman named Bridget whom he calls his wife, from
Thomas John, of New-Castle Co., farmer [4/3]

EDGCOME, Nathaniel, late of Phila., dec'd - accounts with estate
to be settled with Nathaniel Edgcome, son of the dec'd [4/3]

CHIT, Thomas, servant, age c. 35, butcher by trade - runaway from
Zachariah Hutchins, of Phila., butcher [4/10]

DAVID, James, age c. 30 - runaway from house of Thomas Wilson, of New-Hanover, Burlington Co., taking with him a horse belonging to William Wilson (son of Thomas) (4/10)

RICHARDS, Thomas, servant, born in London, tailor by trade - runaway from John Hutchinson, at the falls of Delaware (4/17)

SNAGS, Richard, servant, age c. 30 - runaway from William Iddings, of Nantmeal (4/17)

ALDRIDGE, Mrs., wife of John Aldridge - killed, as was one of her children, by a Negro, who was executed for his crime at Marlborough on Friday last - Annapolis dispatch of April 21 (5/8)

MATTHEW, Roger, of Baltimore Co., Maryland (brother-in-law of Edward Hall) - his Negro slave, age c. 23, was committed to Burlington Goal for stealing (5/8)

BROOKS, John, English servant, blacksmith by trade - runaway from John Copson, of North East, Maryland (5/8)

MABBOT, Richard, servant - runaway from ship Salisbury; reward offered if he is brought to Thomas Sharp or Samuel Bromage (5/15)

RIGBY, George, servant - same as above

TRENCHARD, George, dec'd - his plantation on Alloways Creek, about 3 miles from Salem, offered for sale by Mrs. Mary Trenchard, executrix (5/29)

SLADANE, Alexander, servant - runaway from James Chalmers, of Phila. (6/5)

SERGISSON, William, age c. 20 - runaway from Samuel Worthington, of Phila. (6/5)

TUTHILL, Capt. James, late of Phila., dec'd - accounts with estate to be settled with Joseph Harwood, of Phila., executor (6/5)

WALKER, Thomas, from Northumberland, England, servant, age c. 25 - runaway from Capt. Thomas Colvill, of Cecil Co., Maryland (6/19)

EYRES, William, servant, age 21 - same as above

ROBERTS, Thomas, servant - runaway from Thomas Stackhouse, of Bucks Co. (6/19)

SMITH, Thomas, young contracted servant, stocking-weaver by trade, lately employed as usher in Free School in Prince George's Co. - runaway from James Denune, master of the school (6/19)

BURK, John, servant, age c. 18 - runaway from Thomas Arnold,
    of Bradford, Chester Co. [6/19]

COWNDEN, James, servant, age c. 25 - runaway from Thomas Thorn-
    berry, of Bradford, Chester Co. [6/19]

SHENNAN, John, Irishman, age c. 28 -escaped from William Read,
    Sheriff of New-Castle Co. [7/3]

GRANGER, John, servant - runaway from George Shad, periwig-
    maker, in Front St., Phila. [7/3]

ROBERTS, James, indented servant, age c. 20, paper-maker by
    trade, West-countryman who has been about one year in
    America - runaway from William Bradford's paper-mill at
    Elizabeth Town, New Jersey [7/10]

BLOWDEN, John, servant, age c. 22, shoemaker by trade - runaway
    from Arthur Wells, of Phila. [7/10]

ADAMS, Thomas, late of Phila., innholder, dec'd - accounts with
    estate to be settled with John Bringhurst, of Phila., ad-
    ministrator [7/10]

HODGINS, _____, Irish servant, age c. 28 - runaway from Thomas
    Williams, of New-Castle [7/17]

GUEST, Edward, servant, age c. 22 - runaway from William Ritten-
    housen, of Germantown, paper-maker [7/17]

DAVIS, Thomas, servant, age c. 21 - runaway from Jeremiah El-
    freth, of Phila.; reward is offered for return of servant
    to his master, to John Elfreth, of Bristol, or James Sykes
    at New-Castle [8/7]

GARDNER, Job, a prisoner, born in Scotland, age between 20 and 30 -
    runaway from John Baldwin, High Sheriff of Cecil Co., Md.
    [8/7]

DEMAICK, John, young English servant - same as above

SCOBELL, Henry, dec'd - lands belonging to his estate in Twp. of
    Passian, about 2 miles from Phila., for sale by Charles
    Read and Benjamin Paschall, of Phila. [8/14]

SPROGELL, Lodowick Christian, late of Phila., dec'd - real estate
    near Schuylkill and Germantown for sale by Catharine Spro-
    gell, executrix [8/14]

STACK, Henry, servant - runaway from Benjamin Acton, of Salem
[9/11]

GUNNITT, Isaac, Indian servant - same as above

HILL, Richard, Esq., born in Maryland [whose wife was the widow
of John Delaval and eldest daughter of Thomas Lloyd, Esq.,
once Governor of Pennsylvania], Member of Council, divers
times Speaker of the House and one of the provincial judges -
buried Friday last in Phila. [9/11]

FISHBOURN, William, Esq. - married Sept. 11 in Phila. to Miss
Jane Roberts [9/11]

TEAGUE, Elizabeth, dec'd - accounts with estate to be settled
with Francis Knowles and Henry Hodge, executors [9/11]

BURNET, Governor of Massachusetts - died there Sept. 17 in his
42nd year [9/18]

MACK GUIER, Felix, Irish servant, age c 19 or 20 - runaway from
John Van Horne, of Piscatus [9/18]

REYLY, John, Irish servant, age c. 19 or 20, blacksmith by trade -
same as above

PROWSE, Joseph, age c. 20 - escaped from Phila. Goal [9/18]

MITCHEL, James, who pretends to be a sailor - same as above

BARNHAM, Albert, servant, a sailor - runaway from William Cawtheen, Minister of St. John's Parish in Baltimore Co.,Md.
[9/18]

HEATON, John, servant, age c. 23, who speaks with a Yorkshire
accent - same as above

CHARLTON, Josia, servant, age 27, tailor by trade - runaway from
Ralph Smith, of Annapolis, Maryland [9/28]

HANNA, Andrew, servant, born in Scotland, age c. 21 - runaway from
William Parks, of Annapolis, printer; reward if returned to
his master or to Mr. Marshall, Postmaster in Boston, or william Bradford, of New York, printer, or Andrew Bradford, of
Phila., printer [9/28]

MORGAN, James, apprentice - runaway from Samuel Eastbourn, of Sold-
bury, Bucks Co. [9/28]

BRYAN, Thomas, servant - runaway from Simon Warner, of Alloways
Creek, Salem Co. [10/2]

SPARROW, John, servant - same as above

Corsey, Negro slave, age c. 35 - runaway from Peter Galloway, of Maryland (10/9)

WILSON, James, servant, weaver by trade - runaway from Widow Earlington, of Rockey Hall, East New Jersey (10/23)

BROADEY, Thomas, servant - same as above

CHRISTOPHER, Aristoblus, age c. 30, shipwright by trade - broke out of Burlington Goal (10/23)

MALATO, John, sge c. 40, carpenter by trade - same as above

KENNY, Edward, servant, age c. 18 - runaway from Simon Hadly, Esq., of New-Castle Co. (11/13)

LAMB, Thomas - broke out of Newtown Goal (11/20)

GARLAND, Edward, who pretends to be mate of a ship or a ship-carpenter - same as above

TESDALL, George, labourer - same as above

Hazard, formerly called Robin, a Negro, age c. 15, imported last spring from Barbados by Robert Edgell, merchant - runaway from Richard Brockdon, of Phila., innholder (11/27)

VIPPIN, William, Irish servant, weaver by trade - runaway from Evan Thomas, of Willis Town, Chester Co. (11/27)

DOD, Amy, Irish servant maid, age c. 25 - runaway from Edward Brooks, of Phila., butcher (11/27)

FLORY, Thomas, who died during passage from Ireland to Pa. on board the ship Drogheda Merchant - Capt. Mercer, accused of the murder of Flory, is acquitted by court held in Phila. at the end of November (12/4)

EDWARDS, John, servant, age c. 17 - runaway from John Best, of Chester Co., carpenter (12/4)

MACQUIRE, John, servant, age c. 20 - runaway from Widow Anne John's of the Welsh Tract, New-Castle Co. (12/9)

EGLESTON, Mr., of Newtown, Mass., three-year-old child of - burned to death the latter part of last week - Boston dispatch of Nov. 27 (12/23)

CUSHING, Nathaniel (son of the Hon. Judge Cushing, of Situate),
educated at Harvard, employed in the Secretary's Office and
as Clerk of the Council - died Saturday last in Boston in
his 21st year - Boston dispatch of Nov. 27 (12/23)

BURNSIDES, James, Irishman, age c. 26, shoemaker by trade - broke
out of Burlington Goal (12/23)

Peter, Negro slave, age c. 30 - runaway from Christian Peters,
of Cecil Co., Maryland (12/23)

1730

BRODWAY, Mary - died Saturday last in Phila., aged 100 years and
2 days (1/6)

GILLIAM, William, servant, blacksmith by trade - runaway from
the John Galley, of Dublin, Richard Murphy captain (1/6)

MURRY, Thomas, Irish servant - runaway from Jonathan Cooper, of
Wrights Town, Bucks Co. (1/14)

COCK, Thomas, tailor by trade - murdered by a Negro, who was tried,
convicted and executed last Saturday at Perth Amboy - Perth
Amboy dispatch of Jan. 14 (1/20)

PROUSE, James, age c. 19, born at Brentford, Middlesex Co., Eng.
(son of a corporal in the late Lord Oxford's Regt. of Horse),
who came to Pennsylvania at the age of 12 - condemned to
death but pardoned (1/27)

MITCHEL, James, born at Antrim, Ireland, who at age of 13 was
apprenticed to a bookbinder, served him 4 years, was pressed
on board a man-of-war, the Berwick, returned to England and
then came to America - was arrested on the charge that he
robbed Mr. George Sheed, was condemned to death and then
pardoned (1/27)

DICKINSON, Jonathan, Esq., dec'd - his real estate to be sold
(2/19)

BARTAM, Joseph, servant, age c. 30, tailor by trade - runaway
from the ironworks at French Creek, Chester Co. (2/24)

FORD, Nathaniel, servant, age c. 25, carpenter by trade - same as
above

THOMPSON, George, servant from Yorkshire, age c. 40, carpenter or
wheelwright, imported from York Goal into Pennsylvania by
Capt. Allen Giles - runaway from John Campbell, of Bohemia
Manor, Cecil Co., Maryland (3/3)

MALDIN, Daniel, servant, age c. 22, imported from York Goal into
Pennsylvania by Capt. Allen Giles - runaway from John Winter-
berry, of Cecil Co., Maryland (3/3)

ORPWOOS, Edmond, late of Oxford Twp., dec'd - accounts with estate
to be settled with Francis Knowles or Thomas Gilpin, executors (3/3)

Jenny, Negro slave, age c. 18 - runaway from Martyn Jarvis, at
the Sign of the Hat in Hand, in Second St., Phila. (3/5)

KELSEY, William - executed Saturday last at New-Castle for burglary and burning the New-Castle Goal - New-Castle dispatch
of March 9 (3/11)

KNIGHT, John, late of Phila., dec'd - accounts with estate to be
settled with Hannah Knight, widow and administratrix of the
dec'd (3/11)

OOWELL, William, late of Phila., merchant, dec'd - accounts with
estate to be settled with Simon Edgell, executor (3/19)

GOODMAN, Richard and Samuel, brothers, one a carpenter and the
other a sawyer - runaways from the ship Hume, James Atking
commander, lying in the South River (4/2)

MEDCALF, Joseph, farmer, in his 75th year - married March 10 at
Medfield to Mrs. Hannah Fisher, in her 73rd year (4/9)

ATKINS, Robert, merchant - died Tuesday last at Perth Amboy, New
Jersey - Perth Amboy dispatch of April 4 (4/9)

RICE, Henry, servant, weaver by trade - runaway from Thomas
Robinson, of Solesbury, Bucks Co. (4/16)

HOLLAND, Edward, servant, who formerly lived with John Malts-
bury, at High St. Ferry - runaway from Samuel Throgmorton,
of Freehold, Monmouth Co., New Jersey (4/23)

FLEMING, Arthur, Irish servant, age c. 17 - runaway from Joseph
Lyon, shipwright (5/7)

HEOFORD, John, servant - runaway from White and Taylor (5/14)

CALBERT, Hon. Edward Henry, Esq., second brother of the Lord Proprietor of Maryland, President of the Council, Commissary
General of Maryland - died Friday last at Annapolis - Annapolis dispatch of April 28 (5/21)

CARROLL, Eleanor, of Annapolis, a young maiden lady - died Sunday last at Annapolis - Annapolis dispatch of April 28 (5/21)

GRIMES, John, servant, age c. 21 - runaway from William Parks, of Annapolis, printer (5/28)

MAC CONNEL, Alexander, Irish servant - runaway from Joseph England, of Nottingham, Chester Co. (6/4)

Jenny (daughter of Dr. Cuffy, a free Negro) - runaway from Martyn Jarvis, of Phila. (6/4)

NORRIS, John, servant, age c. 24 - runaway from William Smith, of Phila., shoemaker (6/11)

CURRY, James, apprentice, age c. 19 - runaway (in company with John Norris) from Mrs. Paris, of Phila., brass-founder (6/11)

WILLINGS, David, Irish servant - runaway from Joseph Britain, of Nottingham Twp., Burlington Co., West New Jersey (6/18)

MACKMANNERS, Constantine, Irish servant, tailor by trade - same as above

GRIFFIN, Robert, Irish servant, tailor by trade - runaway from Hannah Pritchett, of Phila. (6/25)

James, Negro slave, age c. 40, who formerly belonged to Sir William Keith - runaway from Stephen Onion & Co., of Principio Ironworks in Maryland (7/9)

MAC GINNIS, James, Irish servant, age 21 - runaway from Richard Sunly, near Wrights Town, Bucks Co. (7/16)

Jack, Negro slave, age c. 25 - runaway from John Plumley, of Bucks Co. (7/23)

BRAISER, Jane, covenanted servant - runaway from Charles Sandiford, lately from Barbados (7/23)

SULLIVAN, Timothy, servant - runaway from James Johnson, near White Clay Creek (7/30)

FORREST, Thomas, servant, age c. 30, skinner by trade - runaway (supposedly in company with William Varnall, absconding debtor) from Jonathan Fisher, of Phila., glover (7/30)

SHIPPEN, Esther, dec'd (devisee in trust of Edward Shippen, late of Phila., merchant, dec'd) - real estate to be sold by Samuel Powell and Samuel Preston, executors of estate of said Esther (8/6)

Pompey, Indian slave, age c. 30, who formerly belonged to Sir
   William Keith - runaway from Stephen Onion, of Principio
   Ironworks (8/6)

HARRIS, Thomas, servant, hatter by trade - runaway from Nicholas Roach, of Phila., hatter (8/20)

PORTER, Abraham, lately dec'd - large tract of land in Gloucester Co. in New Jersey for sale by executors, Mahlon
   Stacy, Jonathan Wright and Thomas Scattergood, of Burlington (8/27)

HUTCHINSON, Sarah - has eloped from her husband, William Hutchinson, of Phila., sawyer (9/10)

BRADSHAW, Samuel, dec'd - real estate in Phila. to be sold by
   Peter Smith (9/24)

HAMBLETON, Michael, servant, age c. 40 - runaway from Robert
   Chapman, of Chesterfield, Burlington Co. (10/1)

CUMMINGS, Robert, Scotch servant, age c. 21, joiner by trade -
   runaway from John Copson, of North-East (10/1)

GIBBS (alias GRIFFITTS), John, servant, age c. 19 - runaway from
   the ship John Frigate, Thomas Smith master (10/1)

SMITH, John, servant, age c. 21, weaver by trade - runaway from
   Peter Rode, of Burlington, brewer (10/1)

HEWLINGS, Mr., a young man - accidentally shot and killed himself near Darby (10/15)

TAMERLIN, Thomas, an East Indian servant - runaway from Charles
   Blakey, at the Sign of the Brigantine, in Water St., Phila.
   (10/15)

DONNE, William - Saturday last in Mayor's Court in Phila. sentenced to be whipped for assault and battery on Frances,
   wife of Roger Thomas (11/5)

CASH, Martha, wife of Leonard Cash - convicted in Mayor's Court
   in Phila. of theft (11/5)

BRADLEY, Jonathan - on Nov. 2 found drowned in a ditch near William Hudson's orchard, in High St., Phila. (11/5)

SEAMAN, Thomas - sentenced to death at Court of Oyer and Terminer in Phila. for burglary and felony (11/5)

CRUMP, John - acquitted in Court of Oyer and Terminer in Phila.
   of charge of murdering his wife Margaret (11/5)

CARTER, Henry, servant, age c. 23, who formerly belonged to John
   Budd - runaway from John Warren, of Wicake, within a mile
   of Phila. [11/5]

DONAHE, Michael, servant, age c. 19 - runaway from Joseph Foster,
   of Bibery Twp., Phila. Co. [11/12]

HALL, Richard, Irish servant, age c. 22 - runaway from James Armitage, Esq., of New-Castle Co. on Delaware [11/19]

SMITH, James, servant, who formerly lived in Newcastle, described as "pretty elderly" - runaway from Robert Cumming, of
   Trenton [11/19]

GLEAVES, Thomas, 8-month-old child of - accidentally burned to
   death in New York City on Wed. last - New York dispatch of
   Nov. 22 [11/26]

ALLISON, Thomas, of New York City - died there Wed. last - New
   York dispatch of Nov. 22 [11/26]

LONG, John [servant of Jonathan Jones, of Kingsess] - accidentally
   drowned last Sunday in Cobb's Creek [12/3]

TYLER, William, born at Long-Ashen, near Bristol in Somersetshire,
   who came to America and is supposed to have been servant to
   George Bowles in Phila. - if he goes to the printer he will
   be sent home if he so desires [12/3]

CORRY, Elizabeth, of Dunory or Chew Magna, Co. of Somerset, who
   came to America, supposed to be given account of by Edward
   Cook, a cooper, living with John Strend, cooper, of Brandywine Hundred in New-Castle Co. - if she goes to the printer
   she may be sent home to her friends [12/3]

HILTON, Andrew, servant, age c. 30 - runaway [in company of Anne
   Pearce, an English woman] from George Parker, near Phila.,
   butcher [12/8]

ENGLISH, Richard, servant, age c. 23, native of Cecil Co., Md. -
   runaway from William Rumsey, of Phila. [12/8]

FORTESCUE, Alexander - found dead last Saturday in a shallop in
   the harbor of Phila. [12/15]

STEVENS, Hon. James, Surveyor-General of North America - died
   Tuesday last in Boston - Boston dispatch of Nov. 30 [12/22]

1731

THOMAS, Elizabeth, of Blockley Twp., age 75 - died Sat. last (1/5)

WENTWORTH, John, Lt.-Gov. of New Hampshire - died Sunday last - Boston dispatch of Dec. 14 (1/12)

ELLERY, Capt., of Cape Ann - drowned "yesterday was three Weeks" in wreck of his schooner when bound to Casco Bay - Boston dispatch of Dec. 14 (1/12)

DOWNING, John, Irish servant, age c. 23 - runaway from John Hood, of Phila., shoemaker (1/12)

Oppekhersa, an Indian King - died lately in the Jerseys (1/19)

RALPH, Joseph - found drowned Thursday last at end of one of the wharves in Phila. (1/19)

POTTS, David, dec'd - John Kensey elected Representative for Phila. in his place (1/19)

SCHUYLER, Arent, proprietor of a rich copper mine in the Jerseys - died Jan. 12 (1/26)

SHIPPEN, William (youngest son of Edward Shippen, Esq., dec'd), late one of the Commissioners of Property in Pennsylvania - died Feb. 1 in Phila. (2/2)

HILL, Richard, Esq., dec'd - accounts with estate to be settled with Lloyd Zachary and Mordecai Lloyd, executors (2/2)

CASH, Caleb, Sr. - his wife, Alice, has eloped from him; debts owed to Caleb Cash, Sr., may be paid to his son, Caleb Cash, Jr. (2/2)

CAHOONE, James, servant, age c. 18 - runaway from Hugh Durborow, of Kent Co. on Delaware; reward for his capture is offered by Hugh Durborow, Jr. (2/2)

ROBERTS, John, dec'd - accounts with estate to be settled with the executors, John White and John Cadwalader (2/16)

PRICHARD, Henry, servant, age c. 22 - runaway from James Wilson, of the Northern Liberties of Phila. (2/24)

DARBY, Francis, Irish servant, age c. 22 - runaway from the snow Dolphin (3/2)

HUGHES, William, English servant, age c. 24 - same as above

TADLOCK, Edward, of Kent Co. on Delaware - on Feb. 14 was lost in the woods near Swatarow Creek and perished from the cold (3/11)

HENDRICKS, James, of Lancaster Co. - on Feb. 25 accidentally
shot and killed his son, aged c. 24 (3/11)

DEALE, Thomas, Irish servant, age c. 22 - runaway from Peter
Wren, of Woodbridge, Middlesex Co., East New Jersey (3/11)

BURREL, Capt., a pilot of Phila. - drowned last week, together
with his son and a servant when fishing in a canoe (3/26)

LLOYD, David, Esq., Chief Justice of the Province of Pennsylvania -
died Tuesday last at his seat in Chester (4/8)

LESTER, William, servant - runaway from John Bayly, of Phila.,
cordwainer (4/8)

ROBERTS, Owen, late of Phila., dec'd - real estate in Chester Co.
for sale by his widow, Ann Roberts (4/22)

BARCLAY, John, Esq. (brother of Robert Barclay, Laird of Ure, in
Scotland, the famous Quaker who wrote Barclay's Appollogy) -
died last week at Amboy, N.J., at an advanced age (4/29)

FELL, Capt. John, master of the Cololina - drowned, along with
his crew, when the ship, bound from Boston to Whitehaven,
was wrecked Feb. 9 in Bantry Bay, Ireland (5/6)

ORANGE, Robert, of Boston - accidentally killed there Friday
last - Boston dispatch of April 15 (5/6)

SMITH, Ralph - drowned Saturday last when going from Phila. to
Delaware Falls (5/6)

WINTHROP, Madam Elizabeth (widow of the late John Winthrop, Gov.
of Connecticut) - died April 24 in her 79th year and was
buried in New London on April 26 (5/13)

BRINDLE, Alexander, Irish servant, age c. 22, weaver by trade -
runaway from Antill Deaver, at the head of Bush River, Baltimore Co., Maryland; in his company went Samuel Brown, an
Englishman, who pretends to be a sailor (5/13)

MAYNARD, Samuel, gentleman, lately dec'd - his executors are
cited to exhibit his will (5/27)

Tobey, Negro slave, age c. 35, who formerly belonged to Joseph
Pidgeon - runaway from Joseph Lynn, of Phila., shipwright
(6/3)

FRENCH, Thomas, servant, age c. 22 - runaway from Thomas Tatnall,
of Chester Co., near Darby (6/3)

BENJAMIN, Mr., of Watertown, Mass. - drowned near the bridge on
Monday last - Boston dispatch of May 27 (6/10)

HANCOCK, Robert, age c. 20 - runaway from the sloop Maryland, of Boston, Edward Sunderland master (6/10)

TELLES, Charles, dec'd - accounts with estate to be settled with Stephen Delancey, administrator, or with Peter Evans, attorney for Delancey (6/10)

DARBY, Francis, servant, age c. 22 - runaway from Thomas Davis, of Bucks Co. (6/10)

BURNET, William, Governor of New York and New Jersey - directed in his will that he be buried next to his wife Mary if he died in New York (6/17)

DAMSEL, Henry, servant - runaway from William Nichols, of Calan, Chester Co., turner (6/17)

M'NAHME, Sarah, servant, age c. 20 - runaway from Joseph Richards, of Phila. (6/24)

GARRETT, Amos, Esq., of Annapolis - his houses and lots there for sale by Amos Woodward and John Galloway, empowered to sell the property by Mrs. Mary Woodward and Mrs. Elizabeth Ginn, of London, England, widows (7/1)

SERGENT, Joseph, of Almsbury, Mass., twelve-year-old daughter of - shot and killed Sunday last by ten-year-old son of Sergent's second wife - Boston dispatch of June 17 (7/8)

CURREN, George, Irish servant - runaway from David Davis, of Goshen, Chester Co. (7/8)

HANSON, Hester (wife of John Hanson, formerly of Upper Dublin, Phila. Co., but now of the City of Phila.) - has eloped from her husband (7/8)

POTTER, Mr., of Concord, Mass. - burned to death June 20 in the conflagration of his house (7/15)

HALL, Joseph, dec'd - plantation at Tacony, near Frankfort, for sale by his executors, Thomas Rutter and Isaac Leech (7/15)

PLUMLEY, Mathew, servant, age c. 19 - runaway from Michael Webster, of Baltimore Co., Maryland (7/15)

ASHMORE, Elizabeth, servant - same as above

WOTTSON, Mary, servant - same as above

WEST, John, servant, whitesmith by trade - runaway from Antell Deaver, of Baltimore Co. (7/15)

TOMPSON, George, age c. 21, shoemaker by trade - runaway from
John Gordon, of Freehold, Twp. of Middletown, East New
Jersey (7/29)

BORDMAN, George, sailor - runaway from ship John Galley, John
Ball commander (7/29)

GILLING, John, sailor - same as above

BAYLEY, Andrew, age between 30 and 40, of Kingsfield, near Brookfield, Mass. - died there last week when hunting (7/29)

GWIN, William Laughlain, servant, age c. 24 - runaway from John
Radford, of Shrewsbury, Monmouth Co., New Jersey (8/26)

TINTSON, Duke, servant, age c. 35, a West-country man, who lately arrived from Nevis - runaway; reward for his capture
offered by Andrew Johnston, merchant, and Robert King,
Esq., both of Perth Amboy, New Jersey (9/2)

JOHNSTON, Col. John (son of Dr. Johnston) - died Monday last in
Monmouth Co., New Jersey (9/9)

REED, Peter, Irish servant, age c. 29, sadler by trade - runaway from William Burge, of Phila. (9/9)

ROE, Stephen, servant, age c. 20, barber and peruke-maker by
trade - runaway from George Sheed, peruke-maker, in Front
St., Phila. (9/9)

TEARNEY, Patrick, Irish servant, age c. 22, tailor by trade -
runaway from James Lewis, of Phila. (9/9)

OWEN, Obediah, age c. 25, a New Englander - broke out of New-
town Goal, Bucks Co. (9/23)

BEMAN, George, Irishman, age c. 24, a felon - same as above

STADING, Francis, Dutch servant - runaway from Samuel Johnson,
of Phila., painter (9/30)

MAC FERSON, Capt. John, age c. 22, born in Dublin, whose parents
now live in Rotterdam - Tuesday last sentenced to death in
Phila. for piracy (10/21 and 28)

GREEN, Paul - same as above

THOMPSON, John - same as above

HARNEY, John - same as above

COLE, John - same as above

CROSLEY, Samuel - Tuesday last fell overboard near Pennypack
    from a passage-boat going from Phila. to Burlington and
    was drowned (10/21)

WOOD, John, servant, age c. 22, born in Birmingham, England,
    carpenter and sawyer by trade, who came from Bristol in
    1730 - runaway from Isaac Norris, of Fairhill (10/28)

MAGUIRE, Thomas, Irish servant, age c. 20 - runaway from
    Richard Thomas, of Whiteland Twp., Chester Co. (10/28)

PIXLEY, Thomas, of Westfield, Mass. - died there Oct. 5 -
    Boston dispatch of Oct. 29 (11/11)

KEHIND, William, servant, age c. 18, a sailor - runaway from
    Edward Clayton, of Bradford Twp., Chester Co. (11/25)

SEWELL, Jonathan, of Boston, merchant - died there Nov. 21
    (12/2)

TODD, Alexander, of Boston, sollicitor - same as above

RICHARDSON, Thomas, servant, age c. 24, tailor by trade - run-
    away from John Hutchinson, of Bucks Co. (12/2)

JAYNE, Richard (who married the Widow Vining), at the Sign of
    the Ship on William Fishbourn's Wharf, in Phila. - all those
    having demands on him are asked to bring in their accounts,
    as he plans to leave the province (12/9)

CAMPION, George, late of Phila., innholder, dec'd - accounts with
    estate to be settled with Mary Campion, widow and ad-
    ministratrix (12/9)

1732

TYLER, Rachel (wife of John Tyler, of Allowes Creek, Salem Co.,
    West New Jersey) - has eloped from her husband (1/4)

GRAHAM, Dr. Hugh, late of Phila., dec'd - persons indebted to
    the estate on account of physic or surgery are to pay Pat-
    rick Baird (1/18); other accounts with estate to be set-
    tled with George M'Call, executor (1/18)

SCOBEL, Henry, dec'd - real estate to be sold at the house of
    Moses Cox, in Moyamensin Twp., by Charles Read, executor
    (1/18)

RASBY, John, servant, a Dutchman, age c. 26 - runaway from
    Daniel West, Master-Collier of Principio Ironworks in
    Maryland (2/1)

PEARSON, Cerlius, servant, age c. 30, hatter by trade - runaway
from ship Mary (lying at Mr. Clymer's wharf, near the end
of Market St, in Phila.), James Brown master (2/29)

MOORE, Prudence (wife of John Moore, Sr., of Thornbury, Chester
Co.) - has eloped from her husband (2/29)

OWEN, Griffith, of Phila., practitioner in physic - died Thursday last in Phila. (3/7)

M'FERSON, Capt. John, condemned pirate - escaped March 9 from
Phila. Goal (3/16)

WELCH, Philip, servant, age c. 19 - runaway from James Ward,
of Monington Twp., Salem Co., New Jersey (3/16)

HARMAN, William, late of Upper Dublin, Phila. Co., dec'd - mills
and land in Dublin Twp., land in Germantown and also land
near Gloucester, West New Jersey, to be sold by Richard Martin, executor (3/16)

BOYD, James, Irish servant - runaway from Henry Peirce, Esq.,
of Concord, Chester Co. (3/16)

WILDMAN, Capt. - drowned Feb. 15, along with his crew, when his
ship, bound from New York to Boston, struck on the Middle
Ground (3/23)

DORCHESTER, John - frozen to death Feb. 15 when travelling to
Springfield, Mass. (3/23)

UMPHRYS, William, of Hempstead, L.I. - his wife last week gave
birth to a daughter; said child's grandfather has a grandmother yet living - New York dispatch of March 27 (3/30)

JOHNSON, John, dec'd - real estate in Newtown, Bucks Co., for
sale by his executors, Euclydus Longshore and Joseph Wildman (3/30)

TAILER, Hon. William, Lt.-Gov. of Massachusetts - buried March 8
in Dorchester, Mass. (4/6)

TIBBIT, Jo. and Tamsen his wife - released on bail at Exeter, N.H.,
on charge of counterfeiting (4/6)

BRIGGS, John, of Burlington Co. - crushed to death Thursday last
when felling a tree (4/6)

HIGGINS, Susannah (wife of Joseph Higgins, of Bucks Co., mason) -
has eloped from her husband (4/6)

COLLET, Simon, servant - runaway from Col. Spotswood, of Spotsyl-
vania, Virginia (4/13)

BICKLEY, Abraham, dec'd - large tracts of land in New Jersey for
sale by his executors, William Hudson, James Steel, George
Fitzwater and Samuel Bickley (4/20)

DEREHAM, Richard (son of Sir Richard Dereham), who was sent to
the West Indies about 20 years ago and has been seen in
Maryland and Pennsylvania - a legacy of £500 Sterling has
been left him (4/20)

THOMAS, Rece, Welsh servant, age c. 30 - runaway from Peter Bond,
of Baltimore Co., Maryland (4/27)

BEALL, George, convict servant, age c. 19 or 20 - same as above

GREY, John, of Harwich, Barnstable Co., Mass. - died last week
when thrown from his horse - Boston dispatch of April 20
(5/4)

BODGE, Mr., of Charlestown, Mass. - died April 12 when fishing
in his canoe (5/4)

WHITMAN, Mr., of North End of Boston, four-year-old child of -
died Sunday last from fall from a window - Boston dispatch
of April 20 (5/4)

GOWEN, John (alias William Taylor), servant - runaway from James
Duncan, of Hackinsack, New Jersey (5/4)

CARPENTER, Nicodemus, servant, age c. 20 - runaway from John Rigley, of Phila. (5/11)

FRENCH, Thomas, English servant, who has been a sailor - runaway
from Thomas Tatnall, of Chester Co. (5/11)

YOUNG, William - drowned Saturday last in the Delaware (5/18)

WITTISIN, William - hanged himself in Twp. of Whitemarsh (5/18)

HALFPENNY, William - murdered near Duck Creek, Kent Co. on Delaware, by Henry Smith (5/25)

CAMBRIDGE, Giles, late of Phila., shopkeeper, dec'd - accounts
with estate to be settled with Alexander Wooddrop, Peter
Lloyd or Samuel Powel, Jr., who are empowered by Sarah Cambridge, widow and executrix of the dec'd (5/25)

OWEN, Dr. Griffith, late of Phila., dec'd - accounts with estate
to be settled with Anne Whipten, executrix (6/1)

M'KINZEY, John, Scotch servant, age c. 30, who has been a soldier in Flanders and speaks Dutch and French - runaway from
Peter Cuff in Phila. (6/1)

BURGAIN, Patrick, Irish servant, age c. 20 - runaway from Jacob
Wright and Richard Anderson, of Whiteland Twp., Chester Co.
(6/15)

FLOOD, John, Irish servant, age c. 20, weaver by trade - same as
above

LEVIT, William, of Exeter, age c. 13 - accidentally shot and
killed Tuesday last by Samuel Scribner, of Exeter, age
c. 13; Scribner's father had been killed about a year before in a similar accident - Boston dispatch of June 19
(6/29)

PINTARD, Anthony, late of Shrewsbury, New Jersey, dec'd - house
where he lived to be sold by his executors, John Pintard and
John Searle (9/29)

COPPIN, Thomas, age c. 14 - accidentally killed May 16 in St.
John's Parish by trying to manage a cow - Charlestown, S.C.,
dispatch of May 27 (7/6)

DENNIS, Christopher, of North Edisto - killed last Wednesday by
two men, one named Robinson, the other Michael Cavino -
Charlestown, S.C., dispatch of May 27 (7/6)

CHAMBERLAIN, Peter, of Mansfield, Conn. - drowned there June 9
in the Mill Pond (7/6)

LANDSDOWN, Thomas, a Bristol man, servant, age c. 26, shoemaker
by trade - runaway from Obediah Eldridge, of Phila., cordwainer (7/6)

DORRINGTON, William, servant, age c. 25 - runaway from William
Overthrow, of Waterford Twp., Gloucester Co., New Jersey,
sawyer (7/6)

HAND, Mrs., of Boston - died there July 9 (7/20)

JEMISON, Robert, of Phila., courier - drowned July 10 in the
Schuylkill (7/20)

DUNN, James, Irish servant, age between 30 and 40 - runaway
from Henry Doughty, of Croswicks, Monmouth Co., East New
Jersey (7/20)

M'DONNAL, John - drowned Tuesday last when trying to swim the
Schuylkill on horseback at Roach's Ferry (7/27)

SCANDELAN, John, servant, cooper by trade - runaway from William
Dickie, of East Sudbury, Chester Co. [7/27]

BOYD, James, Irish servant, age c. 28 - runaway from Henry Pierce, Esq., of Concord, Chester Co. [8/3]

FORRESTER, John, servant, age c. 20 - runaway from Jane Newlin,
of Concord, Chester Co. [8/3]

FITZSYMONS, Maynard (son of Norris Fitzsymons, late of Ireland,
dec'd) - has inherited an estate in Ireland (8/10)

RUSH, Thomas, apprentice, age c. 18 - runaway from Joseph Harrison, of Phila., carpenter [8/24]

RYON, James, Irish servant, age c. 24 - runaway from Peter Hatton, of Concord, Chester Co. [8/31]

POLLOCK, Thomas, servant, from North Britain, age c. 22, who pretends to be a shoemaker - runaway from Obadiah Bonsal, of
Darby, Chester Co. [8/31]

CARTER, Hon. Robert, President of the Council of Virginia - died
Aug. 4, 1732, in his 69th year [9/7]

MACKBRIDE, James, servant, age c. 22 - runaway from Eliacom Anderson, living at Trenton Ferry [9/7]

MOOR, Capt. John, in a schooner from New Hampshire - reported
murdered by Negroes on the coast of Guinea [9/14]

JOHNSTON, Dr. John, of Perth Amboy, New Jersey - died there on
Sept. 6 in his 71st year [9/21]

FORDE, Thomas, servant, born at New-Castle in England, of middle
age, who pretends to be a copper-miner - runaway from John
Leacock at Pool Forge, Phila. Co. [9/21]

HAMBLETON, Edward, young Irish servant - runaway from Thomas May-
berry; he ran away with Thomas Forde [9/21]

FRENCH, Jonathan, servant, age c. 25 - runaway from John Clows,
of Makefield, Bucks Co. [10/5]

PASSMORE, William, dec'd - persons indebted to his estate are to
settle accounts with Joshua Fielding, who intends to leave
Pennsylvania [10/5]

ROGERS, Mr., of Pembroke, widower, age c. 43, father of three children - stabbed to death Thursday last at Brantrey, Mass., by
an Indian belonging to Mr. Howard, of Bridgewater - Boston
dispatch of Sept. 14 [10/12]

SHALCROSS, J., Jr. - run over and killed Oct. 9 by his cart when he was going between Phila. and Frankford (10/12)

WHITE, William, servant, age c. 25 - runaway from Hugh Lawson, at the head of Elk River (10/12)

LEADAM, Susannah (wife of John Leadam, of Hampton Twp., Bucks Co.) - has eloped from her husband (10/19)

TAYLOR, Jeremiah, dec'd - his plantation in Kennet, Chester Co., bounding on Brandywine, for sale (10/19)

HAMMETT, Thomas, in prison at Newport, Rhode Island, for the murder of Catherine Cook - escaped Oct. 10 with the aid of his wife (10/25)

MURREY, John, Irish servant, age c. 24 - runaway from Peter Lycon, of Horsham, blacksmith (10/26)

M'GUIRE, William, Irish servant, age c. 24, shoemaker by trade - runaway from Joseph Reyner, of Chester Co., cordwainer (10/26)

WILSON, Richard - executed Thursday last at Boston for burglary - Boston dispatch of Oct. 23 (11/2)

PERKINS, Mrs. Hannah, of Ipswich, Mass., widow - died there on Oct. 16, aged 91 (11/9)

FULLER, Mrs. Mary, of Ipswich, Mass., widow - died there on Oct. 16, aged 85 (11/9)

SMITH, Mrs. Priscilla, of Ipswich, Mass., widow - died there on Oct. 16, aged 86 (11/9)

WOOD, Mrs. Abigail (wife of S. Wood), of Ipswich, Mass. - died there on Oct. 16, aged 67 (11/9)

DOW, Mary, a maiden, of Ipswich, Mass. - died there on Oct. 16, aged 91 (11/9)

MIDDLETON, Aaron, servant, age c. 26, clockmaker by trade - runaway from Isaac Pearson, of Burlington (11/9)

MARSHALL, Mr., Postmaster of Boston, dec'd - Mr. Boydell is appointed in his place - Boston dispatch of Oct. 30 (11/16)

READ, Christian, woman servant, age c. 20 - runaway (in company of one Ann Bargain) from William Battell, Postmaster in New-Castle (11/23)

BRINTNALL, David, first man that had a brick house in Phila. - died in Phila. in his 77th year (11/30)

MOORE, John, Esq., Collector of H.M.'s Customs for Phila. for
upwards of 30 years - died Saturday last in Phila. in his
74th year [12/7]

SMITH, James, servant, age c. 24, shoemaker by trade - runaway
from Richard Haynes, of Salem, West Jersey [12/7]

GREY, Robert, Irish servant, shoemaker by trade - runaway From
Robert Story, of North-East, Maryland [12/7]

POLLOCK, Robert, supposed to have come to America in 1726 from
the Parish of Mernes in Renfrewshire in North Britain -
will learn of an inheritance if he will come to Patrick
Willson, who lives in Batchelors Hall in the Northern Liberties of Phila., or to Andrew Bradford [12/ 7]

1733

SMITH, John, age c. 34, turner by trade - escaped from custody
of Thomas Hunlake, Sheriff of Burlington Co., New Jersey
[1/11]

Palatines who came in the ship Mary, John Gray commander, who
have neither paid their passage nor given security[the list
is given in English [1/4] and repeated in German [1/11]:Hance
Jacob Stumph; Herman Zin; Johannes Wirth; Hans George
Schmith [Hance Jerich Smith]; Jacob Hauk; Baltus Kluk; Con-
rad Aberman; Peter [Pieter] Werley; Margareta Mihlerin; Wit-
win Sable; Martin Ernst; Johannes Meyer; Philipe [Philip]
Haffner; Philipe Beer; Marks Emler; Cornelius Thiel; Hans
[Hance] Adam Rabendus; Leonard le Gros; Albricht [Albright]
Has; Michael Mintz; Hans Georg [Hance Jurlgh] Ackerbreght;
Gertruide Rosen; the following are described as "not yet
qualified": Jacob Kennama [Kennema]; Jacob Hafmann [Hafman];
Johannes Hoover; Johannes Ever; George Henry Right; Chres-
toffel Pickle; Jonathan Philip Pickle.

Jenney, Negro slave, age c. 21 - runaway from Martin Jervis, of
Phila., shopkeeper [1/11]

BERRY, Withers, of Boston - drowned Monday last when the ferry
overset near Moulton's Point when going from Boston to
Winnisimet - Boston dispatch of Dec. 15 [1/18]

RINDGE, Mr., of Block Island - same as above

RINGLE, William, of Boston, butcher - same as above

HORTON, John, cooper - same as above

MARSHALL, Samuel, glazier - same as above

THOMAS, John, ferryman - same as above

DOEWRA, William, Jr. (son of William Doewra, Sr., dec'd) and
Margaret Bowles (daughter of William Doewra, Sr.) - a deed
supposed to have been executed by them to William Cornwallis, dec'd, and to Andrew Caldwell, dec'd, was never
executed [1/18]

COOPER, James, late of Phila., dec'd - accounts with estate to
be settled with Samuel Cooper and John Cadwalader, executors [1/18]

GREEN, Bartholomew, a deacon of South Church in Boston, princi-
pal printer of Boston for nearly 40 years, born at Cambridge, Mass., on Oct. 12, 1666 (a son of Capt. Samuel
Green, printer, of Cambridge, who arrived with Governor
Winthrop in 1630 in the same ship with the Hon. Thomas Dudley, Esq., and died in Cambridge on Jan. 1, 1701/2 at the
age of 87; he had 19 children, 8 by his first wife and 11
by his second wife, who was a daughter of Elder Clarke, of
Cambridge) - died in Boston on Dec. 28 in his 67th year
[1/30]

JEKYLL, John, for about 27 years Collector of the Port of Bos-
ton - died there Saturday last; Sir Joseph Jekyll, present
Master of the Rolls, was his uncle - Boston dispatch of
Jan. 1 [2/6]

STRETCH, Samuel, apprentice, age c. 18 - runaway from Charles
Hargrave [2/6]

DAVIS, Thomas, servant, born in Maryland or Virginia - runaway
from William Moore, of Moor Hall, Chester Co. [2/12]

CORKER, William, late of Phila., dec'd - accounts with estate
to be settled with Mary Corker and Edward Warner [2/28]

BALTIMORE, Lady - her birthday last Tuesday was celebrated in
Annapolis - Annapolis dispatch of Feb. 9 [3/20]

HUMPHREY, Rev. John - married last Tuesday in Annapolis to Mrs.
Lawrence - Annapolis dispatch of Feb. 9 [3/20]

MEGGEE, Mr., of Phila., nailsmith, two-year-old child of - run
over and killed Saturday last [3/20]

BLOWDEN, John, servant, age c. 25, formerly servant of Arthur
Wells, of Phila. - runaway from William Smith, of Phila.,
cordwainer [3/20]

SEXTON, Andrew, Negro slave, who passes for a cooper or carpenter, formerly slave of James Coots, of Charles Co., Maryland - runaway from Col. Alexander Spotswood in Virginia (3/20)

RUTTER, Thomas, dec'd - plantation in Bristol Twp., about 8 miles from Phila., and also 600 acres of land on Schuylkill, near Mohanatawny, for sale by Thomas Rutter, at Phila. (3/27)

DAVIS, Mary, dec'd - accounts with estate to be settled with Evan Bevan, administrator, in Second St., Phila. (3/27)

SWIFT, John, lately dec'd - accounts with estate to be settled with his executor, Samuel Swift, at Poquestion Mill, Bensalem Twp., Bucks Co. (4/5)

BUCKLEY, Mrs., wife of William Buckley, of Salem Village, Mass. - hanged herself on March 9 (4/12)

FELTS, Bonfield, of Salem, Mass. - last week his wife was delivered of two boys (who soon died) and a girl - Boston dispatch of March 10 (4/12)

HUIS, Capt. John, formerly commander of a ship in England - lately died at an advanced age at his home in Conn. - Newport, R. I., dispatch of March 15 (4/12)

PORT, John, of Rahaway, N.J. - died on Friday - New York dispatch of April 25 (4/26)

KEES, John, servant belonging to Thomas Bacley, of Falls Twp., Bucks Co. - runaway from William Parker, of Phila. (4/26)

CLARKSON, Mary, wife of Thomas Clarkson, of Lewis Town on Delaware, pilot - has eloped from her husband (5/3)

WATHEL, Thomas, late of the Borough of Bristol, Bucks Co., dec'd - accounts with estate to be settled with Joseph Pease, executor (5/3)

MOUNTAINE, Richard, late of Bristol, Bucks Co., dec'd - accounts with estate to be settled with Ennion Williams, administrator (5/3)

BROWN, William (alias William Dorrell), servant, age 21 - runaway from Joseph Richardson, of Perckyomey, Twp. of New Providence, Phila. Co. (5/17)

PARKER, James, apprentice, age c. 19 - runaway from William Bradford, of New York City, printer (5/24)

MEDLEY, John, age 24, buckle-maker by trade - runaway from Richard Floyd, of Gloucester Co. [5/24]

WARDER, Solomon, late of Piles Grove, Bucks Co., dec'd - accounts with estate to be settled with Joseph Warder, executor, at Piles Grove [5/31]

BURTON, Abraham, servant - runaway from Benjamin Howard, on the south side of Patapsco River in Maryland [6/7]

SANDIFORD, Ralph, dec'd - accounts with estate to be settled with the executors, Mathias Aspdin and William Clare [6/7]

COLEMAN, Joseph, dec'd - land in Salem Co., West New Jersey, for sale; apply to Mary Coleman, executrix, at house in Salem, or to Thomas Tresse and William Rawle, of Phila., merchants [6/14]

BAIRD, Robert, servant, age c. 16, who formerly belonged to Capt. Abel Cane and George Mifflin, of Phila. - runaway from Peter Hendrickson, of Christeen Hundred, New-Castle Co. [6/14]

FLAXNEY, Thomas, merchant, dec'd-accounts with estate to be settled with Clement Plumsted or Samuel Powel, executors [6/21]

O'HAVREL, Hugh, Irish servant, age c. 30, weaver by trade - runaway from Capt. Robert Codd [6/28]

JONES, Mary [widow of Edward Jones] at Schuylkill Mill - has 2½ years of time of a servant for sale [6/28]

HART, Rev. Mr., of East Guilford, Conn., son of - thrown by his horse and killed - Boston dispatch of June 14 [7/5]

APPLETON, Mrs. Mary, dec'd - accounts with estate to be settled with Charles Read, one of the executors [7/5]

BYFIELD, Col., late Judge of the Court of Vice Admiralty of Mass. - William Shirley, Esq., has been appointed in his place [7/12]

MILLS, Edward, Sr., schoolmaster, lately dec'd - Samuel Grainger has been appointed in his place by the Society for the Propagation of the Gospel [7/12]

THOMAS, Aaron, West-country servant, age c. 40 - runaway from Richard Clymer, of Phila. [7/12]

GLANDON, Michael, Irish servant, age c. 19 - same as above

PEGG, Daniel, dec'd - his widow offers for sale a team and cart at the house in the Northern Liberties of Phila. [7/12]

ROBINS, Daniel, of Hunterdon Co., New Jersey, born in America, age c. 66 - has 13 children, of whom 11 are married, and 62 grandchildren (7/19)

BERMINGHAM, John, late of Kent Co. on Delaware, dec'd - land adjoining town of Dover offered for sale by Vroneca Bermingham, executris; apply to Jacob Van Bebber, Sr., at St. George's in New-Castle Co. (7/19)

FRARY, William, soldier, age c. 30, born in Suffolk, smith by trade - runaway from Bermuda in an open boat (8/9)

HUNTER, John, soldier, born in Lancashire, age c. 27 - same as above

HAWKINS, Thomas, soldier, born in Cambridgeshire, age c. 21 - same as above

Hazard, Negro slave, born in Guinea - same as above

Will, a young Indian - same as above

WINTER, Robert, servant, age c. 24 - runaway from Mathew Dwait, of Phila., cordwainer (8716)

Charles, Negro slave, country-born, age c. 19, carpenter by trade - runaway (in company with a white servant named Robert Gray, formerly belonging to Dr. James Boswell) from Lingan Wilson, of Upper Marlborough Town, Prince George's Co. (8/16)

HASEY, William, servant, age c. 22 - runaway from Abel Preston, baker (8/23)

DERRINGTON, William, servant, age c. 30 - runaway from Jacob Medcalf, Esq., of Cooper's Ferry, New Jersey (8/23)

GREECSTREET, Benjamin, servant, age c. 24 - same as above

BOGERT, Nicholas, Dutch servant - runaway from John Powell, of Providence Twp., Chester Co. (8/23)

CHAMBLET, Rebecca - last Tuesday sentenced to death in Boston for murdering her bastard male child - Boston dispatch of of Aug. 27 (9/6)

TRULL, Joseph, servant - runaway from Thomas Crispin and Hance Lican (9/6)

NORTON, James, servant - same as above

CLARK, John, Irish servant, age c. 50, gardener by trade - runaway from Benjamin Vining, near Salem, Salem Co., New Jersey (9/6)

HUNNIWELL, Ambrose of Boston, a porter - last week tumbled into the mill-pond and was drowned - Boston dispatch of Sept. 3 (9/6)

HOPKINS, David, supposed to be troubled in his mind, who went away from Nathaniel Pooles, of Phila., shipwright - reward for news of him offered by Reece Jones, at the White Horse, in Market St., Phila., and Robert David, at the Queens Head, in Water St., Phila. (9/13)

HELM, George, Irishman - escaped from the goal of Dover, Kent Co. on Delaware (9/13)

SHANAY, John, Irish servant, age c. 20 - runaway from Samuel Garrat, Jr., near Goshen (9/20)

KORI, Hannah - there is interest in her in England and she is asked to apply to Samuel Johnson or to the printer of the Mercury (9/27)

BROWN, Hannah (pretended wife of John Brown, of Upper Freehold, Monmouth Co., New Jersey, schoolmaster) - John Brown will pay no debts contracted by her in future (10/4)

SMITH, George, Irish servant, age c. 18 - runaway from Jacobus Hegeman, of Somerset Co., New Jersey (10/4)

OVEREND, Joshua, of Derby Ward, Savannah, Georgia - died there June 28, leaving a wife, Mary, in England (10/11)

CRABB, Mary, convict servant - runaway from George Buchanan, of Prince George's Co., Maryland (10/11)

TYZARD, John, convict servant, who was intimate with Mary Crabb - same as above

SPAW, John, convict servant, butcher by trade - runaway from Thomas Stonestreet (10/11)

WALLER, Thomas, native of Yorkshire, carpenter by trade - runaway from Col. A. Spotswood's works in Virginia (10/25)

HARRWOOD, Capt. Samuel, dec'd - accounts with estate to be settled with Charles Hughes, at the Great Last, in Mulberry St. (commonly called Arch St.), Phila. (11/1)

BELL, William, servant, age c. 23, glover by trade - runaway from James Queen, of Nottingham Twp., Chester Co. (11/8)

CHRISTY, Charles, Irish servant, age c. 23 - runaway from Samuel
  Boggs, of Mannington, Salem Co., West New Jersey (11/8)

DAULING, Benjamin, formerly merchant but for some years past the
  Deputy Collector for Boston - died in Boston Nov. 5 (11/15)

MARTIN, Thomas, a very ancient man, many years a schoolmaster in
  Phila. - last Monday fell off a wharf and was drowned (11/29)

HAYNES, George, servant, age c. 28, cooper by trade - runaway
  from the ship Vigor, lately arrived from Bristol, William
  Harris master (12/6)

WOOD, Samuel, servant, who has formerly been in Virginia - same
  as above

WILLIAMS, John, servant - same as above

WIER, Hugh, servant, age c. 30, by trade a flax-dresser, spinster
  and wool-comber - runaway from the Rev. James Anderson, of
  Donegal, Lancaster Co. (12/6)

MILLER, Appelonia (wife of Martin Miller, of Phila.) - has eloped from her husband (12/14)

CAMMOCK, Samuel, Irish servant - runaway; reward offered for his
  capture if he is brought to the Postmaster of Phila. (12/29)

FIELD, Richard, servant, age c. 24 - runaway from Robert Hannum,
  of Birmingham, Chester Co., near Brandywine (12/29)

1734

RICHMAN, William, from Wiltshire, servant, age c. 23, shoemaker
  by trade - runaway from Obediah Eldridge, of Phila. (1/1)

GOARDON, Robert, of Vallenton, Rhode Island - crushed to death on
  Wednesday last by a tree he was felling - Boston dispatch
  of Dec. 10 (1/8)

HUGHS, Robert, servant, age c. 18 - runaway from John Rigley,
  of the Northern Liberties of Phila. (1/8)

SANFORD, Benjamin, master of a sloop belonging to Newport, R.I. -
  last Nov. 21 in the West Indies was knocked overboard by
  the boom and drowned, as reported by Jonathan Conklin, mate
  of the sloop (1/15)

BELL, Mr., an aged man in goal in Boston - died Dec. 24 from a
  wound inflicted by one Amesby, a fellow-prisoner (1/29)

TUFTS, Thomas, Esq., of Medford, Mass. - died Wednesday last in
his sleep - Boston dispatch of Dec. 31 (1/29)

VAN DYKE, Mrs., wife of a silversmith of New York City - died
there Jan. 9 (1/29)

WILCOTSON, Dennis, a stranger employed by Hiah Ashcraft, of Groton, Conn., to assist him in transporting hay by water -
died a few days since, probably murdered by Ashcraft - Boston dispatch of Jan. 7 (2/5)

BOND, Samuel, late of Phila., dec'd - accounts with estate to be
settled with the widow, who is administratrix (2/5)

SALEM (or SOLEM ?), Cornelius, late of New Brunswick, age c. 40 -
broke out of goal of Perth Amboy, New Jersey (2/5)

CLAYTON, Asher, dec'd - his plantation, within a mile of Christiana Bridge, for sale by executors, Mary Clayton and Samuel Bickley (2/19)

CALVERT, Charles, Esq., President of his Lordship's Council and
Commissary General of Maryland - died Saturday last -
Annapolis dispatch of Feb. 6 (2/26)

ROGERS, Terence - sentenced to death Thursday last at an assize
held in Chester for the murder of Edward Swainey (3/5)

MARTIN, D(name illegible), mariner - his dead body found March
4 in the river at Phila. (3/5)

PALMER, Madam Rebecca, late of Phila., dec'd - demands against
her estate to be submitted to George M'Call, of Phila., merchant, who will send them to her husband, Samuel Palmer,
Esq., of Barbados (3/5)

HARRISON, Samuel, late of New York, merchant, dec'd - money
owing him to be paid to William Rawle in Phila., who is impowered to receive the same by the widow, who is administratrix (3/5)

BENTLY, Thomas, servant, age 18 - runaway (in company of a hired-
man named William Mack) from Henry Smith's plantation at Tulpahocken (3/5)

STOICKS, John, age 19, servant of John Varnam, of Dracut, Mass. -
sentenced to die on March 21 for burglary (3/12)

FESSENDEN, Mr., of Cambridge, Mass., who had been married only
a few weeks to his second wife - committed suicide Friday
last by shooting himself - Boston dispatch of Feb. 11 (3/12)

SHEGUIEN, Michael, native of France, age c. 30 - arrested Tuesday last at Boston Neck - Boston dispatch of Feb. 18 (3/21)

HOLYDAY, William, age c. 22, born in Dedain, Artois, France,
soldier - same as above

JOHNSON, Thomas, English servant - runaway from George Robison,
of West Nottingham, Cheshire Co. (3/21)

WORRELL, Mrs. Susannah, dec'd - accounts with estate to be settled with Henry Dexter, Sr., at Schuylkill (3/28)

GALLAWAY, John, servant, age c. 19 or 20 - runaway from Cornelius
Toby, of New-Castle Co. (3/28)

MORS, Capt., of Newport, Rhode Island - died on his voyage from
Jamaica (3/28)

WELLS, Capt. Thomas, of New York - killed about Dec. 18 by some
Indians in the Gulf of Florida (3/28)

CUPIT, Capt. Richard - same as above

TRIP, Samuel - same as above

CRIST, Aaron, of Newport - same as above

MOSS, Capt. Edward, master of a sloop of Newport - died of a
fever on voyage from Jamaica (3/28)

SONMANS, Peter, Esq. (son of Arent Sonmans), who studied at Ly-
den, served in England under King William, was appointed
Member of Council and Ranger of Forests, twice elected Representative from Bergen Co. - buried March 29 in Elizabeth
Town, East New Jersey (3/28)

BELL, James, servant, age c. 18 - runaway from Andrew Robinson
(4/18)

RASPER, John, indented German-born servant, age c. 24, tailor by
trade and likewise a good collier, runaway from John Copson,
of North East or Principio Ironworks (4/18)

WILLIS, William, servant, age c. 27 - runaway from John Black,
of Springfield, Burlington Co. (4/27)

ROOKE, Robert, mate of the ship Ranger, William Haselton master -
Saturday last fell overboard and was drowned (5/2)

BOWEN, Christopher - drowned May 1 at Phila. (5/9)

THOMAS, William, of Pennypack in Dublin Twp., Phila. Co., dec'd -
accounts with estate to be settled with Robert Mason, administrator (5/9)

RAMSDEN, Michael, weaver and wool-comber - dropped down dead Sunday last in Third St., Phila. (5/16)

COOPER, Samuel, late of Phila., dec'd - accounts with estate to
be settled with the widow or with William Cooper, administrator (5/16)

THOMAS, Evan, Welsh servant, age c. 22 - runaway from Thomas
Potts, of Colebrook-Dale Ironworks, Phila. Co. (5/16)

CUNSY, Jo, Negro slave, Pennsylvania-born, age c. 20 - same as
above

REDING, Thomas, peruke-maker, who bound himself about 7 years
ago to Thomas Buttington, of Bradford Twp., Lancaster Co. -
will hear something to his his advantage if he will go to
the Post Office in Phila. (5/23)

RAGAN, Rose (wife of Rockerd Ragan, of Upper Dublin Twp., Phila.
Co.) - has eloped from her husband (5/23)

LOONIN, James, Irish servant, age c. 25 - runaway from James Allcorn, of Marlborough Twp., Chester Co. (5/23)

ROBARDS, Thomas, Welsh servant, age c. 22 or 23 - runaway from
William Ellis, of Waterford Twp., Gloucester Co., West New
Jersey (5/23)

LEE, Anthony, born in Lancashire, England. servant - runaway from
John Leacock, of Pool Forge (5/30)

EFFINGTON, James, servant, born in London, age c. 14 or 15 -
same as above; Lee and Effington ran away in company of a
servant named Samuel Brown (5/30)

BARNS, Thomas, of Brookfield, Mass., age c. 70 - tossed and
killed by a bull a few days ago - Boston dispatch of May 20
(6/6)

GREEN, William, English servant, age c. 25 - runaway from John
Salkeld, of Chester (6/6)

David, Negro slave, age c. 30 - runaway from Alexander Draper,
of Sussex Co. on Delaware (6/6)

GUILMAN, Simon, servant, age c. 40 - runaway from Robert Lawrence, of Monmouth Co., New Jersey (6/6)

JONES, Morgan, Welsh servant, age c. 25, tanner by trade - runaway from Stephen Lewis, of New-Castle, tanner (6/6)

PARROTT, Thomas, servant, born in Buckinghamshire, England, who
    says he was a bone-setter or surgeon in England - runaway
    from John Greeme, at New-Post, Spotsylvania Co., Virginia
    (6/6)

COLSTON, William, servant, born in Yorkshire, age c. 30 - run-
    away from John Lock, of Phila. (6/6)

SANDERS, William, dec'd - accounts with estate to be settled
    with Stephen Armitt, administrator (6/13)

MATTHEWS, Isaac (son of Isaac Matthews, master of the sloop
    Friendship) - on June 14 fell off Mr. Fishbourn's wharf
    in Phila. and was drowned (6/20)

HOY, Ralph, who was drowned June 3 - his body was taken up on
    June 15 at League Island (6/20)

HEMPHILL, Edward, servant - runaway from Robert Chalfin, of Bir-
    mingham, Chester Co. (6/20)

BENNERMAN, James, Scotch servant - runaway from sloop Union,
    Robert M'Cullock master (6/27)

ALDER, Edmond, who lately arrived in Phila. from Bristol in
    the ship of Capt. Bromage - drowned June 28 (7/4)

HAKE, Richard, labourer - died July 3 in Phila. (7/4)

BROOKS, John, late of Phila., baker, dec'd - accounts with es-
    tate to be settled with Elizabeth Brooks, executrix, who
    plans to leave for London, or with John Danby in Third St.
    (7/4)

WORTHINGTON, James, of Byberry - overcome by heat and died on
    July 6 (7/11)

LEE, Jacob, gardener - died July 9 in Phila. from excessive
    heat (7/11)

TOUGH, Arthur, commander of the Bristol Hope - accidentally
    drowned in river at Phila. (7/11)

NEWEL, Thomas, convict Irish servant, age c. 36, shoemaker by
    trade - runaway from the Hon. Thomas Lee, of Potomac (7/11)

PRIESTMAN, James, English convict servant, age c. 40 - same as
    above

WEST, Thomas, English indented servant, age c. 20, barber and
    wig-maker by profession - same as above

HAGAN, Lawrence, English convict servant, age c. 25, butcher by
    trade - runaway from Richard Hill, of Potomac (7/11)

CONNER, Michael, Irish convict servant, age c. 26, husbandman - same as above

PRICKET, Rachel (wife of John Pricket, of Twp. of Chester, Burlington Co., West New Jersey) - has eloped from her husband (7/18)

FISHER, Thomas, servant - runaway from John Hawkins, of Baltimore Co., near Susquehana, Maryland (7/18)

BARD, Col. Peter - died Saturday last at Burlington, New Jersey - Burlington dispatch of July 19 (7/25)

HOWEL, Thomas, who with his wife and two children, Ann and Patrick, came over in 1728 or 1729 in the ship John and Elizabeth, John Yoakley master, bound from Derry, Ireland to New-Castle; if they apply to the printer they will hear something to their advantage (7/25)

BRUNTON, Richard, from Yorkshire, servant, miner by profession - runaway from the plantation of the Hon. John Carter, of Virginia (7/25)

PHILIPS, Charles, servant, smith and farrier - same as above

WARD, Katharine, Scotch servant, age c. 20 - runaway (in company with a carpenter belonging to Capt. Keel) from Thomas Woodward, of Baltimore Ferry Point on Patapsco River (7/25)

DENT, Abigail, of Portsmouth, New Hampshire, age c. 17 - murdered Saturday last, supposedly by two sailors named Thomas Pachal and Thomas Daniels - Portsmouth dispatch of July 12 (8/1)

CAVENAUGH, James, Irish servant - runaway from George Aston, of East Caln Twp., Chester Co. (8/1)

WILTSHIRE, Thomas, English servant, sadler by trade - same as above

COASHER, Josiah, hired-man, born in New England - same as above

ROBERTS, John, dec'd - accounts with estate to be settled with John White, surviving executor (8/8)

NICHOLS, Benjamin, servant, age 18 or 20 - runaway from Edward Jones, of Appoquinimank (being then at Phila.) (8/8)

DAWSON, Mary (alias MURPHEY), born in Ireland, age c. 40, who pretends to be a schoolmistress - runaway from William Alexander, at head of Elk River, Cecil Co. (8/8)

TUCKIE, Richard, belonging to the snow Christian, Samuel Bromage commander - fell overboard Aug. 12 at Phila. and was drowned (8/15)

WHEELER, Mr., of Newport, Rhode Island - died there Aug. 4
    (8/22)

PIERCE, Mr., of Boston, cordwainer, seven-year-old son of -
    injured Monday last and died the next day (5/22)

WADE, Robert, late of Chester Co., dec'd - in his will left
    his plantation in Chester Co., Essex House, to his nep-
    hew (Robert Wade) and his niece (Lydia) (8/22)

COOK, Daniel, of Irish extraction, age c. 34 or 35 - broke open
    the goal of Cecil Co. and escaped from Peregrine Ward,
    sheriff (9/5)

SANDERS, Stephen, age c. 21 - same as above

CHASE, Thomas, dec'd - accounts with estate to be settled with
    Charles Read or John Leacock (9/12)

GORDON, Mrs. (wife of Patrick Gordon, Governor of Pennsylvania),
    who was descended from an honourable family in the southern
    part of Scotland - died Saturday last in Phila. (9/19)

GARWOOD, William, servant, age c. 19 - runaway from James Moyes,
    of Phila., rope-maker (9/19)

BANTOFFS, William, late of Phila., baker, dec'd - accounts with
    estate to be settled with White & Taylor or with William
    Chancellor, administrators (9/19)

ASHTON, Richard, servant, age c. 25 - runaway from Thomas Durninn,
    at the George Inn, in Second St., Phila. (9/26)

SMITHERS, Godfrey, Mulatto, age c. 21 - runaway from Abraham
    Nicholas, of James City Co. in Virginia (9/26)

DOREN, John, Irish servant, age c. 30, who pretends to be a
    maltster and brewer - runaway from Daniel Hornby, of Rich-
    mond Co., Virginia (9/26)

BARD, Peter, late of Burlington, dec'd - accounts with estate
    to be settled with his widow, who is executrix (10/3)

RUTTER, Thomas, late of Phila., dec'd - accounts with estate to
    be settled with Mary Katherine Rutter, by order of Thomas
    Tresse, executor (10/3)

HOWEY, John, Irish indented servant, age c. 21, joiner by trade -
    runaway from Thomas Rigby, of New York City, joiner (10/17)

MILBURN, Leonard, age c. 38 or 40, carpenter and joiner by trade -
    runaway from Robert Buchanan, Esq., High Sheriff of Lancaster
    Co. (10/17)

STAKEPOLE, Lawrence, Irish servant, age c. 20 - runaway from
Ann Cooper, widow, of Deptford Twp., Gloucester Co.
(10/17)

CLYMER, Richard, late of Phila., dec'd - accounts with estate
to be settled with Christopher Clymer, executor (10/17)

Wan, half Indian, half Negro - runaway from Samuel Leonard, of
Perth Amboy, New Jersey (10/24)

DOYLE, John, Irish servant, age c. 22, cooper by trade - runaway from John Bringhurst, of Phila. (10/24)

COFFIN, Ephraim (son of Jonathan Coffin), of Nantucket, age
c. 20 - accidentally drowned early in October at Canso
when he fell from a whaling sloop from Nantucket - Boston
dispatch of Oct. 14 (10/31)

CLARK, Mr., age c. 17, on board a vessel off Cape Sable - shot
and killed accidentally early in October when he was passing a loaded gun to a man on deck - Boston dispatch of
Oct. 14 (10/31)

FRASIER, Mr. - on Oct. 9 murdered his wife in Albany and was
committed to goal there (10/31)

BAKER, John, late of Phila., shopkeeper, dec'd - accounts with
estate to be settled with Benjamin Morgan, of Phila., one
of the executors (10/31)

WARD, Christopher, servant from Yorkshire, shoemaker by trade -
runaway from Major Richard Randolph, of Henrico Co., Virginia (10/31)

ABEL, Thomas, servant - same as above

Derenah, Negro slave woman, age c. 26 - runaway from William
Hayes, near the Sweeds Church, shipwright (11/7)

SPENCE, John, late of Phila., tavernkeeper, dec'd - accounts
with estate to be settled with Jacob Duchee, of Phila., administrator (11/21)

COLLINS, Thomas, transported from England to Annapolis - executed Friday last for house-breaking - Annapolis dispatch of
Nov. 8 (11/28)

LINCH, Charles, shoemaker - same as above

JOHNSON, Thomas, pedlar - same as above

BURK, Ann (wife of Benjamin Burk, of Phila., mariner - has eloped
from her husband (11/28)

COOPER, Samuel, late of Phila., butcher, dec'd - accounts with
    estate to be settled with the widow of the dec'd or with
    William Cooper in Market St. (12/5)

SUPLE, Mary (wife of Bartholomew Suple, of Gloucester Co., West
    New Jersey) - in Sept., 1733, eloped from her husband; she
    ran away with Griffith Pue (12/12)

FISHER, William, dec'd - accounts with estate to be settled with
    Tabitha a..~ William Fisher, administrators (12/17)

GRYER, John, servant - runaway from William Peters, of Ash Town,
    near Concord, Chester Co. (12/24)

PEARCE, John, servant, age c. 25 - runaway from Nathan Beakes,
    of Chester Co. (12/31)

1735

CARY, John, covenanted servant, weaver by trade - runaway from
    Samuel Rickey, of Northampton Twp., Bucks Co. (1/7)

GORDON, Capt. - shot and killed Wednesday last on his ship in
    Rebellion Rd., Charlestown, S.C. - Charlestown dispatch of
    Nov. 2 (1/14)

PARKER, Jacob, of Boston, an ancient man, an East Coaster - died
    of exposure Friday last after his ship ran ashore on Dec. 13
    on a spit at the entrance to Boston Harbor - Boston dispatch
    of Dec. 23 (1/14)

LOWREY, Robert, dec'd - accounts with estate to be settled with
    his widow, Mrs. Sarah Lowrey, or Mr. Alexander Wooddrop,
    executors (1/14)

SELLERS, Thomas, servant, age c. 20, barber by trade - runaway
    from Charles Stagg from the house of Col. Corbin in King
    and Queen St. (1/28)

McBRIDE, Nathaniel, of Marlborough Twp., Chester Co., age c. 23
    or 24, who came from North Ireland about 5 years ago - has
    stolen goods from Nathaniel Jenkins, storekeeper, at New
    Garden, Chester Co. (1/28)

MORRIS, Joseph, servant, age c. 22, tailor by trade - runaway
    from Silas Crispin, of Burlington, tailor (1/28)

POLL, Samuel, of Biddiford, York Co., Mass., millwright - at the
    October Sessions indicted for striking and threatening his
    son Samuel, also of Biddiford, labourer; witnesses were John
    Fravor, William Hyer, Benjamin Remora, William Sibbs and
    Samuel Poll, Jr.; the foreman of the grand jury was Depen-
    dence Picklefield - item from the Boston Gazette (2/11)

HOLLAND, Thomas, block-maker, living near Oliver's Bridge in
Boston - died Tuesday last - Boston dispatch of Jan 16 (2/11)

ADAMS, Matthew, of Boston, ship-chandler and assessor - married
on Jan. 9 Meriel Cotton, daughter of the late Rev. Mr. Cotton, of Sandwich (2/11)

RIDSLEY, James, servant, age c. 25, brass-founder by trade - runaway from John Hyatt, of Phila. (2/11)

MARCELOE, Isaac, apprentice, born on London of French extraction,
formerly apprentice to William Heurtin, of New York City,
goldsmith - runaway from Francis Richardson, of Phila.,
goldsmith (2/11)

CLARK, Valentine, servant, age c. 23 - runaway from Lawrence Ren-
nalds (2/11)

RENEY, Robert, Irish servant, age c. 21 - runaway from Samuel
Parr (who is probably of Phila.) (2/25)

YAWES, Henry, age c. 21 - runaway from William Moods (probably
of Phila.) (2/25)

CUSHING, Benjamin, of Boston, shipwright - fell off the stage
at the shipyard near Charlestown Ferry and died, aged 34,
leaving a widow and four children - Boston dispatch of Feb.
3 (3/4)

EDWARDS, John, late of Annapolis, watchmaker, Scotsman - has run
away, taking the watches of several persons (3/4)

JONES, Reese, late of Phila., innholder, dec'd - accounts with
estate to be settled with his widow and executrix at the
Sign of the White Horse at the upper end of Market St., Phila.
(3/4)

FRANKLIN, James, of Newport, Rhode Island, printer - died there
Tuesday last, aged c. 38 - Boston dispatch of Feb. 10 (3/11)

CHEVER, Mrs., of Manchester - died there a few nights since -
Boston dispatch of Feb. 10 (3/11)

LAMBERT, Thomas, late living at the Falls of Delaware, near Trent
Town, dec'd - a Negro is offered for sale by the executors
of the estate (3/20)

VINING, Mr. Alderman (brother of Benjamin Vining, Esq., Collector
of Salem) - has been knighted - Boston dispatch of Feb. 24
(3/27)

CARIGAN, Mr., of Boston, a porter - drowned Tuesday last when the
    Light-House boat, then between the Long Wharf and the Castle,
    sank - Boston dispatch of March 24 [4/10]

GARRAD, Anthony, English servant, age c. 37 - runaway from William
    Wright, of Conestoga, Lancaster Co. [4/10]

BUNTING, William, late of Willis Town, about 20 miles from Phila.,
    dec'd - real estate to be sold by John Fawkes, administrator
    [4/10]

OWEN, Griffith, dec'd - Anne Whipten, his executrix, is now dead,
    so that all accounts with the estate are to be settled with
    Stephen Armitt [5/1]

ROGERS, Richard (son of Richard Rogers, Clerk of H.M.'s Victualing
    Office on Tower Hill, London), who came to America about 15
    years ago and is supposed to have lived in Rhode Island or on
    Long Island - is requested to send information about his pla-
    ce of abode to George Ross, peruke-maker in Phila. [5/8]

GREGORY, Benjamin, servant, age c. 19, born in East Jersey, who
    works as a carpenter - runaway from Thomas Mercer, of Cecil
    Co., Maryland [5/8]

NENEGRATE, Charles Augustus, chief sachem of the Narragansetts,
    age c. 25 - died at Westerly on April 18, leaving a widow
    and a son aged about 4 months [5/15]

DOWDALL, Andrew, Irish servant, age 28 or 30 - runaway from the
    shallop [lying at Phila.] of Jonathan Rayman, dwelling at
    Duck Creek [5/15]

HAMILTON, James, Scotch convict servant, joiner by trade - run-
    away from Thomas Colvell in Bohemia Manor, Cecil Co., Md.
    [5/15]

HALL, Joshua, convict servant, who speaks North-country and pre-
    tends to be a plowman - same as above

CLARK, Robert, Irish servant, age c. 20, a good scholar - run-
    away from John Whitside, at Duck Creek, New-Castle Co.
    [5/22]

George, Negro slave, a Bermudian, age c. 20 - runaway from Samuel
    Hassell; reward if delivered to the keeper of the Work-
    house in Phila. [5/29]

MATTHEWS, John, servant, age c. 23 - runaway from Edward Harne's
    plantation in the Northern Liberties of Phila. [5/29]

BLYTH, James, foremast-man on the sloop Three Friends, John Rushton master - fell overboard and drowned May 25 off the Capes
of Virginia (6/5)

NORRIS, Isaac, of Fairhill, Esq., Member of Council, often Representative for Phila. Co. in the Assembly, Judge of the Courts
of Quarter Sessions and Common Pleas - died June 4 in the Quaker Meeting House in Germantown (6/5)

LEWIS, Nathan, master of a sloop of Boston, bound from the Bay of
Honduras to Boston - injured last December in a storm and
died at Placentia Harbour (6/12)

BURROWS, Matthew, servant - runaway from Joseph Yard, of Burlington Co. (6/19)

SYMES, John, Esq., High Sheriff of New York Co. - killed Wednesday last in New York City by the bursting of a cannon - New
York dispatch of July 21 (7/24

COURTLANDT, Miss (only daughter of Col. Courtlandt, Member of H.
M.'s Council) - same as above

ROMUR, Alderman, a son-in-law of - same as above

KING, John, a young man from Boston - accidentally killed on July
16, 4 or 5 miles from Phila., when his vehicle overset (7/24)

REDSTRAKE, John, of Penns-Neck, West New Jersey, 3-year-old son
of - died from eating poison mushrooms (7/24)

FINN, William, Irish servant, age c. 23, flax-dresser by trade -
runaway from Philip Doyl, of Gloucester Co. (7/24)

BROWN, David, Scotch servant, age c. 25 - runaway from Daniel
Flexney in Phila. (7/31)

APPLETON, Mrs. Mary, dec'd - two brick tenements belonging to
her estate in Phila. offered for sale by Charles Read and
Caleb Cash, Jr. (7/31)

COGER, Josiah, servant, born in New England - runaway from John
Hannum, of Concord, Chester Co. (7/31)

ROWLANDS, William, Irish servant, age c. 17 runaway from Roger
Bell, of Darby, Chester Co. (7/31)

STEVENS, Capt., of Charlestown, Mass. - drowned when a boat overset at Surinam - Boston dispatch of July 21 (8/7)

JOHNSON, Mrs., of Woodbury, Conn. - burned to death in a fire at
home a few weeks ago - Boston dispatch of July 28 (8/7)

HOLMES, Stephen, mariner, of the ship Penn-Galley, Edward Kirk
commander - drowned Aug. 4 when he fell from Clement Plum-
stead's wharf in Phila. (8/7)

IMLAY, Mary, wife of John Imlay, of Upper Freehold, Monmouth Co.,
New Jersey - her husband will not pay debts contracted by her
in the future (8/7)

MASON, Samson, of Rehoboth, Mass., batchelor, in his 85th year -
married July 14 in Rehoboth , by the Rev. David Turner, to
Abigail Farriss, of Rehoboth, widow, aged c. 45 - Rehoboth
dispatch of July 14 (8/14)

YORK, John, of Boston, a married man, age c. 35 - Tuesday last
was overcome in a well and died - Boston dispatch of July
28 (8/14)

NOBB, John Mack, sailor, age c. 22 or 23 - overcome and died when
trying to rescue Mr. York from the well - Boston dispatch
of July 28 (8/14)

HELBY, Joseph, dec'd - estate in West New Jersey to be sold by
Thomas Lawrence, of Phila., acting on the authority of Mrs.
Sarah Helby, of London, widow and executrix (8/14)

FOREST, William, servant - runaway from Alexander Crukshank, of
Phila., shoemaker (8/21)

ROBINSON, Robert, master of the bilander Oliver - fell overboard
Monday last and was drowned and his body torn to pieces by
by sharks - Charlestown, S.C., dispatch of Aug. 9 (8/21)

DOWTHELL, James - killed by Indians about three weeks ago some
300 miles north of Phila. (8/28)

BALDEN, William - same as above

AXFORD, Hannah, wife of Charles Axford, of Phila. - has eloped
from her husband (8/28)

HOOPER, Samuel, servant, from Devonshire, age c. 23, woolen-
weaver by trade - runaway from James Shelds, of West Bradford, Chester Co. (9/4)

BURCH, Edward, a young merchant, of New London, Conn., just free
from his master - struck dead by lightning on Aug. 31 in
the meeting-house in New London (9/11)

VINING, Benjamin, Esq., Collector of H.M.'s Customs at Salem in
New England - died last week at Salem, New Jersey (9/11);
accounts with estate to be settled with Mary Vining, his
widow and executrix, at Salem, New Jersey (3/9/36)

GORDON, Robert, Esq., Judge of the Courts of New-Castle and
Probate of Wills - died last week (9/11)

DUNN, Jacob, of Phila., age c. 8 - fell into the river last Saturday and was drowned (9/11)

FLANOGIN, Will, Irish servant, age c. 20, miller by trade - runaway from William Beastin, of Cecil Co., Maryland (9/25)

FARRIL, Martin, Irish servant - runaway from Joseph Cumly, of
Manor of Mooreland, Phila. Co. (9/25)

WATKINSON, John, master of a brigantine bound from Piscataqua in
New England to Jamaica - was washed overboard and drowned
on Sept. 6 (10/2)

MOZLEY, Benjamin, Irish indented servant, age c. 18 or 19 -
runaway from William Rumsey, living near the head of Bohemia, Cecil Co., Maryland (10/2)

EASTMAN, Sarah, a young woman - last Friday her dead body was
found floating in the river at Phila. (10/9)

MORREY, Humphry, dec'd - accounts with estate to be settled with
his executors, William Allen and Edward Shippen, who offer
his real estate for sale (10/9)

WILSON, Richard, a Mulatto, age c. 30, shoemaker by trade - runaway from Ann Mason, of Charles Co., Maryland, widow (10/9)

PILLER, Thomas, skipper of a fishing -boat of Boston - drowned
last Thursday se'nnight when boat struck a rock near the
lighthouse - Boston dispatch of Oct. 6 (10/16)

HAMILTON, George - same as above

SAMPSON, Mr. - same as above

MAY, Jane (wife of Joseph May, of Salisbury, Lancaster Co., Pa.)-
has eloped from her husband (10/16)

MATHEWS, Capt. Anthony, eminent merchant and settler of South
Carolina, who first arrived in South Carolina in 1680 -
died in Charlestown, S.C., Saturday last in his 73rd year -
Charlestown dispatch of Aug. 30 (10/23)

DELBEAR, Nicholas, of Rye - died Friday last from a fall from his
horse - Portsmouth, New Hampshire dispatch of Oct. 10 ((10/23)

CHURCH, Joseph, late of New London, mate of the sloop St. Andrew,
bound from St. Christophers to Phila. - knocked overboard in
a storm and drowned on Sept. 15 (10/30)

ALLEN, Elnathan, of Shrewsbury, Mass., age c. 67 or 68 - accidentally killed Oct. 1 when he fell from his cart (11/6)

LURTING, William, age c. 13 (son of the late Col. Lurting, dec'd),
    apprentice to Capt. Farmer - lost his oar Tuesday evening
    last and was driven towards Sandy Hook and presumably driven
    out to sea and lost (11/6)

REYNOLDS, Capt., master of a ship from England - perished Thurs-
    day last when a public house at Patapsco River in Maryland
    burned (11/6)

TIDMARSH, Mr., of Maryland - same as above

WALTON, William, of Maryland - same as above

OVERY, Peter, of Maryland - same as above

LEES, John, of Maryland - same as above

MORGAN, George, late of Phila., dec'd - accounts with estate to
    be settled (11/6)

HOWELL, Mordecai, of Phila. - will pay no debts contracted in
    future by his wife Elizabeth (11/6)

EVERET, Isaac, of Dedham, Mass. - found frozen to death on Thurs-
    day last - Boston dispatch of Nov. 3 (11/13)

WHITE, Mr. - Friday last fell from his flat into the river and
    was drowned (11/13)

TURNER, Mr., of Mansfield - died Oct. 13 when his cart overset -
    Boston dispatch of Oct. 27 (11/13)

OBRIAN, John (alias John Right), Irish servant, age c. 24, who
    pretends to be a butcher - runaway from Ann Roberts, of Twp.
    of Nantmeal, Chester Co. (11/27)

BRINAN, Nell, Irish servant, age c. 25 or 26 - runaway from John
    Breach, of Gloucester Co., West New Jersey (11/27)

BEALL, Henry, servant, age c. 20, who speaks West-country -
    runaway from Catharine Plasay, of Marlborough, Maryland
    (11/27)

HENDRY, John, Irish servant, age c. 22, shoemaker by trade -
    runaway from George House (11/27)

SKYLE, Rachel, wife of William Skyle, of Twp. of Laycock, Lan-
    caster Co., Pa. - has eloped from her husband (11/27)

KAVANAUGH, James, Irish servant, age c. 25, who was formerly
    servant to Joseph Stone, of Lancaster - runaway from John
    Powel, of Lancaster (12/18)

THURSTON, Mrs., of Newbury - died there Monday last - Boston dispatch of Dec. 8 [12/23]

SEWALL, Nicholas, of York - died a few days ago a few hours after he fell from his horse - Boston dispatch of Dec. 8 [12/23].

HYATT, John, of St. George's Hundred (a son of Thomas Hyatt, of St. George's Hundred, New-Castle Co. on Delaware - on Dec. 20 was washed overboard and drowned a little below Marcus Hook [12/30]

1736

ROBERTS, John, dec'd - accounts with estate to be settled with John Danby, of Phila., gentleman, or Rowland Roberts, of North Wales; John White is executor [1/6]

YOUNG, John, master of the brigantine Princess Anne - lately died at sea; his ship, coming from Jamaica, arrived in New York on Saturday last - New York dispatch of Jan. 6 [1/13]

HAGGET, John, Irish servant, hatter by trade - runaway from Samuel Bethel, of the Town of Lancaster [1/20]

READ, William, late of New-Castle, Esq., dec'd - accounts with estate to be settled with John Richardson and Richard Grafton, executors [1/20]

BOYNTON, John, of Newbury Falls, eight children of - died of the distemper between Dec. and Feb. [1/27, 2/10, 3/9]

HATFIELD, Matthias, of Elizabeth Town, New Jersey, son of - died when a tree fell on him - New York dispatch of Jan. 13 [1/27]

LEIGHTON, Samuel, of Kittery - died from a fall on Jan. 25 - Boston dispatch of Dec. 29 [2/3]

APTY, Thomas, plasterer - yesterday at the Red Lyon Tavern in Elbow Lane, on a wager, drank a gallon of "Cyder Royal" and died within a few hours [2/3]

DOLLAN, Peter, dec'd - house and land on south side of Christiana Creek for sale by William Patterson and Reese Jones, administrators [2/3]

BROOK, Henry, Esq., Collector of H.M.'s Customs at Lewis-Town - died Friday last in Phila. [2/10]

RUTTER, John, late of Phila., dec'd - accounts with estate to be settled with Mary Rutter and Samuel Nutt, executors [2/10]

BROWN, Michael, Irish servant, age c. 16, tailor by trade - runaway from Thomas Tarrant, of Dover, Kent Co. on Delaware
[2/10]

BETHUNE, George, Esq., of Boston - died there Jan. 14 [2/17]

KNIGHT, Mr., of Newbury - buried three of his children there on
Monday last - Boston dispatch of Feb. 2 [3/2]

LEE, John, age c. 16 - his body found March 8 in the river where
he was drowned October 28 last [3/9]

BROWN, Edward, Irish servant, age c. 44 - skinner and glover by
trade - runaway from Richard Hughes, innkeeper, at the Sign
of the Three Tons, in Merion, Phila. Co. [3/9]

JEFFERS, Thomas, of New York City - died as result of a stroke
on Wed. last and his wife died on following Friday - New
York dispatch of March 1 [3/16]

COSBY, William, Governor of New York - died there March 10 [3/16]

BROWN, William, of St. Mary's Co., Maryland, seven children of -
perished Dec. 28 when his house burned [3/16]

HORNE, Edward, dec'd - his plantation, near the main road between Phila. and Germantown, about 3½ miles from Phila., is
offered for sale by Elizabeth Horne, executrix [3/16]

SMITH, Mr., of Stanford, Conn., five children of - died of the
distemper in the space of 15 days - Boston dispatch of March
1 [3/23]

MONRO, Lt. Hugh, of the Company of Fusileers in New York City of
which Richard Riggs is captain - died March 9 [3/23]

VERRY, Isaiah, born in Boston, age c. 45 - is desired to make
himself known to John and Richard Billings, who dwell in
Hanover St. and whose shop is on the town dock; his mother,
Mrs. Elizabeth Ruggles, widow, lives in Roxbury and desires
to see him [3/23]

STEWART, John, who came passenger on redemption from Ireland to
the Delaware River in the brigantine John, Robert Hamilton
master - to pay Anthony Pell for passage [3/23]

MILLER, John and wife, who came redemptioners on the same voyage
from Ireland - same as above

GRAGSON, George, who came redemptioner of the same voyage from
Ireland - same as above

THOMPSON, Mary, who came redemptioner on the same voyage from
Ireland - same as above

SLOUS, Robert, who came redemptioner on the same voyage from
Ireland - same as above

BURROWS, Matthew, English servant, age c. 25 - runaway from
Joseph Yard, of Willingborough, Burlington Co. [3/23]

LAWRENCE, Mrs. (wife of a glazier), who kept an inn near Somerset Court House in New Jersey - has been barbarously murdered and her husband injured [4/1]

HARTSHORN, Capt. Richard - lately drowned at mouth of Carendon
River when the boat in which he was going from Charlestown
to Cape Fear overset [4/1]

SMITH, Richard (son of Capt. Smith, of New Jersey) - same as
above

ANDERSON, Hon. John, Esq., President of H.M.'s Council of New
Jersey - died Sunday last at Perth Amboy, New Jersey, in
his 71st year [4/1]

STEVENSON, John, English servant, age c. 30, butcher by trade -
runaway from Lawrence Lawrenceson [4/8]

SCOT, Robert, of Chester Co. - drowned March 20 when going over
John Williams's ferry on the Susquehannah River [4/15]

LLOYD, David, Esq., dec'd - plantation on the Delaware River,
adjoining the Town of Chester, offered for sale by Grace
Lloyd [4/15]

HARWOOD, Rev. Dr. Thomas, lecturer of the Royal Chappel in Boston - died Thursday last - Boston dispatch of April 19
[4/29]

PICKELS, Rachel, wife of Nathan Pickels, of New-Castle Co. upon
Delaware - has eloped from her husband [4/29]

CARROLL, Dominick - drowned April 26 in Maryland when going on
board a ship lately arrived from England [5/6]

CARROLL, Anthony (brother of Dominick) - same as above

WHATNELL, John, born in Cheshire Co., England, age 27 - executed May 5 in Phila. for burglary [5/6]

MCDEIRMAT, Michael, born in Ireland, age 23 - same as above

BURLEIGH, Joseph, late of the Burrough of Bristol, innholder, dec'd - accounts with estate to be settled with John Hall and Joseph Richardson, executors (5/6)

FLOWER, Henry, Esq., late Postmaster of Phila. - died there on Friday last in his 77th year (5/20)

GWYNN, Mr., who fell out of Capt. Trenchard's boat ten weeks ago - his dead body found Saturday last (5/20)

BRACE, James, a young man - drowned last week from Capt. Bond's brig (5/27)

BUTLER, Andrew, owner of a brigantine bound from Dublin for Annapolis Royal - perished for want of water at Pumlico to the westward of Cape Sable; all others on board died except Mrs. Butler - Boston dispatch of May 14 (6/3)

FLOWER, Henry, lately dec'd - accounts with estate to be settled with Thomas Flower and Enoch Flower, executors (6/3)

CARY, Widow, of Bristol - has lost three children in about three weeks - Boston dispatch of May 31 (6/10)

YORK, James, of Stonington, Conn., mother and two children of - burned to death May 24 in conflagration of the house (6/10)

TRENER, Patrick, servant, age c. 13 - runaway from Nicholas Fred, of Birmingham, Chester Co. (6/17)

MOORE, William - accidentally shot and killed on May 14 when hunting deer - Charlestown, S.C., dispatch of May 29 (6/17)

MILLER, William - drowned Sunday last when bathing in the river under Society Hill in Phila. (6/24)

ROMAN, Philip, dec'd - plantation on Chichester Creek and Delaware River, Chester Co., for sale by Jacob Roman and John Taylor, executors (6/24)

SONMANS, Peter, Esq., of Perth Amboy, Middlesex Co., New Jersey, dec'd - his real estate devised to his wife Sarah has been conveyed by her to Samuel Nevill, of London, gentleman (her eldest brother and heir-at-law) and Peter Sonmans, of Perth Amboy, gentleman, Doctor of Physic (6/24)

Bristol, Negro boy, age c. 13 or 14 - runaway from the ship Philadelphia, Nathan Cowman master (6/24)

HAMILTON, John, Scotchman - runaway from the ship Mary and Hannah, Henry Savage master (6/24)

GAMBARTO, Peter - same as above

THOMAS, John, a North-country man, ship-carpenter or caulker by
   trade - runaway from Patrick Creagh, of Annapolis, Maryland
   (7/1)

NEVINSON, Peter, a North-country man, convict servant, smith or
   cutler by trade - same as above

MANNING, Peter, born in New England, having a mother and sister
   living on Block Island - runaway from William Medcalf, of
   Annapolis, Maryland (7/1)

PALMER, Joseph, of Phila., age c. 16 - died Monday last from
   kick of a horse (7/8)

SPURRIER, Theophilus, late of Phila., baker, dec'd - accounts
   with estate to be settled with Edward Nicholas, shopkeeper
   in Second St., Phila., administrator (7/8)

THAYER, David, of Mendon, Mass., three-year-old daughter of -
   died June 20 from bite of a rattlesnake (7/15)

MAC KNAPP, Thomas, servant - runaway from Christian Stone, of
   Lancaster Co. (7/15)

HAWKINS, William, Irish servant, age c. 32, who passes for a
   bricklayer and has been upwards of 10 years in the country -
   runaway from Dr. Hugh Matthews, of Cecil Co., Maryland
   (7/15)

STONEBURNER, Casper, joiner - drowned Sunday last at Phila. when
   he was stepping to the wharf from Capt. Green's ship (7/22)

CARROLL, Anthony, late of Phila., merchant, dec'd - accounts with
   estate to be settled with Andrew Bradford, administrator
   (7/22)

MUMFORD, Mrs. (only daughter of the Rev. Mr. Honyman) - died last
   week in Rhode Island when visiting her parents - Boston dispatch of July 26 (8/5)

GORDON, Patrick, Lt.-Gov. of Pennsylvania and the Counties of New-
   Castle, Kent and Sussex upon Delaware-died Aug. 5 in Phila.
   (8/5); his age was 72 (8/12)

CRUTCHER, John, who bound himself for four years to Ellis Lewis,
   miller, of the Twp. of Kennett, Chester Co. - may hear something agreeable by applying to Capt. Norris on the ship Nelly
   (8/5)

MERRATTY, James, Irish servant, age c. 40 - runaway from Daniel
   Kelly, of Manor of Moorland, Phila. Co. (8/5)

James, a Negro - executed Saturday last in Phila. (8/12)

ROBERDES, Dr. John, late of Burlington, dec'd - his house at
upper end of Market St., commonly called High St., in Burlington for sale; apply to John Roberdes, at the Sign of the
Hat, near Market St. Wharf, Phila., or to Isaac Decow, in
Burlington (8/12)

WILSON, Thomas, English servant, age c. 35, husbandman - runaway
from Joseph Huse, of Kent Island, Maryland (8/12)

JOYNER, John, English servant, age c. 30, who calls himself a
ship-carpenter - runaway from Alexander Spotswood's Ironworks in Virginia (8/12)

HAMILTON, George, English servant, age c. 26, joiner and carpenter by trade - runaway from James Tuff, of Virginia (8/12)

Daniel, Mulatto slave, age c. 35 - runaway from Christopher
Robinson, of Middlesex Co., Virginia (8/12)

M'KEY , John, servant, age c. 22 or 23 - runaway from John Snevely, of Lancaster Co., yeoman (8/19)

BURRIDGE, Thomas, convict servant, age c. 40, tailor by trade -
runaway from David Hugstor, of Kent Island, Maryland (8/19)

GAYLER, Elizabeth (wife of Adam Gayler, of the Northern Liberties of Phila.) - has eloped from her husband and left her
suckling babe (8/19)

CAUGHLAN, Samuel, servant, age c. 32, weaver by trade, who has
been a soldier - runaway from the brigantine Meridian,
Samuel Farra master (8/19)

LEWIS, William, servant to Mr. Tidmarsh - drowned Sunday last
when bathing in the Delaware River (8/26)

TRAVELLE, Thomas, overseer of the copper mines in Lancaster Co. -
found dead in the woods last week (8/26)

MEAD, Samuel, servant, age c. 18 - runaway from Job Harvey, of
Darby, Chester Co. (8/26)

WILLIAMS, John, English servant, age c. 18 - runaway from Robert
Thomas, of Lower Dublin, Phila. Co. (9/2)

CRACKEY, Sam, a free Mulatto - fell from the top of the new works
of the English Church in New York City and died on Sept. 5
(9/9)

POWER, Peter, Irish servant, age c. 35, tobacconist by trade -
runaway from David Evans, of Tulpahacca (9/9)

MORGAN, William, servant, of Welsh descent, age c. 26 - runaway from Thomas Fletcher, of Abington, Phila. Co. (9/9)

GEE, Mrs. (wife of the Rev. Joshua Gee), of Boston - suddenly
died on Saturday last - Boston dispatch of Sept. 6 (9/16)

GORDON, Patrick, Governor of Pennsylvania, dec'd - plantation
known as Traveskan, on Passyunk Road, within 1½ miles of
Phila., for sale by Robert Charles and Abraham Taylor,
executors (9/16)

MAC DANIEL, John, servant, age c. 22, born in Scotland but
lately come from Ireland - runaway from William Roe, of
New Garden, Chester Co. (9/16)

FINLOW, John, labourer - crushed to death Monday last by a tree
that fell on him in the Twp. of Horsham (9/23)

SHEPARD, Thomas, mariner belonging to the ship Princess Augusta -
drowned almost a week ago in Phila. (9/23)

M'GLOUGLIN, Cornelius, servant, age c. 23 - runaway from Darby
Scandland, of Somerset Co. (9/23)

MURPHY, Henry, servant, age c. 40, tanner and cordwainer by trade -
runaway from William Attwood, of Phila. (9/23)

MILLS, George, mate of a sloop at the Long Wharf in Boston - on
Friday last fell down on the deck and died - Boston dispatch
of Aug. 31 (9/30)

FOGO, David, commander of the ship Cambridge - supposed to have
been murdered on board his ship at Phila. on Tuesday last
by one of his men (9/30); his body has been found 12 miles
down the river at Billings Port (10/14)

COWMAN, Capt. Nathan, of Phila., master of the ship Philadelphia -
drowned Aug. 5 when boat in the harbor of Kingston, Jamaica,
overset (10/14)

SUMNER, Capt. Isaac, of Portsmouth - drowned there Friday last
when his boat overset as he was returning from piloting
out Capt. Pain, who was bound for Phila. - Boston dispatch
of Oct. 4 (10/14)

BELCHER, Madam, wife of Governor Jonathan Belcher, of Mass. -
died last Wednesday in Boston - Boston dispatch of Oct. 11
(10/21)

CREMEING, Daniel, Irish servant, age c. 20 - runaway from the
brigantine Salutation, John Carrol master, lately arrived
from Boston (10/21)

PELICAN, Robert, Irish servant lad - same as above

GEOGHEGAN, Thomas, Irish servant, lately come from Ireland, who
pretends to be a schoolmaster - broke out of the Gloucester
Goal; reward for his capture offered by William Tatum,
sheriff (11/11)

CHRISTON, Charles, Irish servant - same as above

COFFEY, Mary, wife of Cornelius Coffey, of Phila. - on Nov. 17
fell into a well when the rope broke as she was drawing
water; she was taken out dead (11/18)

Charles, Negro slave - lately committed to New-Town Goal; he
says his master is Darby Handy, who lives near Gunpowder,
Baltimore Co., Maryland (12/2)

LAWRENCE, Thomas, Irish servant, age c. 28 - runaway from Benjamin Armitage, of Bristol Twp., Phila. Co. (12/2)

SMITH, William, Irish servant, age c. 26 or 28, blacksmith and
farrier by trade, who was formerly a dragoon - runaway from
Henry Young, in Arch St., near the George Inn, Phila. (12/9)

BUTLER, James, young English indented servant, carpenter by trade,
who came last summer with Capt. Bromadge - runaway from
William Fishbourn (12/9)

KERRILL, Morris, Irish servant, plasterer and bricklayer by trade -
same as above

MATTHEWS, James, convict - last Wed. sentenced to death in Williamsburg, Virginia, for horse-stealing - Williamsburg dispatch of Nov. 5 (12/16)

GREENLEY, Elizabeth, convict - sentenced to death last Wed. in
Williamsburg, Virginia, for murder of a fellow-servant -
Williamsburg dispatch of Nov. 5 (12/16)

BOYD, John, Irish servant, age c. 25 - runaway from James M'Cra,
of Northampton, Bucks Co. (12/23)

WILLER, Peter Michael, age 7 - lost in the woods and frozen to
death on Dec. 19 (12/28)

Susan, Negro woman, age between 40 and 50 - runaway from Robert
Field, of Burlington Co., West New Jersey (12/28)

Mc QUATTY, David, Scotch servant, hammerman and refiner by trade,
who fermerly followed shallopping up and down the bay to Egg
Harbour - runaway from Samuell Nutt, of French Creek Ironworks, Chester Co. (1/6)

READ, Charles, Esq., several times Mayor of Philadelphia, Sheriff
of Pennsylvania, Representative for the County, Judge of the
Court of Vice-Admiralty, Member of Council, one of the Commissioners of the Loan Office, Collector of the Port of Burlington, New Jersey - died Thursday last in Phila. in his
51st year (1/13); accounts with estate to be settled with
Sarah Read, administratrix (6/9)

BROWNELL, Thomas (nephew of George Brownell, schoolmaster of
Phila.) - died Monday last in Phila. in his 11th year (1/13)

BOHAM, Sarah, servant, age c. 12 - runaway from John Hethcot, of
Phila., butcher (1/13)

HOW, Mark, of Ipswich, Mass. - a few days ago buried his eighth
child, dead from the throat distemper - Boston dispatch of
Dec. 20 (1/18)

ABBOT, John, of Ipswich - has buried eight children and his
father (age nearly 90), all dead of the throat distemper -
Boston dispatch of Dec. 20 (1/18)

CHAUNCEY, Rev., minister of Hadley, Mass. - his son was burned
to death more than a week ago in the burning of a small
outhouse - Boston dispatch of Dec. 20 (1/18)

HUGHS, Samuel, servant - runaway from John Wall, of Lancaster
(1/18)

McBRIDE, Thomas, servant, age c. 13, imported last fall from Ireland - runaway from Henry Genne, of New-Castle (1/18)

DUNSY, Thomas, Irish servant, age c. 21 - runaway from William
Montgomerie, of Burlington Co., N.J. (1/18)

GRAEME, William, of the Northern Liberties of Phila. - frozen
to death last Tuesday on road to Frankford, about 2 miles
from Phila. (1/25)

AYRES, Joseph, of Bucks Co. - frozen to death last Tuesday night
(1/25)

SHERRARD, Francis - perished Sunday last at upper part of River
Brandywine from fall from his horse (2/3)

HARRY, Anne (wife of John Harry, of Twp. of Amity, Phila. Co.) -
has eloped from her husband (2/3)

TOPP, Joseph, of Phila., master of the snow Warren - died last
fall of smallpox (2/15)

COLLINS, Margaret, late of Phila., widow, dec'd - accounts with
estate to be settled with Miles Strickland and John Walby,
executors (2/15)

WILLIAMS, Richard, of Boston, chimney-sweeper - frozen to death
Tuesday last (2/22)

BELLINGER, Capt., son of - drowned this week at Ashley Ferry -
Charlestown, S.C., dispatch of Jan. 22 (3/8)

EYRE, Mrs. Mary, of Portsmouth, N.H. - last Saturday accidentally fell into the fire and died 16 hours later - Portsmouth dispatch of Feb. 11 (3/8)

HARMAN, Mrs., wife of Col. Harman, of York Co. - accidentally
burnt to death last week - Portsmouth dispatch of Feb. 11
(3/8)

WISE, Rev. Jeremiah, of Berwick, twelve-year-old son of - fell
the fire and survived only 20 hours - Portsmouth dispatch
of Feb. 11 (3/8)

BLAIR, Capt. James, supercargo of the brig Anne, of Edinburgh -
died Feb. 10 in wreck of the brig on a rock at the entrance
to harbor of Scituate, Mass. (3/24)

DALRYMPLE, Pat. (son of Sir John Dalrymple, of Cranston) - same
as above

BANKS, David, mate of the Anne - same as above

FOWLER, David, carpenter on the Anne - same as above

MUCKLE, Robert, boatswain of the Anne - same as above

BEATSON, Richard, sailor - same as above

CAMPBELL, William, sailor - same as above

OLYPHANT, David, sailor - same as above

MACDONALD, Alan, sailor - same as above

HENDERSON, James, sailor - same as above

SUTHERLAND, John, sailor - same as above

HOUSTON, Stuart, sailor - same as above

SANDERS, Charles, passenger - same as above

McPHERSON, John, servant - same as above

SHARP, Henry, servant - same as above

WALKER, Thomas, servant - same as above

CARSSON, Archibald, servant - same as above

DAVIS, Mary, servant - same as above

STEUART, Mary, servant - same as above

EDMINSTOWN, Jenet, servant - same as above

NAIM, Annabell, servant - same as above

YOOL, Mary, servant - same as above

ROBINSON, Mary, servant - same as above

NIMMO, Mary, servant - same as above

LENNOX, Isabel, servant - same as above

HUNTER, Mary, servant - same as above

MILLAR, Helen, servant - same as above

SUTHERLAND, Helen, servant - same as above

PARMENTER, Joseph - died Feb. 20 in his 81st year when at divine
    service at Braintree, Mass., in the church of the Rev. Mr.
    Hancock [3/24]

JACKSON, Mrs., of Marblehead, Mass. - died Feb. 8 when taking
    communion in church [3/24]

SLADES, Christopher, servant, born in England, age c. 20, brought
    up in plantation business in this country 8 years - runaway
    from George Eyres, of Burlington [3/24]

RANDOLPH, Sir John - died Wed. last at his house in Williams-
    burg, Virginia - Williamsburg dispatch of March 4 [3/31]

RUMSEY, Widow - burned to death about 16 days ago, together with
    her granddaughter, when her house in New-Castle caught fire
    and burned to the ground [3/31]

MATTHEWS, John, of Phila., mariner - his wife has eloped from
    him [3/31]

MARSHAL, Lewis, mariner - on March 24 fell from Capt. Searle's ship into the river and was drowned (4/7)

HOUGHTON, John, Esq. - died Feb. 3 at Lancaster in his 87th year, leaving 7 children, 54 grandchildren and 73 great-grandchildren - Boston dispatch of Feb. 15 (4/14)

WADSWORTH, Rev. Benjamin, President of Harvard College - died at Cambridge, Mass., on Wed. last - Boston dispatch of March 21 (4/14)

BURKHARD, Henry, a man in years - on Tuesday last week, when attempting to ride through Perkyeoming at Pawlin's mill, in Phila. Co., fell from his horse and was drowned (4/14)

MAC PETERS, James - broke out of goal of Salem, New Jersey (4/14)

ROBINSON, Henry - same as above

MAC NEIL, John, Irish servant, age c. 21 - runaway from Henry Wynkoop, at Salem, New Jersey (4/14)

GULDING, Christopher - on April 13 went into a cow-house in Market St., Phila., to fodder some cattle and died there (4/21)

EARLE, James (alias "yelloe Jim"), Mulatto, age c. 25, capable at driving a team - runaway from Edward Farmer, of White-marsh, Phila. Co. (4/21)

SPARKS, John, servant, West-country man, age c. 30, butcher by trade - runaway from Pat. Creagh, of Annapolis (4/21)

MAC MULLEN, James, Irish servant, age c. 40 - runaway from William Howel, living at Christiana Bridge (4/21)

PARKER, William, late of Phila., merchant, dec'd - accounts with estate to be settled with his widow and executrix, Hester Parker, in Phila. (4/21)

CASH, Caleb, late of Phila., dec'd - house where he lived in Chestnut St., over against the Three Tuns, is offered for sale by his executors, Caleb Cash and John Beere (5/5)

HOWLET, John, English servant, age c. 20 - runaway from Oba-diah Johnston, of Darby (5/5)

MEAD, Samuel, English servant, age c. 19 - runaway from Job Harvey, of Darby (5/5)

ISAACS, Philip (a lad belonging to Capt. Andrew Sim), who was drowned about a fortnight ago - his body found floating in the river on Sunday last (5/12)

BURK, Patrick, servant, born in Virginia, age c. 30, sadler by
trade - runaway from James Mitchell, of York-Town, Va.
(5/12)

SAVAGE, Richard, servant, tailor by trade - runaway from Reginald Orton, of York-Town, Va. (5/12)

WILEMAN, Henry - last week sentenced by a court in Phila. to
be executed (5/19)

BRADFOARD, Isaac - same as above

CONNER, Catharine (alias SMITH) - same as above

PARKER, Thomas, an Irishman, who was committed for robbing
Jackson's fulling-mill - escaped from gaol of New-Town,
Bucks Co. (5/26)

GRANT, Thomas - same as above

MAC CURDY, Alexander, servant, age c. 19 - runaway from David
Cloyd, of Mill-Creek-Hundred, New-Castle Co. (5/26)

LITTLEFORD, David, from Herefordshire, servant, age c. 40,
who professes to be a miller - runaway from Thomas Yeardley, of Bucks Co. (5/26)

BORN, Neales, late of Lower Dublin Twp., Phila. Co., dec'd -
accounts with estate to be settled with Andrew Toy, administrator (6/2)

JONES, George, servant, age 37 - runaway from Thomas Snooks, of
Phila., bricklayer (6/2)

CONNAL, John, servant, age 23 - runaway from Joseph Flower, of
Phila., joiner (6/2)

WHATLEY, Joseph, an elderly man, who lodged at the George Tavern,
in Second St., Phila. - fell down stairs last Friday and
died of his injuries the next day (6/9)

MAC CLURE, Nathan, servant, age c. 30 - runaway from on board the
St. Andrew at New-Castle - reward for his capture offered by
his master, William Hartley (6/9)

Beck, Negro woman, born in Bermuda, who formerly belonged to Mr.
White, of Phila., merchant - runaway from Thomas Potts, of
Colebrook-Dale Ironworks, at the fair last May (6/9)

DOUGHERTY, John, of Phila. - fell into the river Monday last and
was drowned (6/16)

THOMAS, Samuel, apprentice - runaway from John M'Comb, of Phila.,
tailor (6/16)

MORGAN, George, Welsh servant, age c. 28, joiner by trade - runaway from Edward Annely, of Phila., joiner (6/16)

PITMAN, Capt. Caleb - killed at Salem, Mass., last Saturday -
Boston dispatch of June 7 (6/28)

BLAKE, Mark - found Saturday last hanging on a tree at a small
distance from Phila. (6/23)

ROULT, James, Irish servant, age c. 25, who pretends to be a
linen-weaver and has been about three weeks in the country -
runaway from David Davies, of Goshen, Chester Co. (6/30)

DAVIDS, Thomas, dec'd - his plantation, about 2 miles from Nes-
haminy Meeting-House, offered for sale by Elizabeth Davids
(6/30)

CRASWELL, Jane (wife of Robert Craswell, of Londonderry Twp.,
Chester Co.) - has eloped from her husband (6/30)

VASSAL, Leonard, Esq., of Boston - died there June 20, aged c.
60 (7/7)

WILEMAN, Henry, nailer by trade, age almost 51, born at Hinley
in Staffordshire, England - executed Saturday last in Phila.
for burglary (7/7)

SMITH, Catharine (alias Connor), born in Kings Co., Ireland,
age 23 - same as above

BEVEN, Joseph, age 23, born at Cheshire in England - executed
Saturday last at Chester for robbery (7/7)

WILLICOMB, William, English convict servant, age c. 25, blacksmith by trade - runaway from James Baxter, at Principio
Ironworks, Cecil Co., Maryland (7/7)

BURROWS, Robert, English servant, age c. 30, soap-boiler and
chandler by trade - same as above

HAMILTON, Edward, Irish servant, age c. 26, forgeman by trade -
runaway from Thomas Mayburry, of Poole, Phila. Co. (7/7)

SMITH, Samuel, of Lyme, Conn. - died June 22 when, as he was
greasing the cogs of a grist mill, the wheel drew him and
bruised him (7/14); he left a widow and ten children, the
eldest not more than 17 (7/28)

BIRMINGHAM, James, of Merion - died there Wed. last (7/14)

BUTLER, Michael - Saturday last fell from the brig Hampshire at Phila. and was drowned (7/14)

JOBSON, Samuel, of Phila., skinner - his wife, Winifred, at John Robinson's, near the George, in Second St., Phila., will pay accounts of persons to whom her husband is indebted (7/14)

MAYS, Jane (wife of Joseph Mays, of Pequay, Lancaster Co.) - has eloped from her husband (7/14)

WAYE, Robert, English servant, age c. 30 - runaway from the Caledonia Copper Mines in Phila. Co.; reward for his capture is offered by Jonathan Robeson and Nicholas Scull (7/14)

HARRISON, William, English servant, age c. 28 - same as above

LARBY, Eliphalet - on April 30 murdered by Peter Heckie near Great Cape Capon Creek in Orange Co. - Williamsburg dispatch of June 10 (7/21)

RIDDLE, Thomas - lately killed by his slave in Orange Co. - Williamsburg dispatch of June 10 (7/21)

LAND, Richard - killed by the same slave in Orange Co. - Williamsburg dispatch of June 10 (7/21)

ALEXANDER, Robert, age c. 12 - drowned Sunday last when washing himself in the Schuylkill (7/21)

GROWDON, Joseph, late of Bucks Co., gentleman, dec'd - accounts with estate to be settled with Joseph Growdon, son and administrator of the dec'd (7/28)

Flora, Negro slave, age c. 26 - runaway from Thomas Hatton, near the drawbridge in Front St., Phila. (7/28)

BROWN, Benjamin (youngest son of the late Hon. Col. Brown, of Salem), just come of age - died at the beginning of last week at Salem, leaving his fortune equally divided between his brothers, Samuel and William - Boston dispatch of May 2; dispatch of July 19 states that William Brown has found hidden in Salem 1,093 ounces of silver, including about 6,000 New England shillings (8/4)

MACHON, Samuel, servant, age c. 24, weaver by trade - runaway from William Harrison, of New Hanover, Burlington Co. (8/4)

CATON, William, Irish servant - runaway from Thomas Woodward, of Upper Freehold, Monmouth Co., New Jersey (8/4)

HAMBLETON, Edward, Irish servant, age c. 26 - runaway from Thomas
Maybery, of Pool Forge (8/11)

CROSBE, Faril, Irish servant - runaway from John Leacock, of Pool
Forge (8/11)

MESNARD, Daniel, master-tailor - buried Aug. 14 in New York City
(8/18)

HILDERETH, Benjamin, of New York City, master-tailor - same as
above

KENT, Joseph, age c. 20, formerly servant to Cornelius Low, merchant, of Rariton Landing in Piscataqua - runaway from John
Emley, of Bethlehem, Hunterdon Co., West New Jersey (9/1)

JONES, Evan, age c. 20, servant - same as above

INGLE, Frederick, of Middletown, Chester Co. - crushed to death
by a cart-wheel on Aug. 28 (9/8)

FLOWER, Henry, late of Phila., dec'd - house in Front St. now in
occupation of Thomas Bowling, offered for sale by Thomas and
Enoch Flower, executors (9/15)

READ, Charles, Esq., dec'd - accounts with estate to be settled
with Sarah Read, administratrix (9/22)

PATRICK, William, age c. 19, convict servant, who came from Bristol and speaks West-country - runaway from John Henderson, of
Freehold, Monmouth Co., New Jersey (9/22)

CROWE, Thomas, late of Hull in Yorkshire - Saturday last, when
going on board the snow George and Henry, William Allason
commander, fell into the Delaware River and was drowned (11/3)

MILLER, Barbary, servant, age c. 17 - runaway from John Seger, of
Bohemia River, Maryland (11/3)

DAVIS, Mary (wife of David Davis, of Phila., glover and breeches-
maker) - has eloped from her husband (11/3)

Caesar, Negro slave, age c. 24 - runaway from Alexander Morgan,
of Waterford Twp., Gloucester Co., West New Jersey (11/10)

IMPY, John, servant, age c. 22 - runaway from Henry Smith, of
Tulpahocken, Lancaster Co. (11/24)

QUIGLEY, Matthew, indented servant, of Phila. - died Nov. 29,
apparently from fall from roof of his master's house (12/1)

FINLY, David, Irish servant, blacksmith by trade - runaway from
John Shankland, of Sussex Co. on Delaware (12/1)

HECKIE, Peter - executed Nov. 18 at Williamsburg, Va., for the murder of Eliphalet Larby [12/15]

CONNER, Bryan - same as above

McDOWELL, John, servant, age c. 20 - runaway from William Patterson's shallop, at Phila.; reward for his capture will be paid by Thomas Williams, hatter, in Phila. or at Christiana [12/15]

HARRINGTON, Mrs., age 27 last March, wife of Joshua Harrington, of Westborough, Worcester Co., Mass. - accidentally shot and killed by a servant boy named Ebenezer; she left two children, the eldest aged 3 - Boston dispatch of Nov. 25 [12/22]

GEORGES, John (formerly Secretary to the Duke of Chandois), a Fellow of the Royal Society, who came to Pennsylvania as Private Secretary to the Proprietors and shortly before his death was succeeded by the Rev. Mr. Richard Peters - died Sunday last in Phila. [12/22]

ELLIS, Mrs., wife of Everard Ellis, of Darby - a few days ago gave birth to three daughters; a little more than a year before she was delivered of twins; all the children are alive and well [12/22]

1738

PIERCE, Mr., of Watertown, Mass., son and daughter of - very lately died of fever and flux - Boston dispatch of Dec. 13 [1/3]

DICK, Sir William, captain of one of H.M.'s Independent Companies - lately died at Albany - New York dispatch of Dec. 19 [1/3]

BINGHAM, James, late of Phila., sadler, dec'd - accounts with estate to be settled with Ann Bingham, executrix [1/10]

BROUGHTON, Gov. of South Carolina - lately died in Charlestown, S.C. - New York dispatch of Jan. 2 [1/17]

JOHNSON, Nathaniel, Esq., age c. 21 (son of late Gov. Johnson, of South Carolina, and nephew of Gov. Broughton) - lately died in Charlestown, S.C. - New York dispatch of Jan. 2 [1/17]

WOOD, John - convicted last week in Phila. of burglary [1/31]

PARKER, William, dec'd - real estate on west side of lower end
of Front St. in Phila., near the drawbridge, for sale by
Esther Parker, widow and executrix of the dec'd; she has
impowered Samuel Kirk, of Phila., to receive sums due the
estate (1/31)

CREELY, Peter, Irish labourer - supposed to have been murdered
by John King, of Salem Co., New Jersey (1/31)

JONES, Evan, of Phila., chemist - convicted of manslaughter in
Phila. on Wed. last in the death of a young man, O.R., who
had been his apprentice; the young man died from abuse in
a mock initiation into masonry (2/7)

RION, Morgan, Irish servant, age c. 20 - runaway from Anthony
Noble, of Phila., glazier and painter (2/7)

DUNNING, Thomas, late of Phila., innholder, dec'd - accounts with
estate to be settled with Martha Dunning, executrix and sister of the dec'd; she carries on her brother's business (/21)

GOTT, John, of Wenham, Mass. - on Dec. 5 buried last of his five
children - Boston dispatch of Jan. 24 (2/28)

CROSS, Nathaniel, of Ipswich Hamblets, Mass. - on Dec. 23 buried
last of his seven children - Boston dispatch of Jan. 24 (2/28)

JONES, Dr. Edward - died Friday last at Merion at an advanced age
(2/28)

CORNISH, James, Welsh servant, age c. 21, joiner by trade - runaway from Nicholas Castle, of Phila., ship-joiner (2/28)

Jack, Negro slave - runaway from William Moore, of Moore-Hall,
Chester Co. (2/28)

Will, Negro slave - same as above

Edinburgh, Negro slave - same as above

LOE, Thomas, servant, age c. 21, from Bristol, England, who served
a time in upper part of Chester Co. - runaway from Thomas
Noxon, of New-Castle Co. (2/28)

HANNIGAN, Cornelius, Irish servant, age c. 21 - runaway from Cornelius Johnson, of Aimwell, Hunterdon Co. (3/7)

FANUEIL, Andrew, Esq., body of - buried last Monday in Boston; his
nephew, Peter Fanueil, is heir and sole executor - Boston
dispatch of Feb. 27 (3/30)

PERE, Mr., of Oyster River, New Hampshire, four children of -
consumed in flames on March 3 when house burned - Boston
dispatch of March 6 [3/30]

MATTHEWS, Elizabeth (wife of Nathaniel Matthews, of Douglas Twp.,
Phila. Co.) - has eloped from her husband in company of one
Lewis Jones, who calls himself Doctor of Physic [4/6]

ADAMS, Abraham - on April 5 fell out of a canoe near Perkeyomeny
and was drowned [4/13]

COUCH, Samuel - on April 5 drowned in the Schuylkill when his
canoe overset [4/13]

WOODSEN, Samuel, servant, age c. 20, born at or near Salem -
runaway from Charles Oakford, of Alloways Creek, Salem Co.
[4/13]

TAYLOR, William, servant, this country born, age c. 17 - same as
above

ROOF, Michael, age c. 16 (son of Coonrade Roof, near Mt. Pleasant,
Phila. Co.), a Palatine -went away from his father's house;
reward offered for his return to his father or to Thomas Potts,
at Cole-brook -dale [4/20]

PRITCHARD, Reese, servant, age c. 27 or 28 - runaway from David
Potts, at Forks of Delaware in Bucks Co. [5/4]

Marmaduke, middle-aged Negro slave - runaway from William Hay, of
Chester [5/4]

BELL, Joshua - Tuesday last fell into river from ship Mary and
Hannah and was drowned [5/18]

RYON, Peter, Irish servant, age c. 20 - runaway from Moses Vernon, of Providence, Chester Co., near Chester [5/18]

ADOGAN, Dennis, Irish redemptioner, age c. 20 - runaway from William Lindsay, of Providence, Chester Co. [5/18]

QUIN, Neil, age c. 22, Irish servant to Stephen Cole, of Pequea,
Lancaster Co. - runaway from William Branson's Ironworks
[5/18]

GROWDON, Joseph, Esq., Attorney General of Pennsylvania - died
Monday last in his 32nd year [5/25]

BROWN, John, of Limerick Twp. - died May 21 as result of a fit
[5/25]

RYAN, Edmund, Irish servant, age c. 18 or 19 - runaway, in company of Edmund Butler, from Thomas Cradock, of Milton, Mass., nailor (6/1)

CLIFFORD, Thomas, late of Burrough of Bristol, dec'd - accounts with estate to be settled with Henry Nelson, administrator (6/8)

HOWELL, John, of Phila., mariner - will not pay debts contracted in future by his wife Martha (6/8)

BOND, James, servant, who talks broad West-country, sawyer by trade - runaway from Joseph Lynn, of Phila., shipwright (6/15)

TURNER, Enoch, of New Haven, Conn., age 18 months on May 2 - his size is that of a lad of 16 years - Boston dispatch of June 5 (6/22)

GROWDEN, Joseph, Sr., dec'd - real estate to be sold by Samuel Hazel, Samuel Bulkley and Hannah Growden (6/22)

DEAN, Joshua, London convict servant, age c. 40 - runaway from Alexander Spotswood, Esq., of Germanna, Virginia (6/22)

LINDSEY, John - will not pay debts contracted in future by his wife Rose (6/22)

WILDEERE, Thomas, servant, age c. 22 - runaway from Samuel Hastings (6/29)

MAGUIRE, James, Irish servant, age c. 21 - runaway from Michael Huling (6/29)

COMINS, Thomas, Irish servant, age c. 22 - runaway from Bryan Hughes (6/29)

BROWN, Thomas - on July 5 fell out of a boat into Cooper's Creek and was drowned (7/6)

FISHLY, William, of Lancaster Co. - drowned in Mill-Creek in Bristol, Bucks Co. (7/6)

GROVES, Alexander, physician and surgeon - on July 1, about 13 miles from Phila., had a fit, fell from his horse and died (7/6)

CANNON, William, young apprentice - runaway from Peter Stretch, of Phila., clock-maker (7/6)

Mulatto Jem (alias James Earl) - runaway from Edward Farmer, of Whitemarsh (7/6)

KERREL, Morris, indented Irish servant - runaway from William
    Fishbourn (7/6)

JONES, Mary, who has been servant some four years ago to Peter
    Gardnor, over Schuylkill - runaway from Job Harvey, of Dar-
    by (7/13)

ROGERS, James, dec'd - accounts with estate to be settled with
    William Hellier and John Deverel, administrators (7/20)

DELANEY, Cornelius, servant, sadler by trade - runaway from
    Daniel Bray, of Freehold, Monmouth Co. (7/20)

CRAWLEY, Henry, Irish servant, age c. 16, who pretends to be a
    sailor - runaway from the Caledonia; reward if brought to
    John Robinson in Phila. Co. (7/20)

BILLIN, Abraham, English servant, age c. 27 - runaway from Ab-
    raham Perkins, of Wellingborough Twp., Burlington Co.
    (7/29)

PAYNE, John, merchant, dec'd, who had a store at Robert Moore's,
    near the Court House - accounts with the estate to be set-
    tled with Edmund Iliff and James Day, administrators (8/3)

READ, William - house and wharf to be sold by John Richardson
    and Richard Grafton, executors (8/3)

DUN, Philip, Irish servant, age c. 18, wheelwright and sawyer
    by trade - runaway from William Overthrow (8/3)

WHITACER, Charles, English servant, age c. 25, who speaks West-
    country, sawyer by trade - runaway from James Kirk (8/3)

TODD, Margaret, wife of James Todd, of Phila. Co. - has eloped
    from her husband (8/3)

CROOK, John, servant - runaway from John Holcombe, of Twp. of
    Aimwell, Hunterdon Co., West New Jersey (8/3)

HOOKER, George, of Phila., labourer - on Aug. 18 fell out of a
    boat and was drowned (8/24)

PULLEN, William, servant, age c. 21, who talks West-country -
    runaway from John White, of Phila. (8/31)

KENISON, Philip, now in Cambridge, Mass., Goal under sentence of
    death for burglary - to be executed Sept. 15 - Boston dis-
    patch of Aug. 28 (9/7)

RICE, John - on Sept. 2 fell from the Pennsylvania Packet in the
harbor of Phila. and was drowned (9/7)

HARRIS, John, Welsh servant - runaway from Humphry Brook, of
King William Co., Virginia (9/21)

Abraham, Negro slave, born in Virginia, age c. 25, shoemaker by
trade - runaway from Col. George Braxton, Jr., of King and
Queen Co., Virginia (9/21)

Win'sor, Negro slave, born in Virginia, age c. 20 - same as above

HICKEY, David, age c. 25, who speaks Low Dutch and English -
broke out of Lancaster Goal (10/12)

MURRAY, John, age c. 30 - same as above

TAYLOR, Joseph, age c. 23, miller by trade - same as above

Harry, Negro, age c. 23 - same as above; reward for the four escaped prisoners offered by Richard Lowdon, sheriff at Lancaster

GARLAND, William, Irish servant - runaway from Thomas Blare, of
Bucks Co., near Durham Ironworks (10/19)

FORBES, Thomas, Esq. - buried at Lewes-Town on Sept. 30 (11/9)

SHARP, Anthony the Elder, dec'd, who had conveyed land in New
Jersey to his son, Isaac Sharp the Elder - the land, which
by agreement between said Isaac Sharp the Elder and his
eldest son Anthony was conveyed to Isaac Sharp the Elder,
has been conveyed by him to his sons, Isaac Sharp the Younger
and Joseph Sharp (11/16)

DAVIS, Thomas, sentenced to death - hanged himself Nov. 3 at Newport, Rhode Island (11/23)

LEGRAND, Peter - executed at Bulls Point in Newport, R.I., on
Nov. 3 (11/23)

JESSEAU, Peter - same as above

BOWDOIN, Francis - same as above

WINGATE, Henry, servant, age c. 22 - runaway from William Draper,
of Sussex Co. (11/23)

GRIFFITH, David, servant - has several times run away from
Alexander Mahone, living near Daniel Cooksons, at Pecque
(12/7)

WALTER, Mrs. (wife of Col. Walter, of Island of Jamaica, and
    sister of the late Col. Eely, of Jamaica) died yesterday
    in Boston - Boston dispatch, no date given (12/14)

LAWTON, Priscilla (wife of Job Lawton, Esq., of Newport, Rhode
    Island) - Saturday last injured when her chaise overset
    about a mile from town and she died the next day in her 50th
    year - Newport, R.I., dispatch of Nov. 24 (12/14)

DITTEND, Anthony Francis - executed Nov. 24 at Williamsburg, Va.,
    for murder of Mr. Evans, coach-maker (12/21)

COZENS, Mrs., living within 4 or 5 miles of Glocester Town, Glo-
    cester Co., son of, aged 14 or 15 - murdered Thursday or
    Friday of last week (12/21)

Drunken Frank, woman of York, Pa. - burned to death in her house
    when she was intoxicated (12/21)

OTIS, Solomon, of Barnstable, Mass., daughter of, aged c. 12 -
    fell down and died when running to tell her father that the
    chimney had caught fire - Boston dispatch of Dec. 11 (12/28)

WILSON, John, of Andover, Mass. - in eight days during last month
    buried 8 children who had died of the distemper, of whom
    the eldest was aged 16 or 18 (12/28)

GOMERY, John, Sr., of Germantown, dec'd - accounts with estate
    to be settled with the executors, John Frederick Ax, David
    Endt and Derick Cyser, all of Germantown (12/28)

                              1739

MERIAM, Deacon, of Bedford, Middlesex Co., Mass. - died Monday
    last - Boston dispatch of Dec. 21 (1/23)

HAYES, John, age c. 27 - runaway from Eliazer Umans, of White
    Plains, Westchester Co., New York (1/30)

DUNNING, Thomas and DUNNING, Martha, both dec'd - accounts with
    estates to be settled with Samuel Dunning, executor of es-
    tate of Martha Dunning (2/14)

RICKERBY, Thomas, convict servant, who passes for a sailor -
    runaway from the snow Apelby, George Gibson master, lying
    at Port Tobacco in Maryland (2/22)

HELLEM, Matthew, servant, bricklayer by trade - same as above

MAGEY (alias BROWN), Hugh, servant, tinker by trade - same as
    above

HOOPER, Hon. Robert Letice, late Chief Justice of New Jersey,
a post he held 17 years - buried Thursday last in New York
City - New York dispatch of Feb. 19 (2/28); Robert Morris,
Esq. (son of the governor), is appointed in place of the
late Judge Hooper - Perth Amboy dispatch of March 4 (3/14)

NAILOR, Robert, joiner by trade - broke out of Newtown Goal,
Bucks Co.; reward for his capture is offered by John Hart,
sheriff (2/28)

HAZARD, Mary (widow of Robert Hazard, of South Kingston, and
grandmother of the dec'd George Hazard, Esq., late Deputy
Governor of Rhode Island) - died Jan. 28 in her 100th year;
she had 300 children, grandchildren and great-grandchildren
and left 205 living - Newport, R.I., dispatch of Feb. 9
(3/22)

TUCKET, Daniel, a young man, who lived at the house of John
Boyd in Phila. - murdered March 25 by a Negro (3/29)

JARRAD, Robert, dec'd - accounts with estate to be settled with
William Bell, administrator (3/29)

DEVOE, Peter, French servant, age c. 30 - runaway from James
Davies, of Concord, Chester Co. (3/29)

STUDLEY, Capt., a Jersey man, master of a brigantine owned at
Marblehead, bound to Newbury with cargo of salt from Ali-
cant - drowned March 6 when ship was cast away at Salisbury Beach - Boston dispatch of March 12 (4/5)

STEVILEN, John, servant, age c. 24 - runaway from William Hicklen in Brandywine Hundred, New-Castle Co. (4/5)

BATCHELDER, Joseph, of Hampton in New England, 5 children of
(youngest aged 12) - died of distemper; one daughter, age
c. 21 or 22, is ill but still alive - Hampton dispatch of
March 30 (4/19)

Hannah, Negro slave, born in Barbados - runaway from Thomas Lawrence, of Phila., merchant (4/26)

SMITH, James, who arrived in Phila. about 10 days ago from Cork -
died in Phila. on May 6 (5/10)

LONGACRE, Peter, of Kingsess - found dead in his bed in Phila.
on May 7 (5/10)

JUSTICE, Morton, son of - struck and killed by lightning on
Thursday last at Christiana (5/17)

MADDOCK, Henry - on May 14 fell from a wharf in Phila. into the
    river and was drowned (5/17)

PENNEROY, Daniel, who left Phila. about 12 years ago, probably
    to settle in Maryland or Virginia - will hear something to
    his advantage if he will apply to Edward Evans, cordwainer,
    in Front St., Phila. (5/17)

GEORGES, John, dec'd - two tracts of land on the branches of
    Manakosey Creek, between the forks of Delaware and Bucks
    Co., for sale by Thomas Graeme, administrator (5/17)

JONES, Evan, servant, age c. 20 - runaway from John Emley, of
    Bethlehem, Hunterdon Co., West New Jersey (5/24)

GUIN, Samuel, Irish servant, weaver by trade - same as above

Jack, Negro slave, age c. 21, who formerly belonged to the
    estate of Joseph England, dec'd - stolen from the snow
    Drake, James White master; reward for capture of the run-
    away is offered by Edward Bradley and Co., owners of the
    snow (5/31)

COLLIS, Capt., commander of a sloop belonging to Providence,
    Rhode Island - killed by Spaniards about March 1 (6/7)

WILLIAMS, Joseph, of the sloop of Capt. Collis - same as above

BARBOUR, William, of the sloop of Capt. Collis - same as above

BROWER, Adolph, of Hackensack, young daughter of - last week
    bitten by a rattlesnake when she was gathering strawberries
    and died within a few hours - New York dispatch of June 4
    (6/7)

LAFANT, Jacob, Dutch Palatine servant, age c. 20, who pretends
    to be a butcher - runaway from Harman Richman, of Piles
    Grove, Salem Co. (6/7)

DARBY, Capt. Nath. - perished when his sloop was cast away upon
    the Goodwin Sands (6/21)

TATAM, William, Esq., High Sheriff of Gloucester Co., New Jersey -
    died June 19 at Deptford, Gloucester Co., New Jersey (6/21)

EYRE, Ambrose, servant, age c. 40 - runaway from Andrew Bradford,
    of Phila. (6/21)

LEDREW, Henry, age c. 8 or 9 - drowned June 22 in river at Phila.
    (6/28)

ANNER, Hans, servant, living in Manor of Moorland - drowned June
    23 when washing himself in a mill-pond (6/28)

TRAVETT, John Christian, Palatine servant, who came to Phila.
last fall in Capt. John Stedman's ship from Holland - runaway from David Bush, of Willing Town (6/28)

ROSE, Aquila, dec'd - his son, Joseph Rose, in his printing
office in Market St., Phila., plans to print his late
father's poetical writings (6/28)

Tom, Negro slave, age c. 24 or 25 - runaway from Alexander Wooddrop's plantation at the mouth of Great Hollanders Creek
[7/5]

HILL, Richard, Esq., dec'd - accounts with estate to be settled
with Lloyd Zachary and Mordicai Lloyd (7/19)

KIBLE, Richard, convict servant, who came this year from London
in the Forward Galley and professes to be a carpenter and
joiner - runaway from William Walker, of Westmoreland Co.,
Virginia (7/19)

ELIN, Samuel, convict servant, who came last year from London
in the Forward Galley and professes to be a carpenter and
joiner - same as above

GRIFFITTS, Philip, West-country servant, age c. 30 - runaway
from Richard Ashton, near Paxton, Lancaster Co. (7/19)

SMITH, John, lately dec'd - plantation in Lower Darby, Chester
Co., for sale by Samuel Sellers and Lewis Thomas, executors (7/19)

SHERRON, James - accidentally shot and killed when hunting deer
near Anchocas, Burlington Co. (8/2)

BROWN, John, servant, age c. 21 - runaway from James Paul Heath,
of Cecil Co., Maryland (8/2)

McKUE, John, Irish servant, blacksmith by trade - runaway from
William Aylett and John Bushrod, of Westmoreland Co., Virginia (8/2)

MAN, Francis, servant, born in Huntingtonshire, England, blacksmith by trade - same as above

FITZPATRICK, Daniel, Irish servant, farmer and ditcher by trade -
same as above

FREELOVE, John, servant, gardener by trade - same as above

CARTEY, John, Irish servant, said to be a blacksmith - runaway
from William Aylett, of Westmoreland Co., Virginia (8/2)

MATHES, Jude, Irish convict servant, age c. 25 - runaway from
Coleman Read, living at head of Nomany River, Westmoreland
Co., Virginia (8/2)

SIMMONS, James, Indian trader - supposed to have stolen items of
value from house of Joseph Webb, of Burmingham, Chester Co.
[8/2]

SKELTON, Thomas and Hannah, dec'd - accounts with estates to be
settled with Edward Bradley or White Massey, administrators
(8/16)

PORTER, Andrew, near Nottingham, Chester Co. - killed Friday
last when horse-racing at an auction; his horse passed too
near a tree and he was struck and fell (8/30)

HOWARD, Edmond, servant, age c. 18 - runaway from Jacob Casdorp,
of Phila.; he is supposed to be in company of John Griffiths
and Benjamin Poet, belonging to Edward Wyatt, tailor, and
Jonathan Chambers, belonging to Henry Norwood (8/30)

ASHETON, Robert, dec'd - real estate to be sold by Ralph Asheton,
administrator (8/30)

SHERWIN, James, late of Twp. of Chester, Burlington Co., dec'd -
long list of his neighbors is given (9/13)

NEWMAN, Mrs. Margaret, late of Phila., widow, dec'd - accounts
with estate to be settled with John Newman, executor (9/20)

CARY, Samson, late of Bristol, Bucks Co., dec'd - accounts with
estate to be settled with Samuel Cary, executor (9/20)

JENNINGS, Katherine (wife of Robert Jennings, of New-Castle Co.) -
has eloped from her husband (9/20)

SHARP, Thomas, late of Phila., merchant, dec'd - accounts with
estate to be settled with John Hopkins and John Inglis,
administrators (9/27)

CHASE, Walter, of Newport, Rhode Island - drowned Sunday morning
when boat in which he was going to Seconet struck a rock
and overset; he left a widow and two children - Newport dispatch of Oct. 5 (10/25)

BROWN, Mrs. Cathrine (called "Charity" in newspaper of 11/29/39),
late of Phila., widow, dec'd - accounts with estate to be
settled with Owen Owen, carpenter, in Front St. (11/8)

SHARPAS, William, for about 46 years Town Clerk and Clerk of the
Peace of City and Co. of New York - died there Sunday last
in his 70th year - New York dispatch of Nov. 12 (11/15)

RODE, John Mitchel, servant, a Dutchman, age c. 25, cooper by
trade - runaway from Nathaniel Eavenson, of Thornbury; reward for his capture offered by Ralph Eavenson and John
Newlin, executors (12/13)

PARKER, Samuel, English servant, age c. 17 - same as above

SLAUTER, Joseph, servant, age c. 18 - runaway from Joseph Underwood, of Christiana Hundred, near Brandywine (12/20)

1740

TOWNER, Deborah, of Lyme - died Dec. 5 in her 104th year; she
had four husbands, Jones (by whom she had 7 children),
Crane, Champion and Towner; she left 6 children, 43 grandchildren, 178 great-grandchildren and 26 grandchildrens'
grandchildren - Boston dispatch of Dec. 10 (1/3)

HAGAN, Daniel, Irish servant, age c. 23 - runaway from Andrew
Caldwell, of Pequay, Lancaster Co. (1/3)

JOHNSON, John, servant, peruke-maker by trade - runaway from
William Crosthwaite (1/3)

MORREY, Humphry, dec'd - land in West New Jersey and in Limerick
Twp., Phila. Co., for sale by William Allen and Edward Shippen, executors (1/3)

WOLFRYS, Edeth, age 17 - runaway from Thomas Carvel, of Germantown (1/8)

REDDISH, Nicholas, dec'd - accounts with estate to be settled
with William Cox, administrator (1/29)

MORRIS, Susannah, dec'd - Edward Nicholls, of Phila., had de-
posited with her various items, including two bonds by his
kinsman, John Jones (1/29)

WILDER, Mrs. (wife of Josiah Wilder, of Lancaster, Worcester Co.,
Mass.) - perished, together with her four children, when the
house burned down Wednesday last - Boston dispatch of Jan.
24 (2/26)

COUPHRAM, William - killed in Chester Co. when a tree fell on him
(3/11)

STIRRET, Benjamin - found dead in a small creek in Lancaster Co.
(3/11)

BICKLEY, William, late of Burlington, dec'd - accounts with
estate to be settled with his widow in Burlington (3/11)

CAUGHLAND, Elinor, Irish servant girl - runaway from the Widow
    Rutter, in Market St., Phila. (3/11)

SLACK, John, servant, shoemaker by trade - runaway from William
    Clare, shoemaker (3/20)

THOMAS, Evan, servant, shoemaker by trade - runaway from Joseph
    Davis, shoemaker (3/20)

McQUIRE, Patrick, Irishman, of Bucks Co. - killed Sunday last by
    Nicholas Hentwerk, a Palatine (4/10)

DRIVER, Robert, English servant, age c. 27, butcher by trade -
    runaway from Edward Brooks, of Phila. (4/10)

GAY, Nathaniel, servant, age c. 21, seaman - runaway from Hanse
    Rudulph, near Willington (4/17)

STAMPER, Thomas, of Phila. - will not pay debts contracted in
    future by his wife Dinah (4/17)

PERRY, Frederick, servant, from Somersetshire, England, weaver
    by trade - runaway from ship Young Neptune, Robert Winter
    master (5/15)

(blank), John, servant, age c. 22 - runaway from John Holcolm,
    near Wells's Ferry (5/15)

ENGELBERT, Anthony, Dutchman, stone-cutter by trade - has stolen
    a horse from Walter Shewell, of New Britain, Bucks Co.
    (5/15)

FURLONG, Joseph, Irish servant, age c. 20 - runaway from Thomas
    Smith, of Orange Co. (5/22)

GRACE, Robert, of Phila., merchant - married Monday last to Mrs.
    Nutt (5/29)

ROBERTS, Ann, dec'd - plantation in Twp. of Nantmeal, Chester Co.,
    for sale by Awbrey Roberts, executor (5/29)

DENT, William, age c. 30, bricklayer by trade - said to have
    stolen a mare from Mary Dohartby, of Lancaster Co. (5/29)

NORWOOD, Henry, dec'd - his widow, Elizabeth Norwood, will sell
    a pilot boat at auction on June 10 (5/29)

CARNEE, James, Irish servant, age c. 30 - runaway from Jacob
    Giles, at Susquehannah, Maryland (6/5)

SPOTSWOOD, Alexander, Esq., Postmaster-General of North America -
died Saturday night last, as is reported from Annapolis,
Maryland (6/12)

CALLAGHAM, Daniel, Irish convict servant - runaway from Thomas
Lee, of Potomack, Virginia (6/26)

JONES, Jane, dec'd - house and lot on east side of Second St. in
Phila. for sale by Edward Evans and Susannah Jones, administrators (7/3)

REN, Rogr, servant, who speaks Irish and English - runaway from
Jacob Kirk, of Lampton Twp., Lancaster Co. (7/17)

FITZPATRICK, Thomas, age 29, Irishman, tanner by trade - deserted
from Capt. Gordon's Co. of Col. William Gooch's Regt. of
Foot, quartered in Germantown (7/24)

RYAN, Morgan, age 22, born in Dublin, painter and glazier by
trade - same as above

HUNSMAN, William, age 21, born in Upper Dublin Twp., Phila. Co.,
husbandman by profession - same as above

MECARTNEY, Joseph, age c. 23, Irishman, hatter by trade - deserted from Capt. Thomas Freame's Co. in Col. Gooch's Regt.
(7/24)

PEARSON, Richard, age c. 24, Irishman, mariner - same as above

SMITH, James, age c. 21, Irishman - same as above

PEARSE, Simon, age c. 24, Englishman - same as above

BLACKAL, William, age c. 30, Scotchman - same as above

BROOK, Martin, age c. 40, born in West of England - same as above

BURK, John, late of Bristol, Bucks Co., merchant, dec'd - accounts
with estate to be settled with John Abraham Denormandy and
Joseph Peace, administrators (8/7)

GENTER, William, servant, age c. 20 - runaway from Thomas Hartley, of Buckingham, Bucks Co. (8/7)

SHARP, Thomas, late of Phila., merchant, dec'd - accounts with
estate to be settled with the executor, John Thomas, who
lives at the house of Jonathan Zane in Second St., Phila.
(8/21)

GLASCOW, Hugh - sentenced to death last week for burglary at a
court in New-Castle (8/28)

YOUNG, William - same as above

JENKINS, Robert - sentenced to death last week by a court at
     New-Castle for aiding and assisting in counterfeiting (8/28)

BROWN, Peter, servant, age c. 28, blacksmith by trade - run-
     away from Wm. Salkeld, of Chester, blacksmith (8/28)

BRIMER, Lawrence, age c. 26, Swede by birth, brazier by trade -
     runaway from John Hyatt, of Phila. (10/2)

ELKINGTON, George, late of Northampton, Burlington Co., New
     Jersey - his heir or heirs to apply to the printer to hear
     something of advantage (10/2)

STORY, Mrs., of Boston - perished Monday last when crowd stam-
     peded at meeting-house of the Rev. Mr. Cheekley where they
     had gone to hear the Rev. Mr. Whitefield - Boston dispatch
     of Sept. 29 (10/9)

SHEPERD, Mrs., of Boston - same as above

RUGGLES, Mrs., of Boston - same as above

McCALL, George, a considerable merchant of Phila. - died Monday
     last (10/16)

SOBER, Thomas, late of Phila., merchant, dec'd - accounts with
     estate to be settled with John Sober, executor, next door
     to Mr. Willings in Front St. (10/16)

AHARNS, Andrew, age c. 40, who speaks Low Dutch and some bro-
     ken English - runaway from Edward Shippen and Co. (10/23)

TIMOTHY, Alexander - same as above

DENNIS, John, apprentice, age c. 18 - runaway from Edward Evans
     (10/23)

DENISON, Timothy, servant, age c. 25, who has an Irish brogue -
     runaway from the ship Hannover, Richard Northover comman-
     der, now lying at Capt. Attwood's wharf; reward for his
     capture offered by William Attwood (10/23)

MAHEGAN, Daniel, servant, age c. 25 - same as above

BILES, Samuel, of Nottingham, New Jersey, dec'd - accounts with
     estate to be settled with Mary Cary, now living at the home
     of Elizabeth Biles in Trenton (10/30)

KIGLER, Christopher, Dutch boy, age c. 12 - runaway from Samuel
     Welsh (11/6)

112

MEDCALF, Jacob, formerly High Sheriff of Gloucester Co., New
     Jersey, dec'd - accounts with estate or that of his widow,
     Hannah Medcalf, dec'd, to be settled with the executors,
     Joseph Cooper, of Gloucester, and William Hudson, Jr.
     [11/20]

VANEMAN, John, of Wilmington, New-Castle Co., who was driving
     his cart laden with lime - recently injured by the wheel
     and died [11/27]

MERCER, Thomas, of Goshen, Chester Co., four-year-old child of -
     lately run over and killed by a wagon [11/27]

WILSON, James, of Buckingham, Bucks Co. - same as above

LLOYD, John, Irish servant, age c. 30 - runaway from Walter
     Moore, at Abington [12/18]

McCALL, George, late of Phila., merchant, dec'd - accounts with
     estate to be settled with Ann M'Call, Samuel M'Call, Samuel
     M'Call, Jr., and others, executors [12/18]

CARTER, George, age c. 40, born in White's Parish, 6 miles from
     New Sarum in Wiltshire, baker by trade, who in about 1722
     sailed from Bristol bound for Pennsylvania -   he (or, in
     case of his death, his children) to communicate with John
     Atkinson at the White Lion Tavern, Cornhill, London, or
     with Israel Pemberton, Jr., in Phila. [12/18]

                         1741

DIMSDALE, Sarah, late of Haddonfield, Gloucester Co., New Jer-
     sey, widow, dec'd - accounts with estate to be settled with
     the executors, Joseph Kaighin, in New Jersey, and John Dill-
     wyn, in Phila. [1/1]

Occoris (or Hercules), Negro slave, age 26 or 27 - runaway from
     Andrew Bradford, of Phila., printer [1/8]

DAY, John, English servant - runaway from William Burton, of
     Lewes-Town [1/15]

WILLIAMS, John (alias Henry Welch) - escaped from goal of Phila.
     [2/5]

SWANE, Edward, Irish servant, age c. 16 - runaway from John Hib-
     berd, of Willis-Town, Chester Co. [2/19]

McLACKLIN, Capt. Henry, dec'd - accounts with estate to be set-
     tled with David Bush, administrator, at Wilmington [2/26]

ANDERSON, William, Irish servant, age 18, tailor - runaway from
     John Trimble, of Wilmington, New-Castle Co. [2/26]

BOURNE, Benjamin - drowned Feb. 25 at Thomas Cole's mill in
Burlington Co. when he fell into the stream (3/5)

SCOTT, Thomas, mate of the Phenix, J. Harrison master, from
Liverpool - killed March 2 at Carpenters Wharf in Phila.
when a cannon burst (3/5)

BUNTING, William, of Phila. Co., storekeeper - murdered last
Sunday by two robbers (3/26)

HADLEY, Thomas, servant, age c. 22 - runaway from John Woodward, of Thornbury, Chester Co. (4/2)

HICKS, Benjamin, servant, West-countryman, age c. 26 - runaway
from plantation of Henry Smith at Tulpehocken (4/2)

KALAHAN, Lawrence - on Monday last sentenced to death in Phila.
for murder of William Bunting (4/16)

WILLIAMS, Charles, late of Phila., tailor, dec'd - accounts with
estate to be settled with William Fisher, executor (4/16)

DILL, Alexander, dec'd - accounts with estate to be settled with
Rees Thomas, administrator (4/16)

CUMMINGS, Archibald, Commissary of the Province of Pennsylvania
and Minister of Christ Church in Phila. - died Sunday last
(4/23)

CALAGHAN, Lawrence - executed yesterday in Phila. (4/23)

BETHEL, Samuel, late of Lancaster, Pennsylvania, innholder, dec'd -
accounts with estate to be settled with Peter Woorall, administrator (4/23)

HEART, David, servant, age c. 20, blacksmith by trade - runaway
from William Banford, of Hopewel (4/30)

Caesar, Negro - Friday last sentenced to death at Supreme Court
in New York - New York dispatch of May 4 5/7 postscript)

Prince, Negro - same as above

REES, Thomas, late of Merion, stone-cutter, dec'd - house to be
sold by Mary Rees, executrix (5/7 postscript)

HUSON, John and wife - last week sentenced to death in New York
City for receiving stolen goods - New York dispatch of
May 11 (5/14); John and his wife were hanged but their dau-
ghter Sarah was reprieved (6/18)

KERRY, Margaret - same as above

BULLOCK, John - murdered his wife Monday last in Phila. (5/14)

INGRAY, Nicholas, Irish servant, age c. 26, blacksmith by trade -
runaway from John Dabbin, of Phila., blacksmith (5/14)

MIER, Matthias, of Germantown - on May 15 fell from his horse
in Phila. and died of wounds (5/21)

BARE, Blasius, Dutch servant, age c. 21 - runaway from Frederick Wamburg, of Skippack (5/21)

OLIVER, Christopher, English servant, age c. 22 - runaway from
Samuel Osburn, of Westown, Chester Co. (5/21)

ROGERS, Thomas, servant, age c. 21 or 22, tailor by trade - runaway from ship Adriatick, Christopher Huddy master (5/28)

KEISER, George, Palatine servant, age c. 33, joiner by trade -
runaway from Francis Trimble, of Phila. (5/28)

McCALL, George, late of Phila., merchant, dec'd - real estate,
including plantation called Chevy Chase, for sale by his
executors, Anne McCall, Samuel McCall and Samuel McCall, Jr.
(5/28)

DUFFIELD, Benjamin, late of Phila., dec'd - accounts with estate
to be settled with Joseph Duffield, Edward Bradley and Thomas Whitton, executors (6/4)

ROBINSON, Mary (wife of Charles Robinson, of New-Castle Co.) -
has eloped from her husband (6/4)

Cubba, Negro girl, age c. 14 - runaway from Charles Robinson; a
reward for her capture will be paid by Thomas Griffith, in
Front St., Phila., hatter (6/11)

CARNE, James, Irish servant, age c. 24 - runaway from Capt.
Richard Chapman, of Phila. (6/11)

WOOLINS, Joseph, late of Germantown, miller, dec'd - accounts
with estate to be settled with Samuel Farmer, of Germantown (6/11)

HICKY, John, Irish servant, age c. 40, blacksmith and nailor by
trade, who has been in this country several years and has
lived in Boston - runaway from David Rees and John Moor,
both of Radnor, Chester Co. (6/25)

PITS, David, servant, born in England, nailor by trade - runaway from snow Ann and Mary, Samuel Hudson commander (6/25)

BENNET, Thomas, Irish servant, age c. 19 - runaway from Jonathan
Fisher (7/2)

OWEN, Griffith, late of Phila., practitioner in physic, dec'd -
accounts with estate to be settled with Thomas Say, in
Phila. (7/9)

MARSHALL, Samuel, late innkeeper at New Port on Christiana Creek,
dec'd - inn to be sold by Sarah Marshall, administratrix
(7/9)

WAINWRIGHT, Samuel, lately dec'd - plantation at head of Timber
Creek, Gloucester Co., West New Jersey for sale by Jacob
Reeder, of Newtown, Queens Co., Long Island, executor
(7/23 postscript); one may inquire of Samuel M'Collock on
the premises

HAMILTON, Andrew, Esq. - died Aug. 4; his remains interred the
next day at Bush Hill, his country seat (8/6)

Caesar, Negro slave, this country born, age c. 21 - runaway from
Valentine Robinson, of Brandy Wine Hundred, New-Castle Co.
(8/6)

REICHARD, Michael, Dutch servant, age c. 19 - runaway from Jacob
Neglee, of Oley Twp., Phila. Co. (8/6)

DUMERISQ, Capt. Philip, commander of the Eagle privateer, of
Boston - died at Lisbon - Boston dispatch of Aug. 3 (8/13)

FRY, Peter, late of London, who came to Pennsylvania - will hear
something to his advantage if he will apply to Christopher
Marshall, in Chestnut St., Phila. (8/13)

CONNER, Timothy, Irish servant, age c. 19 - runaway from William
Peters, of Concord Twp., Chester Co. (8/13)

TOMPSON, Martha (wife of Mathew Tompson, of Salisbury Twp., Lancaster Co., yeoman) - has eloped from her husband (8/13)

CHADWICK, William, of Salesbury Twp., Bucks Co. - drowned last
Saturday near shore at Wiccaco (8/20)

PARIS, Elizabeth, late of Phila., chandler, dec'd - accounts with
estate to be settled with George Okill, executor (8/27)

EDWARDS, Mary (wife of Edward Edwards, of St. George's Hundred,
New-Castle Co.) - has eloped from her husband (9/3)

Claus, Negro slave, age c. 45, who speaks Dutch and English, a
fiddler - runaway from Philip French, of New Brunswick,
East New Jersey (9/3)

COWLEY, Mary (widow and administratrix of Matthew Cowley, late
of Phila., skinner, dec'd) carries on her late husband's
business on Society Hill (10/1)

WORMLEY, Henry, late of Phila., baker, dec'd - accounts to be
settled with Eleanor Wormley, executrix [10/1]

SCROGGE, Alexander, servant lately imported from Scotland - runaway from William Montgomerie, of Hunterdon Co., New Jersey
[10/8]

RICHMOND, Capt. John, cammander out of Phila. for more than 30
years - died Oct. 14 in Phila. in his 59th year [10/15]

ROSS, Elizabeth (wife of John Ross, of Hempfield, Lancaster Co.) -
has eloped from her husband [10/22]

Timothy, servant - runaway from John Harris, at Susquehannah
Ferry [10/29]

Thomas, servant - same as above

DELAN...R, minister of Swedish Church at Wikacoe - died Nov. 2
in his 34th year [11/5]

SMITH, William, servant, age c. 20, who says he came from Ireland
about 10 weeks ago - committed to goal in Phila. by Jonathan Robeson, Esq., on suspicion that he is a runaway [11/5]

BULLOCK, John - executed Saturday last in Phila. for murder of
his wife [11/12]

SCHUYLER, John, Esq., Mayor of Albany - has died - New York dispatch of Nov. 16 [11/19]

JEFFERIES, Hannah (wife of Benjamin Jefferies, of East Bradford,
Chester Co.) - has eloped from her husband [11/19]

PAYTON, William, English servant, age c. 23 - runaway from Thomas
Lippincot, near Pensawkin Creek, Burlington Co. [11/19]

KOSTER, Joseph - killed last night in Phila. by Jacob Cvolkt in
a quarrel [11/26]

DAGG, John - on Nov. 20 at Phila. fell overboard from his shallop
into the river and was drowned [11/26]

DE LANCEY, Stephen, of New York City, merchant, born of a family
from Normandy in France - died Nov. 18 in New York City in
his 78th year [12/3]

HEARCOAT, David, English servant, age c. 23, hatter - runaway
from Thomas Griffiths, of Phila., hatter [12/10 and 17]

WOOLSTON, Jonathan, late of Middletown, Bucks Co., dec'd - accounts with estate to be settled with John Woolston and
Samuel Woolston, executors (12/10)

EASTBORN, Benjamin, late of Phila., dec'd - accounts with estate to be settled with Ann Eastborn, administratrix
(12/17)

1742

READ, John, carpenter - house on south side of High St. in
Phila., later occupied by his widow Sarah, to be sold on
execution (1/21)

BROWN, Charity, late of Phila., dec'd - accounts with estate
to be settled with Priscilla Owen (widow of Owen Owen,
house-carpenter), in Front St., Phila., administratrix
(1/21)

FORREST, William, of Phila - on Jan. 13 kicked in the belly by
a horse and died within about 24 hours (2/4)

MARTIN, James, Irish servant, age c. 22, who pretends to be a
weaver - runaway from Folkart Derikson, of Reading Twp.,
Hunderton Co., New Jersey (2/4)

DYCK, Thomas, servant, schoolmaster - runaway from under the
care of Manuel Coryell, Benjamin Canby and Jonathan Ingham, in Solebury Twp., Bucks Co.; he belongs to Edward
Barber and Miner Johnson, both of Hunterdon Co., West
Jersey (2/11)

KILLY, Dennis, lately dec'd - accounts with estate to be settled with George Killy, jacksmith, in Phila., administrator (2/11)

SEARL, Arthur, dec'd - tract of land in Middletown Twp., Bucks
Co., for sale by Thomas Searl, executor (2/11)

WILLIAMS, Charles, dec'd - his new brick house and lot on south
side of Mulbery St. for sale (2/18)

RAWLE, William, late of Phila., merchant, dec'd - John Estaugh,
agent for the Pennsylvania Land Co., who had given his
power of attorney to Rawle, will meet persons who dealt
with Rawle at the house of the Widow Rawle in Water St.,
Phila. (2/18)

NEWMAN, Margaret, dec'd - accounts with estate to be settled with
John Newman (2/25)

RIKARD, Michael, servant, "a High-Dutcher," age c. 20 - runaway
from William Richards, of Oley, Phila. Co. (2/25)

WELDON, John, cordwainer, dec'd - accounts with estate to be settled with Elizabeth Weldon, administratrix (2/25)

TANNER, George, Irish servant, barber and periwig-maker - runaway from George Sheed, of Phila., barber and periwig-maker
(3/4)

DEWEES, Abraham - accidentally shot and killed on March 21 in
Germantown by William Rax; the two men, together with John
Nice and Benjamin Barker, were out after pigeons in German-
town (3/25)

DUNLAP, Elizabeth (wife of James Dunlap, of Piles Grove, Salem
Co., New Jersey) - has eloped from her husband (3/25)

WILLIAMS, Thomas, late of Montgomery, Phila. Co., dec'd - his
plantation for sale by his executors, John Evans, of North
Wales, John Jones, of Montgomery, and John Roberts, of Walt-
pen, all of Phila. Co. (3/25)

HEMMING, Arthur, Irishman - deserted from on board the brig Vernon, Arthur Burrows master, bound for Jamaica (4/1)

STEEL, James, late of Phila., dec'd - accounts with estate to be
settled with Charles Hillyard, Richard Renshaw and Rebecca
Steel (4/1)

THOMSON, Thomas, servant, age c. 20, born in Westmoreland, England - runaway from Jacob Leech, of Chiltinham Twp., Phila.
Co. (4/8)

DE MAREST, Guilliam - lately killed by a falling tree at Hackensack - New York dispatch of April 19 (4/22)

EVANS, Evan - deserted from H.M.'s service; reward for his capture offered by William Thinn (4/22)

DUNN, Timothy - same as above

ROBISON, John - same as above

BROCK, William - same as above

TASKER, David - same as above

TANNER, George, servant belonging to George Sheed, of Phila.,
barber - broke out of the work-house in Phila. (4/22)

DONNEVER, Cornelius, Irish servant, age c. 20 - runaway from
Thomas York, of Germantown, Phila. Co. (4/22)

EGHMOURT, Susanna, wife of Cornelius Eghmourt - has left her husband, who will not pay debts contracted by her in the future (4/22)

SMITH, Thomas - struck and killed by lightning on Saturday last when he was standing under a shed with Thomas Skinner on Society Hill in Phila. (4/29)

BULLOCK, William - yesterday dentenced to death in Phila. for murder of his Negro slave (4/29)

SOLEMN, Mr., daughter of - drowned about 10 days ago, as reported from Brunswick, when a boat bound there from New York City overset (5/6)

JONES, Francis, dec'd - accounts with estate to be settled with Edward Jones, administrator (5/13)

MAGGWIGIN, Patrick - accidentally killed on May 8 at the Ironworks in Douglass Twp., Phila. Co. (5/20)

STOCKDALE, William, dec'd - his plantation at Warminster, Bucks Co., within 3 miles of Horsham Meeting-House, for sale by Israel Pemberton, Jr., of Phila. (5/20)

JERVIS, Martyn, late of Phila., dec'd - accounts with estate to be settled with John Jervis, executor (6/3)

WOOD, Rebecca (wife of Matthew Wood, of Wrights-Town, Bucks Co.) - has eloped from her husband, leaving him with five small children (6/10)

NUTTS, James, son of, aged c. 12 or 14 - swept away by the tide and drowned at Hellgate - New York dispatch of June 14 (6/17)

DUNLAP, Elizabeth (wife of James Dunlap, of Piles-Grove, Salem Co., New Jersey) - states that she did not elope from him as he claims but was forced to flee from him for safety of her life (6/17)

COX, James, passenger on ship Adventure, Josiah Cocks master - drowned April 30 when ship ran ashore on Isle of Sable - Boston dispatch of June 14 (7/1)

HYLAND, William - killed June 29 at the side of Percomini Creek when his wagon overset as he was coming from the Ironworks to Phila. (7/1)

HEDRICK, Philipina (wife of Casper Hedrick, of Phila.) - has eloped from her husband (7/1)

TAYLOR, Joseph, an ancient man of Phila. - found dead on July 5,
    overcome by heat, on road between Schuylkill Falls and
    Germantown (7/8)

MAHANY, John, Irish servant, age c. 22 - runaway from Daniel
    Willis, of Northampton, Burlington Co., West New Jersey,
    farmer (7/8)

OGLEBY, James, Irish servant - runaway from John Harry, of White-
    marsh, Phila. Co. (7/29)

FOSTER, Joseph, of Newark, New Jersey, who formerly taught
    school there - hanged himself Thursday last - New York
    dispatch of July 30 (8/5)

MORAN, Thomas, Irish-born servant, age c. 30 - runaway from
    Richard Porter and Archibald Morrison, both of Readings
    Town, Hunterdon Co., New Jersey (8/5)

KEASEY, William, servant, born in Ireland, age c. 30 - same as
    above

DAVIS, Joseph, of Phila. - died Sunday last, aged 93, and on
    Tuesday last his wife died (8/12)

FISHBOURN, William, dec'd - accounts with estate to be settled
    with Jane Fishbourn, executrix (8/12)

MURPHY, John, Irish servant, age c. 32 - runaway from Francis
    Garrigues, of Phila., carpenter (8/12)

ROURKE, Hugh, Irish servant, age c. 18 - runaway from Joseph
    Grove(r), of Frederick Twp., Phila. Co. (8/12)

JACKSON, Sarah (alias LEDDON), wife of Richard Jackson, of
    Gloucester Co. - husband will not pay debts contracted
    by her in future (8/12)

PEGG, Daniel, dec'd - four water lots fronting his estate for
    sale in Phila. (8/26)

SIMMONS, Weldon, of Phila., shipwright - states he is falsely
    accused by Isabella Chalmer of defrauding her orphan
    children of seven years' rent (8/26)

EDGECOMB, Nathaniel, of Phila., dec'd - accounts with estate to
    be settled with his widow Susannah Edgecomb (9/2)

JONES, John, late of Phila., baker, dec'd - accounts with estate
    to be settled with the executors, Elizabeth Jones, Charles
    Jones, Wight Massey and Enoch Flower (9/9)

LACEY, Thomas, late of Phila., dec'd - accounts with estate to
be settled with the Widow Lacey, who has a bake-house in
Chestnut St., with two bolting-mills to let (9/9)

BRISTOLL, Thomas, dec'd - house and lot at corner of Fourth and
Sasafrax Streets in Phila. for sale by Dan. Bristoll and
also a house and lot in Front St. (9/16)

M'CARLIN, James, a young servant, tailor by trade - runaway from
Anthony Dushane, store-keeper, near St. George's, New-Castle
Co. (9/16)

SIMS, Lydia (wife of William Sims, of Phila.) - has eloped from
her husband (9/16)

WORMLY, Henry, late of Phila., baker, dec'd - accounts with estate to be settled with William Hodge, in Walnut St. (9/23)

Mingo, Negro lad, age c. 16 or 17 - runaway from Thomas Mayburry,
of Marlborough Twp., Phila. Co. (10/7)

LANGHORNE, Hon. Jeremiah, Esq., Chief Judge of Pennsylvania -
died Monday last (10/14)

JORDAN, Robert - died Oct. 5 (10/14)

FOMBARK, Leonard, Dutch servant, age c. 24, shoemaker by trade -
runaway from Jacob Slough (or Slouch), of Manheim Twp.,
Lancaster Co. (10/14)

MOOR, Roger, Irish servant, age c. 22 - runaway from William
Walker, at the forks of Neshameny, Bucks Co. (10/14)

CLARE, William, late of Phila., cordwainer, dec'd - accounts
with estate to be settled with John Clare and Esther Clare
(10/21)

WRIGHT, Capt. Edward, dec'd - accounts with estate to be settled
with Thomas Lawrence and Edward Shippen, administrators
(10/21)

TOOL, John, Irish servant - runaway from George Munrow, of
Evesham Twp., Burlington Co. (10/21)

BRADFORD, Andrew, first publisher of the American Weekly Mercury - died Nov. 24; his widow, Cornelia Bradford, hopes
that customers will excuse the omission of last week's
paper (12/2)

DENNY, Capt. D., of Leicester, a child of - accidentally scal-
ded to death last Wednesday - Boston dispatch of Nov. 22
(12/9)

WOODDROP, Alexander, late of Phila., merchant, dec'd - accounts
with estate to be settled with Joseph Sims, one of the
executors [12/16]

1743

DARREL, John, Jr., one of the Castle men - drowned last Tuesday
when he fell off the wharf at Boston and was drowned - Boston dispatch of Dec. 13 [1/4]

PARKER, Mrs. Ann - died Monday last in Boston at a neighbor's
house near the Rev. Mr. Checkley's meeting-house - Boston
dispatch of Dec. 27 [1/27]

DAWSON, John, of Phila.-on Jan. 26 found burnt to death on his
own hearth [1/27]

THOMAS, Rees, of Merion, an early settler of Pennsylvania - died
Jan. 28 at an advanced age [2/10]

CURRIER, Richard, of Haverhill, Mass., age c. 15 - burned to
death on night of Jan. 22 when house of Dr. Brown in
Haverhill burned to the ground - Boston dispatch of Jan. 31
[3/1]

BROWN, Dr., two-year-old child of - same as above

FLEMMING, Andrew, of Groton, Mass. - sentenced at Court of
Assizes held in Charlestown, Mass., to sit upon the gallows
in Cambridge and to be flogged and imprisoned for incest
with his daughter Elizabeth - Boston dispatch of Feb. 7
[3/1]

GILLION, Francis, of Phila. - being disturbed in mind and some-
what in drink hanged himself last night [3/10]

RAKESTRAW, William, late of Phila., dec'd - haircloths continue
to be made and sold as formerly by Grace Griscom in the
house of the dec'd at the upper end of Front St. [3/10]

BRADFORD, Andrew, late of Phila., dec'd - accounts with estate
to be settled with Cornelia Bradford, executrix [3/10]

WHETMORE, Izratiab, of Middletown, Conn. - died there Tuesday
last, aged 86 last March; he left two brothers, one a year
and a half older and the other a year and a half younger -
Middletown dispatch of Jan. 17 [3/30]

SUCDUN, Ann (wife of George Sucdun, of Abington, Phila. Co.) -
has eloped from her husband [4/7]

SWENEY, Cornelius, Irish servant, age c. 24 - runaway from Jo-
    seph Allison, of New-London Twp., Chester Co. (5/5)

BRIDGHAM, Dr. Joseph, of Plympton, wife of - a few days ago was
    delivered of twins for the fourth time; she has had eight
    children in about three years (6/9)

WILLOCK, Hannah (née FORBUS), wife of Alexander Willock, of
    Solesbury Twp., Bucks Co. - has eloped from her husband.
    Richard Bright, master of arms to the ship Wilmington,
    states that said Hannah had to flee from the abuses and
    threats of her husband (6/16)

NORTHOVER, Capt. Richard, master of the ship Hanover Pink, of
    Bristol, which was lately cast away - arrived May 8 at
    Providence, Rhode Island, in his long-boat from Crooked
    Island and Friday last married Miss Elizabeth Barnard, of
    Jamaica, who had been a passenger in his ship bound to
    England - Providence dispatch of May 16 (6/23)

M'DONAL, Michael - last week at Gloucester, West New Jersey,
    was sentenced to death for the murder of Richard Filpot,
    of Great Egg-Harbour in September last (6/23); executed
    Monday last (6/30)

WALL, Joseph, servant - runaway from Henry Smith, of Tulpe-
    hacken (6/23)

COLSON, Edward, servant - same as above

HOWELL, David, an Englishman, age c. 25, who served his time
    with Samuel Sellers, near Darby, Chester Co. - stole goods
    from Bartholomew Saplee, of Billens-Port, Gloucester Co.,
    West New Jersey (6/23)

LYNCH, Head, Esq., Post-Master General of America - died Mon-
    day last at his house in Caroline Co. - Williamsburg, Va.,
    dispatch of June 10 (7/14)

DERICKSON, Cornelius, of Jamaica, Long Island, aged almost 80,
    a cooper, member of the Dutch Church, having a daughter
    living somewhere up Hudson River - hanged himself on June
    26 on the road going from Jamaica to Flushing (7/14)

STOQUI, Mrs., an ancient gentlewoman of New York City - acci-
    dentally run over and killed Monday last by a chaise driven
    by a Negro slave - New York dispatch of July 11 (7/14)

HILL, Mrs., a widow, of Rehoboth, Mass. - committed suicide on
    June 30, according to a private letter (7/14)

GOOCH, William, Jr., dec'd, son of - died July 1 - Williamsburg, Va., dispatch of July 1 (7/14)

MURFY, James, Irish servant, age c. 20 - runaway from Samuel Tamplan, hammerman at Spring Forge, near Oly Twp., Phila. Co. (7/21)

FENNIFY, Margaret, husband of - on April 14 was struck overboard by boom of ship and drowned at almost the same hour that said Margaret was executed at Cambridge for the murder of her bastard child - Boston dispatch of July 18 (7/28)

SNED, Mary, dec'd - brick house and lot in High St., adjoining David Evans's, for sale by Edward Brooks, in Second St., administrator (7/28)

NEAVE, Joel (brother of Samuel Neave, of Phila., merchant) - died Tuesday last in Phila. (8/4)

LEDAIN, Capt. Charles, of Boston, merchant - killed by three Portuguese seamen on a schooner not many leagues from Surinam - letter from Surinam dated July 1 and printed in a Boston dispatch of Aug. 1 (8/11)

JACKSON, Capt. Newark, of Boston, master of a schooner - same as above

ELLIS, William, commander of H.M.'s ship Gosport - died Friday last in New York City and his remains were buried there on Saturday - New York dispatch of Aug. 15 (8/18)

HIVES, John, of Phila., cutler - Tuesday night fell from a window in Second St., fractured his skull and died the next day (8/18)

HATSON, Peter, from New England, age 26 - entered orphanage in Phila. on Oct. 8, 1741 (8/25)

HOLMES, Han., from East Jersey, age 18 - entered orphanage in Phila. on Sept. 25, 1740 (8/25)

CHANLER, Sam., from South Carolina, age 10 - entered orphanage in Phila. on Sept. 9, 1740 (8/25)

ONEAL, William, from Ireland, age 30 - entered employ of the orphanage in Phila. on Sept. 4, 1740 (8/25)

MILLS, Grace, from New England, age 24 - entered employ of the orphanage in Phila. on May 3, 1741 (8/25)

CUTLER, Capt. John, commander of a snow of Boston - murdered
by some Portuguese when he was trading in the River Leona
in Guinea - Boston dispatch of Aug. 15 [8/25]

ABEEL, John (son of David Abeel, of New York City, merchant) -
last Saturday one of his arms was shattered when a gun went
off as he was taking it from a canoe - New York dispatch
of Aug. 22 [8/25]

PRESTON, Samuel, Esq., Treasurer of the Province of Pennsylvania -
died Sunday last in Phila. at an advanced age and on Monday his remains were interred in the Quaker Burying-Ground
[9/15]; accounts with his estate to be settled with Samuel
Preston Moore and Preston Carpenter, executors [5/24/1744]

EYRES, Phineas, a noted pilot of New York - drowned Dec. 3 when
his boat overset as he was going to pilot a sloop out of
the Hook - New York dispatch of Dec. 12 [12/21]

1744

COOPER, Rev. William, pastor of a church in Boston - died Dec. 13
in Boston in his 50th year - Boston dispatch of Dec.13
[1/12]

BAYNTON, Peter, Esq., late of Phila., merchant - drowned Thursday last when a small sloop in which he was going from
Phila. to Burlington overset [3/1]

STAPLEFORD, John, a young man, just married, who had served an
apprenticeship with Baynton - same as above

CLARK, John, of Conanicut, wife of - a few days ago was delivered of three children - Newport, R.I., dispatch of
Feb. 3 [3/7]

CHADWICK, William, late of Solebury, Bucks Co., dec'd - real
estate for sale by his brother, John Chadwick, who lately
came from England and intends to return there in the
spring [3/7]

WHITE, Peter, dec'd - accounts with estate to be settled with
Timothy Matlack and Richard Summons, executors, at house
of Joseph Ruckel in Burlington [4/19]

ARMSTRONG, John, an Indian-trader - murdered by some Delaware
Indians in the back part of Lancaster Co. [4/26]

FISKE, Capt., master of a sloop belonging to Boston - killed
last winter by Spaniards in the Bay of Honduras - Boston
dispatch of April 23 [5/3]

126

NEAL, Valentine, Irish servant lad - runaway from William Bullock, of New-Hanover Twp., Burlington Co., West New Jersey (5/24)

HANNIS, William, dec'd - accounts with estate to be settled with
John Kearsley, Andrew Hannis and Barthol. Penrose, executors
(5/31)

LICET, John (commonly called "Twig"), English servant, age c. 21,
brass-founder or brazier by trade - runaway from Matthias
Kairlin, of Concord Twp., Chester Co. (5/31)

RATSAY, Robert, late commander of the ship King David, of New
York - died March 26 - Newport dispatch of June 29 (7/12)

FORRIST, Samuel, servant, age c. 22 - runaway from David Marshall, of Duck Creek, Kent Co. (7/12)

JONES, John, apprentice lad - runaway from James Davis, of
Phila., carpenter (7/12)

JONES, Morgan, Welsh servant, age c. 20 - runaway from George
Emlen, of Phila. (7/12)

GOODSON, Andrew, English servant - runaway from Timothy Matlack, of Haddonsfield, Gloucester Co. (7/12)

COLLEMORE, William, servant - runaway from Abraham Carlisle,
of Phila. (7/12)

EDWARDS, Thomas, apprentice, age c. 15, born in this country -
runaway from Joseph Clark, of Phila., baker (7/19)

GREAR, George, journeyman hatter in New York City - found murdered last Saturday in street where he lived - New York
dispatch of July 30 (8/2); coroner's jury decided he fell
out of a window when walking in his sleep - New York dispatch of Aug. 6 (8/9)

STEVENS, John, late of Ash Swamp, East New Jersey - Friday se'n-
night sentenced to death for counterfeiting - New York dispatch of Aug. 13 (8/16); executed Aug. 7 (8/30)

BAYARD, Mrs. (wife of Samuel Bayard, of New York City, merchant) -
died last Friday in New York City; her remains were interred
Sunday last in the family vault - New York dispatch of Aug.
13 (8/16)

CRUGER, John, Esq., Mayor and vendue-master of New York City -
died Aug. 13 in New York City (8/16)

BOLTON, Robert, dec'd - accounts with estate to be settled with
Edward Shippen, administrator (8/16)

KENNEY, Capt., commander of a schooner of Boston - killed by a
Frenchman - Boston dispatch of Aug. 20 (8/30)

MORISON, Sarah (wife of John Morison, of Phila.) - her husband
will not pay debts contracted by her in future (9/13)

RICHARDS, Capt. Samuel, master of a sloop bound from New York
to Piscataqua - shot and killed by men of a privateer sloop -
Boston dispatch of Sept. 24 (10/4)

GRANT, Capt. - died as result of gunpowder explosion - Newport,
R.I., dispatch of Sept. 28 (10/11)

CODDINGTON, Mr. - same as above

TAYLOR, Mr. - same as above

WARTON, George - drowned Thursday when coming from Chester in a
flat at mouth of Chester Creek (10/11)

MILLER, Mary (wife of Boltis Miller, of East Bradford, Chester
Co.) - has eloped from her husband (10/11)

DYKE, Thomas, servant, age c. 25 - runaway from Thomas Maybury,
of Green-Lane Forge, Phila. Co. (11/8)

SHAE, Francis, Irish servant, age c. 26 - same as above

Sibba, Negro woman, age c. 23, lately bought from Capt. William
Bell, of Phila. - runaway from John Morgan, of Carnarvon
Twp., Lancaster Co. (11/22)

ALLEN, Capt. - killed by an Indian - Boston dispatch of Nov. 19
(11/29)

SLEIGH, Mrs., ancient gentlewoman of New York - Friday last fell
into fire and perished - New York dispatch of Oct. 3 (12/6)

FOLGER, David, master and owner of a sloop - drowned when sloop
sank near Horseshoe Shoal as it was going from Nantucket to
mainland on Oct. 20; his son was also drowned (12/14)

SWAIN, Richard - drowned Oct. 20 when the above-mentioned sloop
sank (12/14)

ELLOTT, Elizabeth (wife of Moses Ellott, of Chichester) - has
eloped from her husband (12/28)

1745

PERDUE, William, first lieutenant - killed on board the schooner
George, William Dowell commander, in engagement with French
ship (1/15)

CASEY, Josiah, second lieutenant - same as above

RESS, Lawrence, private - same as above

OWEN, Evan, private - same as above

GUERNSEY, John, private - same as above

SHENIGER, Jacob, private - same as above

DONAVAN, James, private - same as above

BARRY, John, private - same as above

ALEXANDER, William, Esq., Collector of Customs for the Port of
    Phila. - died suddenly last Wed. night in Phila. [1/23]

FINLY, William, servant, age c. 26 - runaway from John Jackson,
    of East Caln, in the Great Valley, Chester Co. [1/23]

FRANKLIN, Josiah, of Boston, tallow-chandler and soap-maker -
    died Jan. 16, aged 87 - Boston dispatch of Jan. 17 [2/12]

OSBORNE, James, age c. 18, apprentice to Capt. Griffith - shot
    and killed last Monday at Newport, R.I., by Samuel Banis-
    ter, Jr., when Peleg Brown, High Sheriff, was attempting
    to take possession of a house occupied by Banister - Bos-
    ton dispatch of Jan. 31 [2/26]

MULLEN, William, of Lewis-Town, pilot - drowned Jan. 24 when
    boat overset as he was returning from Capt. Meas's ship
    [3/5]

NUNES, Moses, of Lewis- Town, pilot - same as above

BELL, Capt. William, of Phila. - died Sunday last in Phila.;
    his remains were interred on March 4 [3/5]

NAYLCR, Charles, servant - runaway from John Comeggs and An-
    thony Roe, living in Queen Ann's Co., Maryland [4/4]

CONKLYN, Capt., commander of a privateer - killed when at-
    tempting to cut a vessel out of a harbor on the Spanish
    Main - Newport, R.I., dispatch of March 22 [4/12]

CORTRECHT, Mr. - crushed to death Monday last between the sloop
    Amelia and Mr. Van Zent's wharf in New York City - New
    York dispatch of April 22 [4/25]

CROTTY, William, servant, age c. 18 or 19 - runaway from Isaac
    Vanhorne, of Salisbury Twp., Bucks Co. [4/25]

COOMBE, Anne (wife of Benjamin Coombe, of Bristol) - has
    eloped from her husband (5/2)

SIBBALD, George (brother of Capt. Sibbald, of Phila.) - drowned
    March 27 when a small schooner belonging to Capt. Ferris
    sank near Fleet's Bay, a little above the mouth of the
    Pappahanock - Williamsburg, Va., dispatch of April 18
    (5/9)

PACKE, Graves (son of Mrs. Sarah Packe, of Williamsburg), age
    c. 18 - same as above

FRETZEL, John Harmon, Dutch servant, age c. 24, and his wife
    Gertrude - runaways from Robert Meads's plantation in the
    Northern Liberties of Phila. (5/23)

PLUMSTED, Hon. Clement, Member of Council and Alderman of Phila.-
    died Sunday last in Phila. (5/30)

BEVAN, Rees, who came from Antigua with Capt. Kollock to see a
    brother - his body was found Saturday last floating in the
    river at Phila. (6/6)

EDWARDS, Thomas, apprentice, age c. 16 - runaway from Joseph
    Clark, of Phila., baker (6/6)

BRYAN, James, Irish apprentice, age c. 18 - runaway from Nicholas
    Fenuel, of Phila., cordwainer (6/6)

MITCHELL, Elizabeth (wife of George Mitchell, of Phila., inn-
    holder) - has eloped from her husband (6/20)

EVANS, Peter, formerly Collector of the Port of Phila. - died
    Friday last in Phila. (6/20)

HARRISON, Col. Benjamin, of Berkley, Charles City Co., Va.,
    for many years representative of his county in the Assembly -
    killed last Friday, as were his two daughters, when light-
    ning struck his house - Williamsburg dispatch of July 18
    (8/22)

TREBY, Mrs. and two of her children - drowned last Tuesday when
    boat of a Mr. Brooks overset - New York dispatch of Aug. 19
    (8/22 postscript)

MOOR, Mary, a High Dutch woman, child of - same as above

MICK, Rudolph, Dutch servant, age c. 35 - runaway from Henry
    Teringer, of Hanover Twp. in Falconar Swamp, Pa. (9/19)

TRAUT, George, late of Germantown, dec'd - his house at upper
end of Germantown, Phila. Co., will be sold at auction by
John Frederick Ax and Richard Robb, executors (9/26)

COOK, John, servant, age c. 19 - runaway from Francis Morgan, of
Carnarvon, Lancaster Co. (10/10)

COX, Thomas, of New York City, butcher-accidentally shot and
killed Monday last in a public house by a young gentleman from the privateer Clinton - New York dispatch of
Oct. 28 (10/31)

ELLSWORTH, Theophilus, of New York City - Friday last fell off
the wharf near Mr. Cannon's and was drowned - New York dispatch of Nov. 18 (11/21)

WILLIAMS, Francis, Welsh servant - runaway from the brig Kouli -
Kan at Phila. (11/21); reward for his capture offered by
James Templeton, of Phila. (12/17)

EVANS, David, of Phila. - died there last week, aged 77 (12/5)

SHARP, Thomas, late of Phila., merchant, dec'd - accounts with
estate to be settled with Walter Goodman, of Phila., merchant, attorney for John Thomas, sole executor (12/5)

REA, James, servant, age c. 18 - runaway from Joseph Rogger, of
Winsen Twp., Chester Co. (12/10)

PARKER, Gabriel (son of Col. Parker, of Calvert Co., Maryland) -
died Friday last in Prince George's Co., Maryland - Annapolis dispatch of Dec. 6 (12/17)

BELL, William, second lieutenant of the privateer schooner
George, Capt. Dougall commander - killed in October in engagement with a French ship (12/24)

1746

COOGDILL, John, servant - runaway from Samuel Morris, of Whitemarsh (1/8)

BROWN, Capt. William, of New York City, master of the sloop
Bumper - knocked overboard by the boom and drowned on a
voyage from Jamaica to New York - New York dispatch of
Jan. 15 (1/21)

PRICHARD, Samuel, who lived about 8 miles from John Harris's
ferry on Susquehannah and had been jailed for forgery and
fraud - escaped from the constable in Donegall, Lancaster
Co. (2/11)

132

A

ABBOT/ABBOTT
  John 89
  Robert 16
ABEEL
  David 125
  John 125
ABEL
  Thomas 73
ABERMAN
  Conrad 60
ACKERBREGHT
  Hans Georg 60
ACTON
  Benjamin 43
ADAMS
  -- Rev. 11
  Abraham 39
  Matthew 75
  Thomas 42
ADOGAN
  Dennis 99
AHARNS
  Andrew 111
ALDER
  Edmond 70
ALDERBURGH
  Richard 15
ALDRIDGE
  -- Mrs. 41
  John 41
ALEXANDER
  Robert 14, 15, 95
  William 71, 128
ALLCORN
  James 69
ALLEN
  -- Capt. 127
  Elnathan 79
  John 20
  Richard 5
  William 26, 79, 108
ALLISON/ALLASON
  Joseph 122
  Thomas 49
  William 96
AMESBY
  -- Mr. 66
ANDERSON
  Eliacom 58
  James 8, 33, 66

  John 5, 83
  Richard 57
  William 112
ANNELY
  Edward 94
ANNER
  Hans 105
ANNIS
  John 20
APPLETON
  Mary 63, 77
APTY
  Thomas 81
AQUITTIMAUG
  John 25
ARCHER
  John Rose 19
ARMIT/ARMITT
  Elizabeth 30
  Stephen 70, 76
  Thomas 30
ARMITAGE
  Benjamin 88
  James 9, 49
ARMSTRONG
  John 125
ARNETT
  Alexander 16
ARNOLD
  Thomas 42
ASHCRAFT
  Hiah 67
ASHTON/ASHETON
  Ralph 38, 107
  Richard 72, 106
  Robert 32, 107
  Thomas 28
  William 16, 21
ASHMORE
  Elizabeth 52
ASHWOOD
  John 3
ASKEW
  John 30
ASPOIN
  Mathias 63
ASTON
  George 71
ATKING
  James 46

ATKINS
  Robert 46
ATKINSON
  John 112
  Samuel 29
ATTWOOD
  -- Capt. 111
  William 87, 111
AUSTIN
  John 39
AX
  John Frederick 103, 130
AXFORD
  Charles 78
  Hannah 78
AYLETT
  William 106
AYMET
  John 14
AYRES
  Absalom 1
  Joseph 89
        B
BACKER
  -- 37
BACLEY
  Thomas 62
BACON
  Butts 27
BADCOCK
  Henry 7, 11
BAILY/BAYLEY/BAYLY/BEALEY
  Andrew 53
  John 13, 39, 51
  Thomas 1
BAIRD
  Patrick 54
  Robert 63
BAKER
  John 73
BALDWIN/BALDING/BALDEN
  Ezekiel 11
  John 42
  William 17, 22, 78
BALL
  John 27, 35, 53
BALTIMORE
  -- Lady 61
BANFORD
  William 113

BANISTER
  Samuel, Jr. 128
BANKS
  David 90
BANNET
  William 28
BANTOFF/BANTOFFS/BANTOFT
  William 31, 32, 72
BARBER
  Edward 117
  Peter 23
BARBOUR
  William 105
BARCLAY
  John 31, 51
  Robert 51
BARCROFT
  Ambrose 10
BARD
  Peter 71, 72
BARE
  Blasius 114
BAREFORD
  William 36
BARGAIN
  Ann 59
BARKER
  Benjamin 118
BARNARD
  Elizabeth 123
BARNES/BARNS
  Henry 14
  Thomas 3, 69
BARNHAM
  Albert 43
BARROW
  George 17
BARRY
  John 128
  Mathias 23
  Richard 31
BARTAM
  Joseph 45
BASS
  Elizabeth 29
  Jeremiah 26
BATCHELDER
  Joseph 104
BATTELL
  William 40, 59

BATTIN
  John 9
  William 9
BAVENSON
  Richard 10
BAXTER
  James 94
BAYARD
  -- Mrs. 126
  Samuel 126
BAYNTON
  Peter 125
BEAKE
  Samuel 13
BEAKES
  Nathan 74
BEALL
  Henry 80
BEASTIN
  William 79
BEATSON
  Richard 90
BEAUMONT
  William 10
BECKET
  Joseph 12
BEER/BEERE
  John 92
  Philipe 60
BELCHER
  -- Madam 87
  Jonathan 87
BELL
  -- Mr. 66
  Henry 22
  James 68
  John 39
  Joshua 99
  Roger 77
  William 65, 104, 127, 128,
    130
BELLINGER
  -- Capt. 90
BEMAN
  George 53
BENJAMIN
  -- Mr. 51
BENNERMAN
  James 70

BENNET
  John 16
  Thomas 114
BENTLY
  Thomas 67
BERRY
  Withers 60
BEST
  John 44
BETHEL
  Samuel 81, 113
BETHUNE
  George 82
BEVAN/BEVEN
  Evan 62
  Joseph 94
  Rees 129
BICKLEY
  Abraham 56
  May 18
  Samuel 27, 56, 67
  William 108
BILES
  Elizabeth 111
  Samuel 111
  Thomas 40
BILLET
  William 26
BILLIN
  Abraham 101
BILLINGER
  Thomas 20
BILLINGS
  John 82
  Richard 82
BINGHAM
  Ann 97
  James 2, 97
BINGLY
  Thomas 11
BIRMINGHAM/BERMINGHAM
  James 95
  John 64
  Vroneca 64
BISSELL
  William 25
BISSET
  David 32
  Margaret 32

BLACK
  John 68
BLACKAL
  William 110
BLADES
  William 14
BLAIR/BLARE
  James 90
  Thomas 102
BLAKE
  Mark 94
  Samuel 9
BLAKEY
  Charles 48
BLANCHET
  John 33
BLOWDEN
  John 42, 61
BLYTH
  James 77
BODGE
  -- Mr. 56
BOELS
  Thomas 38
BOGERT
  Nicholas 64
BOGGS
  Samuel 66
BOHAM
  Sarah 89
BOLTON
  Everard 33
  Margaret 33
  Robert 126
BOMARZEEN
  -- Col. 21
BOND
  -- Capt. 84
  Honsey 7
  James 100
  Joseph 30
  Peter 56
  Samuel 7, 31, 67
BONDE
  Thomas 37
BONHAM
  Samuel 13
BONSAL
  Obadiah 58

BOON
  Richard 20
BOORE/BOURE
  Thomas 32
BORDMAN
  George 53
BORNE/BORN
  George 11
  Neales 93
BOSTICK
  William 4
BOSTOCK
  George 18
BOSWELL
  James 64
BOURNE
  Benjamin 113
BOWDOIN
  Francis 102
BOWEL
  Elizabeth 31
  William 31
BOWEN
  Christopher 68
  Richard 38
BOWLES/BOWELS/BOWLS
  George 32, 49
  Margaret 61
  Samuel 38
BOWLING
  Thomas 96
BOYD
  James 55, 58
  John 88, 104
  Patrick 5
BOYDELL
  -- Mr. 59
BOYNTON
  John 81
BRACE
  James 84
BRADFORD/BRADFOARD
  -- Mr. 1
  Andrew 37, 38, 43, 60, 85
    105, 112, 121, 122
  Cornelia 121, 122
  Isaac 93
  William 42, 43, 62

136

BRADLEY
  Edward 107, 114
  Edward & Co. 105
  John 17
  Jonathan 48
BRAGGINTON
  William 25
BRAISER
  Jane 47
BRANDRIFF
  Timothy 38
BRANSON
  William 36, 99
BRAXTON
  George, Jr. 102
BRAY
  Daniel 101
BRAZIL
  Michael 39
BREACH
  John 80
BRIDGHAM
  Joseph 123
BRIGGS
  Ezra 20
  John 55
BRIGHT
  John 14
  Richard 123
BRIGHTWELL
  John 38
BRIMER
  Lawrence 111
BRINAN
  Nell 80
BRINDLE
  Alexander 51
BRINGHURST
  John 42, 73
BRINKLEY
  James 14
BRINTNALL
  David 59
BRISTOLL
  Dan. 121
  Thomas 121
BRITTAIN/BRITAIN
  Joseph 36, 47
BROADEY
  Thomas 44

BROCK
  William 118
BROCKDON
  Richard 44
BROCKENBURY
  John 30
BRODERICK
  Darby 37
BRODWAY
  Mary 45
BROMAGE/BROMADGE
  -- Capt. 70, 88
  Samuel 41, 71
BROME
  John 3
BROMLEY
  John 29
BROOK/BROOKE
  Elizabeth 6
  Henry 81
  Humphry 102
  Martin 110
BROOKS
  -- Mr. 129
  Edward 4, 44, 109, 124
  Elizabeth 70
  John 41, 70
BROUGHTON
  -- Gov. 97
BROWER
  Adolph 105
BROWN
  -- Col. 95
  -- Dr. 122
  Benjamin 95; Cathrine 107
  Charles 13
  Charity 107, 117
  David 77
  Edward 82
  George 21
  Hannah 65
  Henry 2
  Hugh 33
  Hugh (alias of Hugh Magey) 103
  James 55
  John 14, 23, 29, 65, 99, 106
  Michael 82
  Peleg 128
  Peter 111

Ruth 21
Samuel 51, 69, 95
Thomas 21, 31, 100
William 62, 82, 95, 130
BROWNELL
George 89
Thomas 89
BRUNTON
Richard 71
BRUSTALL
Richard 20
BRYAN
James 129
John, Sr. 33
Thomas 43
BRYANT/BRIANT
-- Mr. 131
John 31
BUCHANAN
George 65
Robert 72
BUCKLEY/BUCKLY
-- Mrs. 62
Joseph 28, 32
William 62
BUDD
John 49
BULKLEY
Samuel 100
BULL
Richard 36
Sarah 36
BULLOCK
John 114, 116
Thomas 33
William 119, 126
BUNTING
William 76, 113
BURCH
Edward 78
BURGAIN
Patrick 57
BURGE
William 53
BURK
Ann 73
Benjamin 73
John 42, 110
Patrick 93
Richard 23

BURKHARD
Henry 92
BURLEIGH
Joseph 84
BURN
Roger 37
BURNET
-- Gov. 43
-- Mrs. 7
Mary 35, 52
William 35, 52
BURNS
Thomas 26
BURNSIDES
James 45
BURREL
-- 18
-- Capt. 51
BURRIDGE
Thomas 86
BURROUGH
William 21
BURROWS
Arthur 118
Edward 17, 22
John 26
Matthew 77, 83
Robert 94
Samuel 9
BURTON
Abraham 63
William 112
BUSH
David 106, 112
BUSHROD
John 106
BUTLER
-- Mrs. 84
Andrew 84
Edmund 100
James 88
John 21, 40
Michael 95
BUTTINGTON
Thomas 69
BYERLY
Thomas 23
BYFIELD
-- Col. 63
BYNG
Thomas 25

C

CADWALADER
  John 18, 50, 61
CAHOONE
  James 50
CALAGHAN/CALLAGHAM/KALAHAN
  Daniel 110
  Lawrence 113
CALCORD
  Peter 22
CALDER
  Thomas 15
CALDWELL
  Andrew 61, 108
CALLSEY
  William 39
CALVERT
  Charles 67
  Edward Henry 46
CAMBRIDGE
  Giles 56
  Sarah 56
CAMMOCK
  Samuel 66
CAMPBELL
  John 29, 45
  William 90
CAMPION
  George 7, 54
  Honsey 7
  Mary 54
CANBY
  Benjamin 117
CANE
  Abel 63
CANNON
  William 100
CAPER
  Joseph 25
  William 29
CARABSERT
  -- Capt. 21
CAREY
  Roger 37
CARIGAN
  -- Mr. 76
CARLETON
  Edward 11
CARLISLE
  Abraham

CARNE/CARNEE
  James 109, 114
CARPENTER
  Nicodemus 56
  Preston 125
  Samuel 24
CARR
  James 19
  Peter 15
CARROLL/CARROL
  Anthony 83, 85
  Dominick 83
  Eleanor 47
  James 3
  John 87
CARSSON
  Archibald 91
CARTER
  George 25, 112
  Henry 49
  John 71
  Morris 4
  Robert 58
  William 17
CARTEY
  John 106
CARUTHERS
  Nathaniel 16
CARVEL
  Thomas 108
CARVER
  James 38
  Robert Mullard 26
CARY
  -- Widow 84
  John 74
  Mary 111
  Samson 107
  Samuel 107
CASDORP
  Jacob 107
CASE
  Robert 19
CASEY
  Josiah 128
CASH
  Alice 50
  Caleb, Sr. 50, 92
  Caleb, Jr. 50, 77, 92

Leonard 48
Martha 48
CASSELL
  Arnold 21
  John 21
CASTLE
  Nicholas 98
CATON
  William 95
CAUGHLAN
  Samuel 86
CAUGHLAND
  Elinor 109
CAVENAUGH
  James 71
CAVINO
  Michael 57
CAWTHEEN
  William 43
CAYWOOD
  -- Capt. 24
CEADLES
  Joseph 10
CHADWICK
  John 125
  William 115, 125
CHALFIN
  Robert 70
CHALMER
  Isabella 120
CHALMERS
  James 41
CHAMBERLAIN/CHAMBERLIN
  -- Mr. 7
  Peter 57
  Richard 16
CHAMBERS
  Jonathan 107
CHAMBLET
  Rebecca 64
CHAMPION
  -- Mr. 108
  Deborah 108
CHANCELLOR
  William 5, 16, 24, 72
CHANDOIS
  Duke of 97
CHANLER
  Sam. 124

CHAPMAN
  John 10
  Richard 114
  William 12, 37
CHARADON
  Clement 34
CHARLES
  Robert 87
CHARLTON
  Josia 43
CHASE
  Thomas 72
  Walter 107
CHAUNCEY
  -- Rev. 89
CHEEKLEY
  -- Rev. 111, 122
CHEESEMAN
  Edward 18
CHENEY
  Thomas 38
CHEVER
  -- Mrs. 75
CHILD
  Cephas 28
CHIT
  Thomas 40
CHOISE
  Garrett 2
  Jane 2
CHRISTON
  Charles 88
CHRISTOPHER
  Aristoblus 44
CHRISTY
  Charles 66
CHURCH
  Charles 14
  Joseph 79
CLARE
  Esther 121
  John 121
  Peter 27
  William 63, 109, 121
CLARK
  -- Mr. 73
  John 65, 125
  Joseph 126, 129
  Robert 20, 76
  Valentine 75

CLARKE
  -- Elder 61
CLARKSON
  Mary 62
  Thomas 62
CLASSON
  Nicholas 37
CLAYPOLE
  George 17
CLAYTON
  Asher 67
  Edward 54
  Mary 67
  Richard 33
CLIFF
  John 14
CLIFFORD
  Thomas 100
CLOWS
  John 58
CLOYD
  David 93
CLYMER
  -- Mr. 55
  Christopher 73
  Richard 63, 73
COASHER
  Josiah 71
COATS
  John 25
  William (or COUTS)
COCK
  Thomas 45
COCKS
  Josiah 119
CODD
  Robert 63
CODDINGTON
  -- Mr. 127
CODGDILL
  John 130
COFFEY
  Cornelius 88
  Mary 88
COFFIN
  Ephraim 73
  Jonathan 73
COGER
  Josiah 77

COGSHALL
  -- Mr. 16
COLE
  John 8, 53
  Thomas 113
COLEBY
  -- Ensign 16
COLEMAN
  Joseph 13, 17, 63
  Mary 63
COLLEMORE
  William 126
COLLET
  Robert 28
  Simon 56
COLLINS/COLLINGS
  John 31
  Joseph 7
  Margaret 90
  Nicholas 3
  Thomas 32, 73
COLLIS
  -- Capt. 105
COLSON
  Edward 123
COLSTON
  William 70
COLVILL/COLVELL
  Thomas 41, 76
COMEGGS
  John 128
COMINS
  Thomas 100
CONALLY
  William 36
CONKLIN/CONKLYN
  -- Capt. 128
  Jonathan 66
CONNAL
  John 93
CONNER/CONNAR/CONNOR/CONOR
  Bryan 97
  Catharine 93, 94
  Lawrence 37
  Michael 71
  Timothy 115
  William 10
CONRON
  Edward 39

COOK
-- Mr. 131
Catherine 59
Daniel 72
Edward 49
Gregory 33
John 130
Richard 40
COOKE
Edward 10
William 12
COOKSON
Daniel 102
COOMBE
Anne 129
Benjamin 129
COOMBES
Thomas 12
COOPER
Ann 73
James 26, 61
Jonathan 45
Joseph 112
Mary 26
Samuel 61, 69, 74
William 28, 69, 74, 125
COOTS
James 62
COPPIN
Thomas 57
COPSON
John 10, 34, 36, 41, 48,
  68
CORBETT/CORBET
John 3, 7
CORBIN
-- Col. 74
CORKER
Mary 61
William 28, 61
CORMELE
Benjamin 3
CORNISH
Andrew 39
James 98
CORNWALLIS
Penelope 24
Thomas 24
William 24, 61
CORRY
Elizabeth 49

CORTRECHT
-- Mr. 128
CORYELL
Manuel 117
COSBY
William 82
COTTMAN
Benjamin 9
COTTON
-- Rev. 75
Meriel 75
COUCH
Samuel 99
COULTON
Henry 1
Marmaduke 2
COUPHRAM
William 108
COURIER
Reynolds 23
COURTLANDT
-- Col. 77
-- Miss 23
COURTS
William 23
COWLEY
John 3
Mary 115
Matthew 115
COWMAN
Nathan 87
COWNDEN
James 42
COX
James 119
Moses 54
Thomas 130
William 9, 34, 108
COZENS
-- Mrs. 103
CRABB
Mary 65
CRACKEY
Sam 86
CRADOCK
Thomas 100
CRAIGE
Archibald 37
CRANE
-- Mr. 108
Deborah 108

CRANSTON
  John 23
CRASWELL
  Jane 94
  Robert 94
CRATHO
  John 19
CRAWLEY
  Henry 101
CREAGH
  Patrick/Pat. 18, 19, 27,
    85, 92
CREELY
  Peter 98
CREMEING
  Daniel 87
CRISPIN
  Silas 74
  Thomas 64
CRIST
  Aaron 68
CROOK
  John 101
CROSBY/CROSBE
  Adam 39
  Charles 37
  Faril 96
  John 28
CROSLEY
  Samuel 54
CROSS
  Nathaniel 98
CROSSET
  Thomas 34
CROSTHWAITE
  William 108
CROTTY
  William 128
CROUDERS
  James 30
CROWE
  Thomas 96
CRUGER
  John 126
CRUKSHANK
  Alexander 78
  Richard 40
CRUMP
  John 48
  Margaret 48

CRUTCHER
  John 85
CUFF
  Peter 57
CUFFY
  -- Dr. 47
CUMLY
  Joseph 79
CUMMINGS/CUMMING
  Archibald 113
  Robert 48, 49
CUNLIFF
  John 35
CUNSY
  Jo. 69
CUPIT
  Richard 68
CURREN
  George 52
CURRIER
  Richard 122
CURRY
  James 47
CURTIS
  John 23
CUSHING
  -- Judge 45
  Benjamin 75
  Nathaniel 45
CUTLER
  John 125
CUTTS
  George 19
CYPHERS
  Elizabeth 32
CYSER
  Derick 103
D
DABBIN
  John 114
DAGG
  John 116
DALRYMPLE
  Sir John 90
  Pat. 90
DAMSEL
  Henry 52
DANBY
  John 19, 70, 81
"Dancing Hannah" (alias of
  Hannah Travis) 1

DANIELS
  Thomas 71
DANIS
  David 10
DARBOROW
  Daniel 11
DARBY
  Francis 50, 52
  Nath. 105
DARREL
  John, Jr. 122
DAULING
  Benjamin 66
DAVID
  James 41
  Robert 65
DAVIDS
  Elizabeth 94
  Thomas 94
DAVIES
  David 94
  James 104
  William 10
DAVIS
  Benjamin 22
  David 52, 96
  Edmund 5
  James 7, 126
  John 8
  Joseph 109, 120
  Lewis 24
  Mary 62, 91, 96
  Philip 14
  Thomas 27, 42, 52, 61, 102
  William 33
DAWSITT
  Philip 26
DAWSON
  John 122
  Mary 71
DAY
  Humphrey 40
  James 101
  John 112
  William 29
DEALE
  Thomas 51
DEAN
  Joshua 100

DEAVER
  Antill/Antell 51, 52
DEBNY
  Lewis 5
DE LANCEY/DELANCEY
  Stephen 52, 116
DELAN ...R
  -- Rev. 116
DELANEY
  Cornelius 101
DELAVAL
  John 43
DELBEAR
  Nicholas 79
DEMAICK
  John 42
DE MAREST
  Guilliam 118
DEMPSY
  Vallentine 34
DENHALL
  Benjamin 2
DENHAM
  Thomas 38
DENISON
  Timothy 111
DENNIS
  Christopher 57
  John 20, 111
  Samuel, Jr. 11
DENNY
  D. 121
DENORMANDY
  John Abraham 110
DENT
  Abigail 71
  William 109
DENUNE
  James 41
DE PEYSTER
  Elizabeth 6
DEREHAM
  Richard 56
  Sir Richard 56
DERICKSON/DERIKSON
  Cornelius 123
  Folkart 117
DERRINGTON
  William 64

DERRYMAN
    Mary 35
DESKELE
    -- Mr. 12
DEVEREL
    John 101
DEVOE
    Peter 104
DEWEES
    Abraham 118
DEXTER
    Henry, Sr. 68
DICK
    Sir William 97
DICKER
    Samuel 13
DICKIE
    William 58
DICKINSON
    John 32
    Jonathan 11, 17, 39, 45
DICKS
    Peter 3
DIGGS
    -- Col. 18
DILL
    Alexander 113
DILLWYN
    John 112
DIMSDALE
    Sarah 112
DOBSON
    Richard 23
DOD
    Amy 44
DOEWRA
    Margaret 61
    William, Sr. 61
    William, Jr. 61
DOHARTBY
    Mary 109
DOLLAN
    Peter 81
DONAHE
    Michael 49
DONAVAN
    James 128
DONNE
    William 48

DONNEVER
    Cornelius 118
DORCHESTER
    John 55
DOREN
    John 72
DORRELL
    William [alias of William
       Brown] 62
DORRINGTON
    William 57
DOUBLE
    John 25
DOUDALL
    -- Major 5
DOUGALL
    -- Capt. 130
DOUGHERTY
    John 93
DOUGHTY
    Henry 57
DOUGLASS
    Archabald 2
DOW
    Mary 59
DOWDALL
    Andrew 76
DOWELL
    William 46, 127
DOWNING
    John 50
DOWTHELL
    James 78
DOYLE/DOYL
    John 73
    Philip 77
DRAPER
    Alexander 69
    William 102
DREW
    John 15
DREWRY
    David 11
DRIVER
    Robert 109
    Samuel 1
"Drunken Frank" 103
DRYSDALE
    -- Major 28

DUCHEE
    Jacob 73
DUDLEY
    -- Judge 15
    Thomas 61
DUFFIELD
    Benjamin 114
    Joseph 114
DULANY
    Matthew 7
DUMERISQ
    Philip 115
DUMMOND
    Duncan 37
DUN
    Philip 101
DUNBAR
    George 19
DUNCAN
    Bridget 40
    James 65
DUNGANNON
    Peter 21
DUNLAP
    Elizabeth 118, 119
    James 118, 119
DUNN
    Jacob 79
    James 57
    Timothy 118
DUNNING
    Martha 98, 103
    Samuel 103
    Thomas 98, 103
DUNSY
    Thomas 89
DURBOROW
    Hugh 50
    Hugh, Jr. 50
DURNINN
    Thomas 72
DUSHANE
    Anthony 121
DWAIT
    Mathew 64
DYCK/DYKE
    Thomas 117, 127

E
EARL
    James (alias of Mulatto Jem) 100
EARLE
    James 92
    John 8
EARLINGTON
    -- Widow 44
EASTBORN/EASTBOURN
    Ann 117
    Benjamin 117
    Samuel 43
EASTMAN
    Sarah 79
EATON
    Edward 14
    Moses 9
EAVENSON
    Nathaniel 108
    Ralph 108
EADGECOMB/EDGCOME
    Nathaniel 40, 120
    Susannah 120
EDGELL
    Robert 44
    Simon 46
EDGO
    John 19
EDMINSTOWN
    Jenet 91
EDMONDS
    Deborah 36
    Roger 36
EDWARDS
    Edward 115
    Evan 28
    John 29, 44, 75
    Mary 115
    Thomas 126, 129
EELY
    -- Col. 103
EFFINGTON
    James 69
EGHMOURT
    Cornelius 119
    Susanna 119

EGLESTON
-- Mr. 44
ELDRIDGE
Obediah 57, 66
ELFORD
John 31
ELFRETH/EFFRETH
Jeremiah 27, 42
John 42
ELIN
Samuel 106
ELKINGTON
George 111
ELLERY
-- Capt. 50
ELLIS
-- Mrs. 97
Everard 97
Robert 19
William 69, 124
ELLOTT
Elizabeth 127
Moses 127
ELLSWORTH
Theophilus 130
ELRINGTON
Elizabeth 17
Frances 17
EMANS
John 10
EME
William 13
EMLEN
George 126
EMLER
Marks 60
EMLEY
John 96, 105
EMMIT
-- Capt. 36
EMPSON
Ebenezer 8
ENDT
David 103
ENGELBERT
Anthony 109
ENGLAND
Joseph 47, 105
ENGLE
Frederick 28

ENGLISH
Richard 49
ENOCKS
Henry 27
ENSWORTH
James 27
ERNST
Martin 60
ESTAUGH
John 117
EVANS
David 2, 86, 124, 130
Edward 105, 110, 111
Evan 6, 118
John 29, 118
Peter 52, 129
EVER
Johannes 60
EVERET
Isaac 80
EVOLKT
Jacob 116
EYRE
Ambrose 105
Mary 90
EYRES
George 91
Phineas 125
William 41
F
FAIRMAN
Benjamin 34
FALCONER
Alexander 3
FANUEIL/FENEUIL/FENUEL
Andrew 24, 98
Nicholas 129
Peter 98
FARE
Thomas 1
FARINTON
George 33
FARMER
-- Capt. 80
Edward 3, 92, 100
Samuel 114
FARRA
Samuel 86
FARREL/FARRIL
Edmond 27
Martin 79

FARRISS
  Abigail 78
FAULKNER
  Alexander 7
FAWKES
  John 76
FELL
  John 51
FELTS
  Bonfield 62
FENNIFY
  Margaret 124
FENTON
  John 2
FERGUSON
  Samuel 36
FERRY
  William 34
FESSENDEN
  -- Mr. 67
FIELD
  Richard 66
  Robert 88
FIEZ
  Thomas 3
FILPOT
  Richard 123
FINLOW
  John 87
FINLY
  David 96
  William 128
FINN
  William 77
FISHBOURN
  -- Mr. 70
  Jane 43, 120
  William 30, 43, 54, 88,
    101, 120
FISHER
  Hannah 46
  Jonathan 47, 114
  Tabitha 74
  Thomas 71
  William 74, 113
FISHLY
  William 100
FISKE
  -- Capt. 125

FITZGERALD/FITZ GERALD
  -- Mr. 7
  John 14
  Rowland 17
FITZPATRICK
  Daniel 106
  Thomas 110
FITZSYMONS
  Maynard 58
  Norris 58
FITZWATER
  George 56
FLANOGIN
  Will 79
FLAXNEY
  Thomas 63
FLEMING/FLEMMING
  Andrew 122
  Arthur 46
  Elizabeth 122
  John 7
FLETCHER
  Robert 34
  Thomas 34, 87
FLEXNEY
  Daniel 77
FLOOD
  John 57
FLORY
  Thomas 44
FLOWER
  Enoch 84, 96, 120
  Henry 7, 84, 96
  Joseph 93
  Thomas 84, 96
FLOYD
  Richard 63
FOGO
  David 87
FOLGER
  David 127
FOMBARK
  Leonard 121
FORBES
  Thomas 102
FORBUS
  Hannah 123
FORD/FORDE
  Nathaniel 45
  Thomas 58

FORLONG
  Peter 16
FORMAN
  Joseph 36
FOREST/FORREST/FORRIST
  Samuel 126
  Thomas 47
  William 78, 117
FORRESTER
  John 58
  William 17
FORTESCUE
  Alexander 49
FORTUNE
  William 30
FOSTER
  Joseph 49, 120
FOULKS
  John 9
FOWLER
  David 90
FOX
  William 3
FOY
  Edward 30
FRAME
  Alexander 34
FRANCIS
  Isaac 19
FRANKLIN
  James 75
  Josiah 128
FRANSH
  Manuel 11
FRARY
  William 64
FRASIER
  -- Mr. 73
FRAVOR
  John 74
FREAME
  Thomas 110
FRED
  Nicholas 84
FREELOVE
  John 106
FRENCH
  Aves 40
  Charles 7

  Jonathan 58
  Philip 115
  Thomas 51, 56
FRETZEL
  Gertrude 129
  John Harmon 129
FRY
  -- Major 11
  Peter 115
FULLER
  Mary 59
FURLONG
  Joseph 109
      G
GAAR
  Solomon 8
GALLOWAY/GALLAWAY
  John 52, 68
  Peter 44
GAMBARTO
  Peter 85
GAMMON
  Philip 30
GARDNER/GARDNOR
  Job 42
  Peter 101
GARLAND
  Edward 44
  Sylvester 8, 33
  William 102
GARRAD
  Anthony 76
GARRETT/GARRAT
  Amos 35, 52
  Samuel, Jr. 65
GARRETSON
  Elizabeth 8
GARRIGUES
  Francis 120
GARWOOD
  William 72
GATAN
  Nicholas 33
GAUGH
  William 3
GAY
  Nathaniel 109
GAYLER
  Adam 86
  Elizabeth 86

GEE
-- Mrs. 87
Joshua 87
GENINGS
-- Mr. 7
GENNE
Henry 89
GENTER
William 110
GEOGHEGAN
Thomas 88
GEORGES
John 97, 105
GERLACH
John Ierich 14
GIBBENS/GIBBIN/GIBBON
David 33
John 24
William 24
GIBBS
James 9, 37
John 48
GIBEONS
David 38
GIBSON
Benjamin 12
George 103
GILEAD
Matthew 6
GILES
Allen 45, 46
Jacob 109
GILLIAM
William 45
GILLING
John 53
GILLION
Francis 122
GILPIN
Thomas 46
GINN
Elizabeth 52
GLANDON
Michael 63
GLASCOCK
Gregory 17
Thomas 17
GLASCOW
Hugh 110

GLEAVES
Thomas 49
GOARD
Solomon 36
GOATLY
Henry 3
GOMERY
John, Sr. 103
GOMEZ
Jacob 8
GOOCH
William 110
William, Jr. 124
GOODMAN
Richard 46
Samuel 46
Walter 130
GOODSON
Andrew 126
GORDON/GOARDON
-- Capt. 74, 110
-- Mrs. 72
John 53
Patrick 72, 85, 87
Robert 66, 79
GOTT
John 98
GOULDING
Joseph 24
GOURE
John 34
GOWEN
John 56
GRACE
Robert 109
GRAEME
Thomas 105
William 89
GRAFTON
Richard 81, 101
GRAGSON
George 82
GRAHAM
Hugh 54
GRANGER/GRAINGER
John 42
Samuel 63
GRANT
-- Capt. 127

Hector 131
Thomas 25, 93
GRAY
 Jeffery 4
 Robert 64
GREAR
 George 126
GREECSTREET
 Benjamin 64
GREEME
 John 70
GREEN
 -- Capt. 85
 -- Widow 3
 Bartholomew 61
 Paul 53
 Samuel 61
 William 69
GREENLEY
 Elizabeth 88
GREGORY
 Benjamin 76
GREY
 John 56
 Robert 60
GRIFF
 Thomas 33
GRIFFIN/GRIFFING
 Robert 47
 Thomas 10
GRIFFINS
 Joseph 7
GRIFFITH/GRIFFITHS/GRIFFITS/
GRIFFITTS
 -- Capt. 128
 David 102
 John 107
 John (alias or John Gibbs) 48
 Philip 106
 Thomas 114, 116
GRIGG
 James 2
GRIMES
 John 47
GRISCOM
 Grace 122
GROVE(R)
 Joseph 120

GROVES
 Alexander 100
GROWDEN/GROWOON
 Hannah 100
 Joseph 95, 99
 Joseph, Sr. 100
GRUBB
 Henry 30
GRYER
 John 74
GUBB
 Nathaniel 31
GUERNSEY
 John 128
GUEST
 Edward 42
GUILMAN
 Simon 69
GULDING
 Christopher 92
GUMLY
 Nathan 9
GUNNITT
 Isaac 43
GWYNN/GWIN/GUIN
 -- Mr. 84
 Samuel 105
 William Laughlain 53
 H
HADLEY/HADLY
 Samuel 4
 Simon 44
 Thomas 113
HAFFNER
 Philipe/Philip 60
HAFMANN/HAFMAN
 Jacob 60
HAGAN
 Daniel 108
 Lawrence 70
HAGGET
 John 81
HAILY
 -- Capt. 33
HAKE
 Richard 70
HALFPENNY
 William 56

HALL
    Aquila 39
    Archibald 28
    Edward 41
    John 28, 84
    Joseph 52
    Joshua 76
    Richard 49
HALLIWELL
    -- Mr. 6
HAMILTON/HAMBLETON
    Andrew 115
    Edward 58, 94, 96
    Elizabeth 6
    George 79, 86
    James 76
    John 6, 84
    Robert 82
HAMLIN
    Michael 9
HAMMETT
    Thomas 59
HANCOCK
    -- Rev. 91
    Robert 52
    Stephen 21
HAND
    -- Mrs. 57
    James 5
HANDY
    Darby 88
HANNA
    Andrew 43
HANNAM/HANNUM
    John 9, 77
    Robert 66
HANNIGAN
    Cornelius 98
HANNIS
    Andrew 126
    William 126
HANSON
    Hester 52
    John 52
    Jonathan 16
HARDING
    Samuel 7, 10
HARDMAN
    Edward 10
    Thomas 2

HARGRAVE
    Charles 61
HARMAN
    -- Col. 90
    -- Mrs. 90
    William 55
HARMSON
    Henry 16
HARNE
    Edward 76
HARNEY
    John 53
HARNUS
    Morris 14
HARRADINE
    Andrew 18
HARRINGTON
    -- Mrs. 97
    Joshua 97
HARRIS
    Charles 14
    James 15
    John 40, 102, 116, 130
    Richard 8
    Robert 13, 24
    Thomas 48
    William 66
HARRISON/HARISON
    Benjamin 129
    J. 113
    John 11
    Joseph 58
    Samuel 67
    Sapins 29
    William 38, 95
HARRY
    Anne 89
    John 89, 120
HART
    -- Rev. 63
    John 104
HARTLEY
    Thomas 110
    William 93
HARTSHORN/HARTSHORNE
    Richard 83
    Thomas 131
HARVEY
    Job 86, 92, 101
    Nathaniel, Sr. 20

HARWOOD/HARRWOOD
  Joseph 41
  Samuel 65
  Thomas 83
HAS
  Albricht 60
HASELTON
  William 68
HASEY
  William 64
HASSELL
  Samuel 76
HASTINGS
  Samuel 100
HATFIELD
  Matthias 81
HATSON
  Peter 124
HATTON
  Peter 58
HAUK
  Jacob 60
HAWKINS
  John 71
  Thomas 64
  William 85
HAWLEY
  Joseph 3
HAY
  William 99
HAYES/HAYS
  John 23, 103
  William 11, 29
HAYNES
  George 66
  Richard 60
HAYWARD
  Thomas 12
HAZARD
  George 104
  Mary 104
  Robert 104
HAZEL/HAZELL
  Samuel 100
  Thomas 15
HEARCOAT
  David 116
HEART
  David 113

HEATH
  James 10
  James Paul 106
HEATHCOTE
  Caleb 4
  Gilbert 4
HETHCOT
  John 89
HEATON
  John 43
HECKIE
  Peter 95, 97
HEDFORD
  John 46
HEDRICK
  Casper 119
  Philipina 119
HEGEMAN
  Jacobus 65
HELBY
  Joseph 78
  Sarah 78
HELLEM
  Matthew 103
HELLIER
  William 101
HELM
  George 65
HEMMING
  Arthur 118
HEMPHILL
  Edward 70
HENDERSON
  James 90
  John 96
HENDRICKS
  -- Mr. 30
  James 61
HENDRICKSON
  Peter 63
HENDRY
  John 80
HENRY
  John 36
HENTWERK
  Nicholas 109
HERBERT
  William 39
HERNE
  Launcelot 38

HERRING
  Benjamin 20
HEURTIN
  William 75
HEWLINGS
  -- Mr. 48
HIBBERD
  John 112
HICKEY/HICKY
  David 102
  John 114
HICKLEN
  William 104
HICKS
  Benjamin 113
HIGGINS/HIGGONS
  Alexander 19
  Joseph 55
  Susannah 55
  Timothy 24
HILDERETH
  Benjamin 96
HILL
  -- Mrs. 123
  Hannah 31
  John 36
  Richard 12, 31, 37, 43
    50, 70, 106
  Thomas 6, 22
HILLTON/HILTON
  Andrew 32, 49
HILLYARD/HILLIARD
  Benjamin 9, 15
  Charles 118
HINCHARD (see KENCARD)
  John 15
HIRST
  Samuel 30
HIVES
  John 124
HODGE
  Henry 43
  William 121
HODGES
  Joseph 38
HODGINS
  -- Mr. 42
HOLCOMBE/HOLCOLM
  John 101, 109

HOLLAND
  Robert 46
  Thomas 75
HOLM
  Benjamin 2
HOLMES
  Han. 124
  Stephen 78
HOLT
  Samuel 32
HOLYDAY
  William 68
HONYMAN
  -- Rev. 85
HOOD
  John 50
HOOKER
  George 101
HOOPER
  Robert Letice 104
  Samuel 78
HOOVER
  Johannes 60
HOPKINS
  Alexander 2
  David 65
  John 107, 131
  Nicholas 25
HORNBY
  Daniel 72
HORNE
  Edward 82
  Elizabeth 82
HORNEY
  James 131
HORSMAN
  Mary 36
HORTON
  John 60
HOSKINS/HOSKIN
  Ruth 33, 39
HOUGHTON
  John 92
HOUSE
  George 34, 39, 80
HOUSTON
  Stuart 90
HOW
  Mark 89

HOWARD
  -- Mr. 58
  -- Benjamin 63
  Edmond 107
HOWELL/HOWEL
  Ann 71
  David 123
  Elizabeth 80
  John 100
  Martha 100
  Mordecai 80
  Nicholas 1, 4
  Patrick 71
  Thomas 71
  William 92
HOWEY
  John 72
HOWLET
  John 92
HOY
  Ralph 70
HUDDY
  Christopher 114
  Martha 5
HUDSON
  Samuel 114
  William 48, 56
  William, Jr. 34, 112
HUFF
  Samuel 4
HUGGET
  Thomas 14
HUGH
  Ann 17
  Owen 17
  William 16
HUGHES/HUGHS
  Bryan 100
  Charles 65
  Hugh 12
  John 10
  Richard 13, 82
  Robert 66
  Samuel 89
  William 50
HUGSTOR
  David 86
HUIS
  John 62

HULING
  Michael 100
HULL
  John 34
HUMPHREY/HUMPHRY
  John 32, 33, 61
HUNLAKE
  Thomas 60
HUNNIWELL
  Ambrose 65
HUNSMAN
  William 110
HUNT
  Edward 3
  Martha 3
  Obadiah 8
  William 9, 11, 13
HUNTER
  -- Mr. 28
  John 64
  Mary 91
HUSE
  Joseph 86
HUSON
  Ann 3
  John 113
  Sarah 113
HUTCHINS
Zachariah/Zechariah 9,
  27, 40
HUTCHINSON
  John 41, 54
  Sarah 48
  William 48
HUTTON
  John 27
HYATT
  John 2, 75, 81, 111
  Thomas 81
HYDE/HIDE
  Daniel 15
  William 23
HYER
  William 74
HYLAND
  William 119
HYNES
  John 27
HYNSON
  Thomas 16

I
ILIFF
  Edmund 101
IMLAY
  John 78
  Mary 78
IMPY
  John 96
INGHAM
  Jonathan 117
INGLE
  Frederick 96
INGLIS
  John 107
INGRAY
  Nicholas 114
ISAACS
  Philip 92

J
JACKSON
  -- Mrs. 91
  John 17, 28, 128
  Joseph 33
  Newark 124
  Richard 120
  Sarah 120
  Stephen 32, 33
JACOBS
  Caleb 18
JARRAD
  Robert 104
JARVIS/JERVIS
  John 119
  Martin/Martyn 46, 47,
    60, 119
JAYNE
  Richard 54
JEFFERIES
  Benjamin 116
  Hannah 116
JEFFERS
  Thomas 82
JEKYLL
  John 61
  Sir Joseph 61
JEMISON
  Robert 57
JENKINS
  Nathaniel 74
  Robert 111

JENNINGS
  -- Capt. 4
  John 30
  Katherine 107
  Robert 107
JESSEAU
  Peter 102
JOB
  -- Capt. 21
JOBSON
  Samuel 95
  Winifred 95
JOHN
  Anne 44
  Thomas 40
JOHNSON
  -- Gov. 97
  -- Mrs. 77
  Andrew 17
  Cornelius 98
  James 47
  John 34, 55, 108
  Joshua 32
  Miner 117
  Nathaniel 97
  Reyner 1
  Samuel 53, 65
  Thomas 68, 73
JOHNSTON
  -- Dr. 7, 53
  Andrew 53
  John 53, 58
  Joseph 131
  Obadiah 92
JONES
  -- Mr. 108
  Charles 120
  Deborah 108
  Edmund 12
  Edward 22, 27, 63,
    71, 98, 119
  Elizabeth 120
  Evan 96, 98, 105
  Francis 119
  George 93
  Griffith 2
  James 34
  Jane 110
  John 7, 17, 31, 34, 108,
    118, 120, 126

Joseph 6, 34
Lewis 99
Mary 63, 101
Morgan 38, 69, 126
Reece/Reese 65, 75, 81
Samuel 35
Susannah 110
Thomas 3, 4, 5, 14
William 14
JORDAN
Dominicus 14
Robert 121
JOYCE
John 16
JOYNER
John 86
JUERY
James 16
JUSTICE
Morton 104
JUSTUS
John 32

          K
KAIGHIN
Joseph 112
KAIRLIN
Matthias 126
KANN
Conrad 35
Mariana 35
KAVANAUGH
James 80
KEARSLEY
John 126
KEASEY
William 120
KEEL
-- Capt. 71
KEES
Andrew 11
John 62
KEHIND
William 54
KEISER
George 114
KEITH
Sir William 16, 22, 47, 48
KELLY
Daniel 85

KELSEY
William 46
KENCARD (see HINCHARD)
John 15
KENEDY
Patrick 37
KENISON
Philip 101
KENNAMA
Jacob 60
KENNEY/KENNY
-- Capt. 127
Edward 44
KENSEY
John 50
KENT
Joseph 96
KENTON
Henry 30
KERRILL/KERREL
Morris 88, 101
KERRY
Margaret 113
KERSEY
John 19
KEWES
Peter 14
KEYLL
John 15
KIBLE
Richard 106
KIGLER
Christopher 111
KING
-- Capt/ 34
George 35
John 77, 98
Robert 53
KIRK/KIRKE
Edward 78
Jacob 110
James 101
John 6
Samuel 2
KLUK
Baltus 60
KNIGHT
-- Mr. 82
Hannah 46
John 18, 46
Joseph 27

KNOWLES
  Francis 43, 46
  John 33
KOLLOCK
  -- Capt. 129
KORI
  Hannah 65
KOSTER
  Joseph 116
KURES
  Peter 15

L
LACEY/LACY
  -- Widow 121
  Abraham 14
  Samuel 7
  Thomas 121
LAFANT
  Jacob 105
LAHUR
  Peter 19
LAMB
  Thomas 44
LAMBERT
  Thomas 74
LAMPERY
  Richard 6
LAND
  Richard 95
LANDON
  Richard 37
LANDSDOWN
  Thomas 57
LANGHORNE
  Jeremiah 121
LARBY
  Eliphalet 95, 97
LASEY [alias THORNTON]
  John 4
LASLEY
  George 23
LAUGHTON
  Francis 13
LAWRENCE
  -- Mrs. 61, 83
  Robert 69
  Thomas 26, 78, 88,
    104, 121

LAWRENCESON
  Lawrence 83
LAWS
  Samuel 9
LAWSON
  Edward 13
  Hugh 59
LAWTON
  Job 103
  Priscilla 103
LEA
  Roger 18
LEACOCK
  John 58, 69, 72, 96
LEADAM
  John 59
  Susannah 59
LEBBY
  Joseph 15
LEDAIN
  Charles 124
LEDDEL
  Joseph 25
LEDDON
  Sarah [alias of Sarah
    Jackson] 120
LEDREW
  Henry 105
LEE
  Anthony 69
  Jacob 70
  John 7, 20, 82
  John [alias of Reyner
    Johnson] 1
  Thomas 70, 110
LEECH
  Isaac 31, 52
  Jacob 118
  Thomas 31
  Tobias/Toby 5, 31
LEES
  John 80
LEGRAND
  Peter 102
LE GROS
  Leonard 60
LEICESTER
  Thomas 5
LEIGHTON
  Samuel 81

LEMMONS
  Francis 5
LENNOX
  Isabel 91
LEONARD
  James 32
  John 33
  Samuel 73
LERNER
  Edmund 3
LESTER
  William 51
LETCHER
  James 36
LEVIS
  Samuel 21
  William 21
LEVIT
  William 57
LEWIS
  S Vanderspeigel 131
  Ellis 37, 85
  James 53
  John 29
  Nathan 77
  Samuel 1
  Stephen 69
  Thomas 31
  William 86
LICET
  John 126
LINDSAY/LINDSEY
  John 100
  Rose 100
  William 99
LINNECER
  Thomas 13
LIPPINCOT
  Thomas 116
LISLE
  Mary 11
  Maurice 11
LITLE
  William 131
LITTLEFORD
  David 93
LLOYD
  David 51, 83
  Grace 83

  John 24, 112
  Mordecai/Mordicai 50, 106
  Peter 56
  Philemon 19
  Thomas 43
LOCK
  John 70
  William 3
LOCKHART
  Alexander 33
LOE
  Thomas 98
LOFTUS
  Lefon 19
LOGAN
  James 11
LONG
  John 49
LONGACRE
  Peter 104
LONGSHORE
  Euclydus 55
LONGSTREAT
  Theophilus 31
LOONIN
  James 69
LOVEWELL
  -- Capt. 24
LOW
  Cornelius 96
LOWDON
  Hugh 12, 16
  Richard 102
LOWE
  Nicholas 39
LOWREY/LOWRY
  Robert 74
  Sarah 74
  Thomas 40
LUDWELL
  -- Col. 2
  Phillip 1
LURTING
  -- Col. 80
  William 80
LYCON/LICAN
  Hance 64
  Peter 59
LYELL
  Fenwick 26

LYNCH/LINCH
  Charles 73
  Cornelius 12
  Head 123
LYNN
  Joseph 51, 100
LYON
  Joseph 46

        Mc
MACABOY
  Francis 18
MACKANDRES
  Edmund 10
McBRIDE/MACKBRIDE
  James 58, 89
  Nathaniel 74
MACCABEE/MAKEE
  John 1
McCALL/M'CALL
  Ann/Anne 112, 114
McCALL/M'CALL/MACKALL
  George 54, 67, 111, 112,
    114
  Nathaniel 6
  Samuel 112, 114
  Samuel, Jr. 112, 114
M'CARLIN
  James 121
[McCARTNEY]/MECARTNEY
  Joseph 110
MACK CELLICK
  Peter 38
MAC CLURE
  Nathan 93
MACCOLESTER
  Alexander 30
M'COLLOCK/M'CULLOCK
  Robert 70
  Samuel 115
M'COMB
  John 94
MAC CONNEL
  Alexander 47
M'COY
  Neal 38
M'CREA/M'CRA
  James 88
  William 131

MAC CURDY/M'CURDEY
  Alexander 93
  James 11, 15
MACDANIEL/MAC DANIEL
  John 32, 87
  Robert 16
McDEIRMAT
  Michael 83
MACDEWELL
  -- Sergt. 21
M'DONNAL/M'DONAL
  John 57
  Michael 123
MACDONALD/Mac DONNALD
  Alan 90
  George 8
Mc DOWELL/M'DOWELL
  John 97
  William 39
[McGEE]/MEGGEE
  -- Mr. 61
MAC GINNIS
  James 47
M'GLOUGLIN
  Cornelius 87
M'GUIRE/MACK GUIER/MACQUIRE/
    MAGUIRE
  Felix 43
  James 100
  John 44
  Patrick 109
  Thomas 54
  William 59
MACKINTOSH
  Joseph 1
M'KEY
  John 86
M'KINZEY
  John 57
MAC KNAPP
  Thomas 85
McKUE
  John 106
McLACKLIN
  Henry 112
MACKMANNERS
  Constantine 47
MAC MULLEN
  James 92

M'NAHME
  Sarah 52
MAC NEIL/MAC NAYLE
  John 31, 92
MAC-NEMAR
  Francis 4
MACKNISH
  George 16
[McNULTY]/MAKANULTIE/
  MACANOULLY
  Dennis/Denith 9, 12
MAC PETERS
  James 92
McPHERSON/MAC FERSON/M'FERSON
  John 53, 55, 91
McQUATTY
  David 89
MACWARD/MAC-WARD
  Grace 3
  Miles 4, 5
[McWIGGIN]/MAGGWIGIN
  Patrick 119

    M
MABBOT
  Richard 41
MACHON
  Samuel 95
MACK
  William 67
MADDOCK
  Henry 105
MAGEY
  Hugh 103
MAGILL/MAGIL
  Daniel 9, 12
MAGUIRE (see McGUIRE)
MAHANY
  John 120
MAHEGAN
  Daniel 111
MAHONE
  Alexander 102
MALATO
  John 44
MALDIN
  Daniel 46
MALLARY
  Ebenezer 7

MAN
  Francis 106
  John 34
MANASSIS
  Amos 20
MANLESTER
  John 39
MANNING
  Peter 85
MANTHORPE
  Samuel 28
MARCELOE
  Isaac 75
MARKHAM
  Joanna 29
  William 29
MARLE
  Thomas 5
MARPOLE
  David 19
MARSHALL/MARSHAL
  -- Mr. 43, 59
  Alexander 35
  Christopher 115
  John 18, 35
  Lewis 92
  Samuel 60, 115
  Sarah 115
  Thomas 10
MARTIN
  D. 67
  Daniel 7
  James 117
  Richard 38, 55
  Thomas 66
MASON
  Abigail 78
  Ann 79
  Robert 69
  Samson 78
  William 40
MASSEY
  White/Wight 107, 120
MASTERSON
  Hugh 22
MATHES
  Jude 107
MATLACK
  Timothy 125, 126

MATTHEW
  Roger 41
MATTHEWS/MATHEWS
  Anthony 79
  Elizabeth 99
  Hugh 85
  Isaac 70
  James 88
  John 76, 91
  Nathaniel 99
MATTOCKS
  Edward 34
MAY
  Charles 16
  Jane 79
  Joseph 79
MAYBERRY/MAYBERY/MAYBURY
  MAYBURRY
  Thomas 58, 94, 96, 121, 127
MAYNARD
  John 37
  Samuel 51
MAYS
  Jane 95
  Joseph 95
MEAD
  Samuel 86, 92
MEADE
  Robert 129
MEAS
  -- Capt. 128
MEDCALF
  Hannah 46, 112
  Jacob 64, 112
  Joseph 46
  William 85
MEDLEY
  John 63
MERCER
  -- Capt. 44
  Thomas 76, 112
MEREDITH
  William 13
MERIAM
  -- Deacon 103
MERRATTY
  James 85
MERVIN
  Samuel 4
MESNARD
  Daniel 96

MEYER
  Johannes 60
MICK
  Rudolph 129
MIDDLETON
  Aaron 59
  Richard 5
MIER
  Matthias 114
MIFFLIN
  George 63
MIHLERIN
  Margareta 60
MILBURN
  Leonard 72
MILLAR
  Helen 91
MILLER
  -- Mrs. 82
  Appelonia 66
  Barbary 96
  Boltis 127
  John 23, 82
  Martin 66
  Mary 127
  Robert 34
  William 84
MILLS
  Edward, Sr. 63
  George 87
  Grace 124
  Samuel 31
MILNER
  Nathaniel 10
MINNEMAN
  William 1
MINTZ
  Michael 60
MIRANDA
  -- Mr. 7
MITCHELL/MITCHEL
  Elizabeth 129
  George 129
  James 43, 45, 93
MOGG
  -- Capt. 22
MOLSON
  Richard 2
MONRO
  Hugh 82

MONTGOMERIE
  William 89, 116
MOODS
  William 75
MOORE/MOOR
  -- Capt. 25
  Eleanor 8
  John 21, 22, 23, 58, 60,
    114
  John, Sr. 55
  Mary 129
  Prudence 55
  Richard 29
  Robert 101
  Roger 121
  Samuel Preston 125
  Simon 21
  Thomas 14
  Walter 112
  William 28, 61, 84, 98
MORAN
  Thomas 120
MORE (alias BROWN)
  Thomas 31
MORFFEE
  William 38
MORGAN
  Alexander 20, 96
  Benjamin 73
  Evan 34
  Francis 130
  George 80, 94
  James 43
  John 127
  William 87
MORREY
  Humphry 79, 108
MORRILL
  Thomas 26
MORRIS
  James 23, 33
  Joseph 74
  Robert 104
  Samuel 130
  Susannah 108
MORRISON/MORISON
  Archibald 120
  John 127
  Sarah 127
MORS
  -- Capt. 68

MOSES
  Titus 20
MOSS
  Edward 68
MOUNTAIN/MOUNTAINE
  Philip 19
  Richard 62
MOYES
  James 72
MOZLEY
  Benjamin 79
MUCKLE
  Robert 90
MUGGLEWAY
  Charles 31
MULHOLLAND
  Arthur 31
MULLEN
  Edward, Jr. 26
  William 128
MULLOWNY
  Patrick 28
MUMFORD/MUMFORT
  -- Mrs. 85
  Tom 15
MUNDAY
  Henry 12
MUNDON
  Stephen 13
MUNROW
  George 121
MURPHY/MURFY/MURPHEY
  Henry 87
  James 124
  John 120
  Margaret 33
  Mary (alias of Mary
    Dawson) 71
  Richard 45
MURRAY/MURRY/MURREY
  John 23, 59, 102
  Thomas 45
  Timothy 32

N
NAILOR/NAYLOR/NAYLER
  Charles 128
  John 24
  Robert 104
NAIM
  Annabell 91

NEAL/NEALE
   Jacob 15
   Valentine 126
NEAVE
   Joel 124
   Samuel 124
NEGLEE
   Jacob 115
NELSON
   Henry 100
NENEGRATE
   Charles Augustus 76
NEVILL/NEVIL
   Samuel 84
   Walter 21
NEVINSON
   Peter 85
NEWBERRY
   William 5
NEWELL/NEWEL
   Joseph 27
   Thomas 70
NEWLIN
   Jane 58
   John 108
NEWMAN
   George 39
   John 107, 117
   Margaret 5, 107, 117
NICE
   John 118
NICHOLAS
   Abraham 72
   Charles 5
   Edward 85
NICHOLLS/NICHOLS/NICOLLS
   Benjamin 71
   Edward 108
   John 16
   Joshua 37
   William 32, 52
NIMMO
   Mary 91
NISBITT
   James 35
   Sarah 35
NOBB
   John Mack 78
NOBLE
   Anthony 98
   William 4

NORRIS
   -- Capt. 85
   Isaac 17, 35, 54, 77
   John 47
NORTHOVER
   Elizabeth 123
   Richard 111, 123
NORTON
   James 64
   Ruth 21
NORWOOD
   Elizabeth 109
   Henry 107, 109
NOTT
   Samuel 36
NOXON
   Thomas 98
NUNES
   Moses 128
NUTT
   -- Mrs. 109
   Samuel 81, 89
NUTTS
   James 119

                  O
OADE
   Joseph 21
OAKFORD
   Charles 99
OBRIAN
   John 80
OGLEBY
   James 120
O'HAVREL
   Hugh 63
OKILL
   George 115
OLIVER
   Arthur 35
   Christopher 114
   Mary 35
OLYPHANT
   David 90
ONEAL
   William 124
ONION
   Stephen 9, 32, 38, 47, 48
ORANGE
   Robert 51

ORPWOOD
  Edmond 46
ORTON
  John 5
  Reginald 93
OSBORNE/OSBURN
  James 128
  Nicholas 16
  Samuel 114
OTIS
  Solomon 103
OUGHTOPAY
  Daniel 7
OULDISWORTH
  Stephen 23
OVER
  Thomas 8
OVEREND
  Joshua 65
  Mary 65
OVERTHROW
  Ham 26
  William 57, 101
OVERY
  Peter 80
OWEN
  Evan 34, 36, 128
  Griffith 55, 56, 76, 115
  James 18
  Mary 34, 36
  Obediah 53
  Owen 107, 117
  Priscilla 117
OXFORD
  Lord 45

      P
PACHAL
  Thomas 71
PACKE
  Graves 129
  Sarah 129
PAGE
  Adam 7
  Man 25
PAIN
  -- Capt. 87
PAINTER
  Nicholas 23, 24

PALMER
  -- Capt. 13
  John 6
  Joseph 85
  Rebecca 67
  Samuel 67
PARIS
  -- Mrs. 47
  Austin 4
  Elizabeth 115
PARK/PARKE
  Nicholas 31
  Thomas 23
PARKER
  -- Col. 130
  Ann 122
  Esther 98
  Gabriel 130
  George 49
  Hester 92
  Jacob 74
  James 62
  Samuel 108
  Thomas 93
  William 7, 62, 92, 98
PARKS
  William 37, 43, 47
PARLER/PARLOUR
  Sarah [alias SARTIN] 29
  Thomas 17
PARMENTER
  Joseph 91
PARNEL
  James 25
PARR
  Samuel 75
PARROTT
  Thomas 70
PASCHALL/PASCHAL
  Benjamin 11, 30, 42
  Thomas 18
PASSMORE/PASMORE
  John 37
  William 58
PASTOW
  Richard 2
PATRICK
  William 96

PATTERSON/PATERSON
-- Mr. 27, 28
James 1
William 81, 97
PATTISON
Sarah 35
PAWLEY
George 7
PAYNE
John 101
PAYTON
William 116
PEACE
Joseph 62, 110
PEARCE/PEARSE
Anne 49
Daniel 16
John 74
Simon 110
William 25
PEARSON
Abel 4
Cerlius 55
Henry 31
Isaac 59
Richard 110
PECKFORD
Richard 35
PEECOCK
John 3
PEELE
Samuel 37
PEGG
Daniel 63, 120
PEIRCE
Henry 55
PEIRSON
Samuel 2
PELICAN
Robert 88
PELL
Anthony 82
PEMBERTON
Israel 2, 3
Israel, Jr. 112, 119
James 2
PENHOOK
Samuel 1
PENNEROY
Daniel 105

PENNINGTON
Edward 131
PENROSE
Barthol. 126
PERDUE
William 127
PERE
-- Mr. 99
PERKINS
Abraham 101
Hannah 59
PERRY/PEREY
Elisha 23
Frederick 109
Micajah 7
PETERS
Christian 45
Rice/Rese 24, 30
Richard 97
Thomas 24, 30
William 74, 115
PHILIPS/PHILLIPS
(a pirate) 18, 19
Charles 71
PICKELS
Nathan 83
Rachel 83
PICKFORD
Richard 37
PICKLE
Chrestoffel 60
Jonathan Philip 60
PICKLEFIELD
Dependence 74
PIDGEON
Anna 40
Joseph 40, 51
PIERCE
-- Mr. 72, 97
Henry 58
PIKE
John 3
PILE
Ralph 23
PILLER
Thomas 79
PINTARD
Anthony 57
John 57

PIPER
  Henry 6
  Matthew 6
PITMAN
  Caleb 94
PITS
  David 114
PIXLEY
  Thomas 54
PLASAY
  Catharine 80
PLUMFIELD
  Clement 38
PLUMLEY
  John 47
  Mathew 52
PLUMSTEAD/PLUMSTED
  Clement 63, 78, 129
POET
  Benjamin 107
POLL
  Samuel 74
  Samuel, Jr. 74
POLLARD
  Anne 26
POLLATTO
  John Baptist 19
POLLOCK
  Robert 60
  Thomas 58
POOLES
  Nathaniel 65
PORT
  John 62
PORTER
  Abraham 22, 48
  Andrew 107
  Richard 120
POTTER
  -- Mr. 52
  William 17
POTTS
  David 50, 99
  Thomas 69, 93, 99
POWELL/POWEL
  Evan 6
  John 64, 80, 131
  Samuel 19, 47
  Samuel, Jr. 56, 63
  Sarah 131
  Thomas 13

POWER
  Peter 86
PRAT
  Richard 33
PRESTON
  Abel 64
  Richard 39
  Samuel 47, 125
PRICE
  Edward 33
  Thomas (alias of Thomas
    Fare) 1
PRITCHARD/PRICHARD
  Henry 50
  John 29
  Obadiah 9
  Reese 99
  Samuel 130
PRICKET
  John 71
  Rachel 71
  William 12
PRIDE
  Abraham 7
PRIESTMAN
  James 70
PRIOR/PRYER
  Thomas 7, 31
PRITCHETT
  Hannah 47
PROUSE/PROWSE
  James 24, 45
  Joseph 43
PUE
  Griffith 74
PUGH
  Henry 38
PULLEN
  William 101
PURNEL
  James 38
PYLE
  Joseph 6, 9, 10
  Ralph 10
  Robert 10

          Q
QUEEN
  James 65
QUIGLEY
  Matthew 96

QUIN
  Neil 99
QUITTAMOG
  John 15

      R
RABENOUS
  Hans Adam 60
RADFORD
  Andrew 1
  John 53
RAGAN
  Rockerd 69
  Rose 69
RAKESTRAW
  William 122
RALLE
  M. 21
RALPH
  Joseph 50
RAMSDEN
  Michael 69
RANDOLPH
  Sir John 91
  Richard 73
RANSON
  Joshua 20
RASBY
  John 54
RASPER
  John 68
RATSAY
  Robert 126
RAVENCROFT
  Thomas 2
RAWLE
  Francis 32
  Franck 31
  Martha 31, 32
  William 32, 63, 67, 117
RAWLINSON
  Mary 39
RAX
  William 118
RAYMAN
  Jonathan 76
RAYMOND
  John 11
REA
  James 130

READ/READS
  -- Mr. 6, 10
  Charles 18, 30, 42, 54,
    63, 72, 77, 89, 96
  Christian 59
  Coleman 107
  John 117
  Peter 8
  Sarah 89, 96, 117
  William 13, 42, 81, 101
REDDISH
  Nicholas 108
REDING
  Thomas 69
REDMAN
  Joseph 10
  Sarah 10
REDSTRAKE
  John 77
REDWOOD
  Henry 8
REED
  Peter 53
  William 37
REEDER
  Jacob 115
REES
  David 114
  Mary 113
  Thomas 113
REEVE/REEVES
  David 13
  Thomas 13
REICHARD
  Michael 115
REID
  James 39
REMORA
  Benjamin 74
REN
  Rogr 110
RENEY
  Robert 75
RENSHAW
  Richard 118
RESCARRICK
  George 23
RESE
  Edward 25

RESS
  Lawrence 128
REYNER
  Joseph 59
REYNES
  Daniel 26
REYNOLDS/RENALDS/RENNALDS/
RENOLDS
  -- Capt. 80
  John 4
  Lawrence 22, 26, 28, 75
  Philip 18
  Robert 38
RHODES
  Benjamin 28
RICE
  Henry 86
  Jacob 1
  John 102
  Owen 13
RICHARDS
  Joseph 52
  Samuel 127
  Thomas 41
  William 117
RICHARDSON
  Anna 2
  Francis 75
  John 10, 81, 101
  Joseph 62, 84
  Joshua 39
  Thomas 54
RICHMAN
  Harman 105
  William 66
RICHMOND
  John 116
RICKARD
  Michael 117
RICKERBY
  Thomas 103
RICKEY
  Samuel 74
RIDDLE
  Thomas 95
RIDMAN
  Thomas 27
RIDSLEY
  James 75

RIGBY
  George 41
  Thomas 72
RIGGS
  Richard 82
RIGHT
  George Henry 60
  John (alias of John
    Obrian) 80
RIGLEY
  John 56, 66
RIKARD
  Michal 117
RILEY/RYLEY/REYLY
  -- Dr. 5
  Dennis 35
  James 28
  John 43
  Margaret 36
  Patrick 36
RINDGE
  -- Mr. 60
RINGLE
  William 60
RITTENHOUSEN
  William 42
RIVEA
  David 11
ROACH
  Nicholas 48
ROBB
  Richard 130
ROBERDES/ROBARDS
  John 86
  Thomas 69
ROBERTS
  Ann 27, 51, 80, 109
  Awbrey 109
  Edward 18
  James 42
  Jane 43
  John 27, 50, 71, 81, 118
  Owen 5, 26, 27, 51
  Rowland 81
  Thomas 1, 41
ROBESON
  John 18
  Jonathan 95, 116
ROBINS
  -- Ensign 24

Daniel 64
ROBINSON
-- Mr. 57
Andrew 18, 21, 27, 68
Charles 114
Christopher 86
Henry 92
James 12
John 2, 95, 101
Mary 91, 114
Robert 78
Thomas 18, 46
Valentine 115
ROBISON
George 68
John 118
RODE
John Mitchel 108
Peter 48
ROE
Anthony 128
Stephen 53
William 87
ROGERS
George 26
James 101
John 36
Morgan 18
Richard 76
Terence 67
Thomas 114
William 18
ROGGER
Joseph 130
ROLPH/ROLFE
Josiah 6
Thomas 10
ROMAN
Jacob 84
Philip 84
ROMUR
-- Alderman 77
ROOF
Coonrade 19
Michael 99
ROOKE
Robert 68
ROSE
Aquila 21, 106
Joseph 106

ROSEN
Gertruide 60
ROSS
-- Rev. 6
Elizabeth 116
George 76
John 116
ROTHWELL
Henry 5
ROULT
James 94
ROURKE
Hugh 120
ROWLANDS
William 77
ROZER
Notley 4
RUCKEL
Joseph 125
RUDDOCK
Joseph 16
RUDULPH
Hanse 109
RUDYARD
John 31
RUGGLES
-- Mrs. 111
Elizabeth 82
RUMSEY
-- Widow 91
William 49, 79
RUSH
Thomas 58
RUSHTON
John 77
RUTTER
-- Widow 109
John 5, 38, 81
Mary 81
Mary Katherine 72
Thomas 5, 52, 62, 72
RYAN/RYON/RION
Edmund 100
James 58
Morgan 98, 110
Peter 99
Thomas 36

SABLE
  Witwin 60
SALEM (or SOLEM)
  Cornelius 67
SALKELD
  John 69
  Wm. 111
SALTONSTALL
  Gurdon 22
SAMPSON
  -- Mr. 79
SANDERS
  Charles 90
  Stephen 72
  William 70
SANDIFORD
  Charles 47
  Ralph 63
SANFORD
  Benjamin 66
SAPINTON
  Thomas 1
SAPLES
  Bartholomew 123
SARTIN
  Richard 29
SAVAGE
  Henry 84
  Richard 93
SAY
  Thomas 115
SCANDELAN
  John 58
SCANDLAND
  Darby 87
SCANK
  Garet 12
SCATTERGOOD
  Thomas 48
SCHMITH/SMITH
  Hans George 60
SCHOWTHRIP
  Thomas 23
SCHUYLER
  Arent 50
  John 116
  Peter 17
SCOBELL/SCOBEL
  Henry 30, 42, 54

SCOLLARD
  -- Capt. 26
SCOTT/SCOT
  Robert 83
  Thomas 113
SCRANTON
  -- Capt. 11
SCRIBNER
  Samuel 57
SCROGGE
  Alexander 116
SCULL
  Nicholas 95
SEAMAN
  Thomas 48
SEAMORE
  Thomas 32
SEARLE/SEARL
  -- Capt. 92
  Arthur 117
  John 57
  Thomas 117
SEGER
  John 96
SELLERS
  Samuel 106, 123
  Thomas 74
SERGENT
  Joseph 52
SERGISSON
  William 41
SEWALL/SEWELL
  -- Judge 15
  Jonathan 54
  Nicholas 81
SEWERS
  John 29
SEXTON
  Andrew 62
SHADICK
  Edward 39
SHAE
  Francis 127
SHALCROSS
  J., Jr. 59
SHANAY
  John 65
SHANKLAND
  John 96

SHARP
  Anthony 102
  Anthony, Sr. 102
  Henry 91
  Isaac, Sr. 102
  Isaac, Jr. 102
  Joseph 102
  Thomas 41, 107, 110, 130
SHARPAS
  William 107
SHAUGHNESAY
  Thomas 5
SHAUNY
  Thomas 5
SHEAD/SHEED/SHAD
  George 12, 19, 42, 45,
    53, 118
SHEFFIELD
  Nathaniel 19
SHEGUIEN
  Michael 68
SHELDS
  James 78
SHENIGER
  Jacob 128
SHENNAN
  John 42
SHEPARD
  Thomas 87
SHEPERD
  -- Mrs. 111
SHEPHARD
  Robert 27
SHEPPARD
  Aemy 33
SHERBURN
  John 29, 38
SHERRARD
  Francis 89
SHERRIN
  David 20
SHERRON
  James 106
SHERWIN
  James 107
SHEWELL
  Walter 109
SHIPPEN
  Edward 47, 50, 79, 108,
    111, 121, 126
  Esther 47

  William 50
SIBBALD
  -- Capt. 129
  George 129
SIBBS
  William 74
SIM
  Andrew 92
SIMMONS
  -- Capt. 7
  James 107
  John 1
  Weldon 120
SIMPSON
  Samuel 20
SIMS
  Joseph 122
  Lydia 121
  William 121
SINTON
  William 17
SITCH
  John 34
SKELTON
  Hannah 107
  Richard 3, 12
  Thomas 107
SKINNER
  Thomas 119
SKYLE
  Rachel 80
  William 80
SLACK
  John 109
SLADES
  Christopher 91
SLOANE
  Alexander 41
SLAUTER
  Joseph 108
SLEIGH
  -- Mrs. 127
SLOUGH/SLOUCH
  Jacob 121
SLOUS
  Robert 83
SMART
  James 27

SMITH
-- Capt. 83
-- Mr. 82
Catharine (alias of Catharine Connor) 93, 94
Clodius 22
George 30, 65
Henry 56, 67, 96, 113, 123
James 49, 60, 104, 110
James (alias SPURLING) 25
John 6, 18, 48, 60, 106
Joseph 26
Joseph, Jr. 16
Priscilla 59
Ralph 43, 51
Richard 83
Samuel 26, 94
Thomas 41, 109, 119
Thomas (alias of Thomas Wright) 34
William 1, 15, 25, 37, 47, 61, 88, 116
SMITHERS
Godfrey 72
SMOUT
Edward 33
SMYTH
Lawrence 34
SNAGGS/SNAGS
Richard 36, 41
SNED
Mary 124
SNEVELY
John 86
SNOOKS
Thomas 93
SOBER
John 111
Thomas 30, 111
SOLEMN
-- Mr. 119
SOMPER
Joseph 16
SONMANS
Arent 68
Peter 68, 84
Sarah 84
SOWOD
Joseph 13

SPARKS
John 92
SPARROW
John 44
SPAW
John 65
SPENCE
John 73
SPOTSWOOD
-- Col. 8, 56
Alexander/A. 62, 65, 86, 100, 110
SPRIGGS
-- Capt. 21
SPRING
John 29
SPROGELL
Catharine 42
Lodowick Christian 42
SPURLING
James (alias James Smith) 25
SPURRIER
Theophilus 85
SQUIBB
Robert 23
STACK
Henry 43
STACKHOUSE
Thomas 41
STACY
Mahlon 48
STADING
Francis 53
STAGG
Charles 74
STAKEPOLE
Lawrence 73
STAMPER
Dinah 109
Thomas 109
STANBURY
Nathan 9
STAPLEFORD
John 125
STEDMAN
John 106
STEEL
James 118
Rebecca 118

STELL
  James 27, 56
STELLE
  Gabriel 7, 15, 24, 29
STEVENS
  -- Capt. 77
  George 25
  James 49
  John 126
  Joseph 15
STEVENSON
  John 83
STEVILEN
  John 104
STEWARD
  James 34
STEWART/STEUART
  John 82
  Mary 91
STILL
  Gabriel 10
STIRRET
  Benjamin 108
STOCKBRIDGE
  Samuel 12
STOCKDALE
  William 119
STOICKS
  John 67
STONE
  Christian 85
  Joseph 80
STONEBURNER
  Casper 85
STONESTREET
  Thomas 65
STOQUI
  -- Mrs. 123
STORY
  -- Mrs. 111
  Robert 60
STOTTE
  -- Mr. 12
STRAHAM
  David 2
STREND
  John 49
STRETCH
  Peter 100
  Samuel 61

STRICKLAND
  Miles 90
STUDLEY
  -- Capt. 104
STUEFIELD
  William 13
STUMPH
  Hance Jacob 60
STURGUS
  Joseph 40
SUCDUN
  Ann 122
  George 122
SULLEVAND
  James 14
SULLIVAN
  Timothy 47
SUMMONS
  Richard 125
SUMNER
  Isaac 87
SUNDERLAND
  Edward 52
SUNLY
  Richard 47
SUPLE
  Bartholomew 74
  Mary 74
SUTHERLAND
  Helen 91
  John 90
SUSTTON
  Josias 40
SUTTON
  John 8
SWAIM
  James 4
SWAIN/SWANE
  Edward 112
  Richard 127
SWEETSER
  Jos. 15
SWENEY/SWAINEY
  Cornelius 123
  Edward 67
SWIFT
  John 62
  Samuel 62
SWINDALL
  Jonathan 18

SWINYARD
 John 26
SYKES
 James 23, 42
SYMES
 John 77
SYMMONDS
 -- Capt. 23

T
TADLOCK
 Edward 50
TALBOT
 John 35
 Katherine 26
 Robert 26
TAMERLIN
 Thomas 48
TAMPLAN
 Samuel 124
TANNER
 George 118
TARRANT
 Thomas 82
TASKER
 David 118
TATNALL
 Thomas 51, 56
TATUM/TATAM
 William 88, 105
TAYLOR/TAYLER/TAILER
 -- Mr. 28, 127
 Abraham 87
 Alexander 2
 Jeremiah 59
 John 84
 Joseph 120
 Joseph, Jr. 30, 102
 Philip 4, 10
 William 25, 55
 William [alias of John
  Gowen] 56, 99
 White & 72
TEAGUE
 Elizabeth 43
TEARNEY
 Patrick 53
TELLES
 Charles 52
TEMPLETON
 James 130

TERBURY
 William Farmer 40
TERINGER
 Henry 129
TERNAN
 Thody 40
TESDALL
 George 44
THAYER
 David 85
THIEL
 Cornelius 60
THINN
 William 118
THOMAS
 Aaron 63
 Edmund 8
 Elizabeth 50
 Evan 44, 69, 109
 Frances 48
 John 19, 61, 85
  110, 130
 Lewis 106
 Rece/Rees 56, 113,
  122
 Richard 54
 Robert 86
 Roger 48
 Samuel 94
 William 69
THOMPSON/TOMPSON/THOMSON
 Edward 24
 George 45, 53
 John 32, 53
 Martha 115
 Mathew 115
 Mary 83
 Thomas 27, 118
THORNBERRY
 Thomas 42
THORNTON
 John [alias of John
  Lasey] 4
 William 19
THROCKMORTON/THROGMORTON
 John 19, 29
 Samuel 46
THURSTON
 -- Mrs. 81
THWAIRS
 James 28

TIBBIT
  Jo. 55
  Tamsen 55
TICHUM
  Richard 28
TIDMAN
  Thomas 27
TIDMARSH
  -- Mr. 80, 86
TILGHMAN
  Richard 2
TIMOTHY
  Alexander 111
TINTSON
  Duke 53
TOBY
  Cornelius 68
TODD
  Alexander 54
  James 101
  Margaret 101
TOMKINS
  John 13
TOMLINSON
  Thomas 29
TOMSON
  Christopher 38
  James 15
  Neal 16
TOOL
  John 121
TOPP
  Joseph 90
TOTTERDEL
  -- Capt. 8
TOUGH
  Arthur 70
TOWNER
  -- Mr.
  Deborah 108
TOWNSEND
  Grace 35
TOWNSHEND
  Joseph 12
TOY
  Andrew 93
TRAUT
  George 130
TRAVELLE
  Thomas 86
TRAVETT
  John Christian 106

TRAVIS
  Hannah 1
TRAYNER
  Eleaner 5
TREBY
  -- Mrs. 129
TRENCHARD
  -- Capt. 84
  George 41
  Mary 41
TRENER
  Patrick 84
TRENT
  William 22
TRESSE
  Hugh 5, 18, 21
  Mary 5
  Thomas 5, 18, 63, 72
TRIMBLE
  Francis 114
  John 112
TRIP
  Samuel 68
TROUGHER
  Joseph 6
TRULL
  Joseph 64
TUCK
  Lawrence 9
TUCKET
  Dahiel 104
TUCKIE
  Richard 71
TUFF
  James 86
TUFFO
  Henry 9
TUFTS
  Thomas 67
TUNBROLL
  Robert 8
TURCY
  Henry 30
TURNER
  -- Mr. 80
  David 78
  Enoch 100
  Francis 21, 26
TUTHILL
  James 41
TYLEE
  Nathaniel 36

TYLER
  John 54
  Rachel 54
  William 49
TYZARD
  John 65

    U
UMANS
  Eliezer 103
UMPHRYS
  William 55
UNDERWOOD
  Joseph 108
UNGLE
  Charles 25

    V
VANABLE
  Joseph 16
VAN BEBBER
  Jacob, Sr. 64
  James 2
VAN BURKELOO
  Abel 3
VANDERSPEIGEL
  William 131
VAN DYKE
  -- Mrs. 67
VANEMAN
  John 112
VANHIST
  Ranier 5
VAN HORNE/VANHORNE
  Isaac 128
  John 43
VAN ZENT
  -- Mr. 128
VARNAM
  John 67
VARNALL/VARNILL
  William 4, 10, 47
VASSAL
  Leonard 94
VAUGHEN
  Valentine 18
VERNON
  Moses 99
VERRY
  Elizabeth 82
  Isaiah 82

VINING
  -- Alderman 75
  -- Widow 54
  Abraham 22
  Benjamin 22, 65, 75, 78
  Mary 78
VIPPIN
  William 44
VRESSHER
  John Mattuse 4

    W
WADE
  Lydia 72
  Robert 72
WADSWORTH
  Benjamin 92
WAINWRIGHT
  Samuel 115
WAKLEY
  Shadrach 4
WALBY
  John 90
WALDRON
  -- Capt. 8
WALKER
  John 20
  Thomas 2, 41, 91
  William 106, 121
WALL
  Ann 20
  John 89
  Joseph 123
  Richard 20
WALLER
  Thomas 65
WALTER
  -- Col. 103
  -- Mrs. 103
WALTERS
  John 13
WALTON
  William 80
WAMBURG
  Frederick 114
WANTON
  -- Col. 11
WARD
  Christopher 73
  James 55
  Katharine 71

Peregrine 72
William 4
WARDER
  Joseph 63
  Solomon 63
WARNE
  Samuel 40
  Stephen 18
WARNER
  Edward 61
  Simon 43
WARREN
  John 49
WARTON
  George 127
WATERS
  Richard 131
WATHEL
  Thomas 62
WATKINS
  John 15
  Thomas 35
WATKINSON
  John 79
WATMORE
  James 29
WATSON
  Isaac 36
  Nathan 14
WAUGHOP
  Thomas 5
WAYE
  Robert 95
WEBB
  Elizabeth 1
  Joseph 107
  Richard 1
  William 9
WEBSTER
  Michael 52
WELCH
  Henry (alias of John
    Williams) 112
  Philip 55
WELDON
  Elizabeth 118
  Jacob 26
  John 118
WELLERD
  -- Mr. 15

WELLS
  Arthur 42, 61
  Joseph 22
  Thomas 68
WELSH
  Samuel 111
WENTWORTH
  Benjamin 38
  John 50
WERLEY
  Peter 60
WEST
  Charles 31
  Daniel 54
  James 32
  John 52
  Robert 25, 39
  Thomas 70
WESTON
  Edward 17
WESTRON
  John 24
WESTWOOD
  Elijah 26
WEYMAN
  Richard 4
WHATLEY
  Joseph 93
WHATNELL
  John 83
WHEELER
  -- Mr. 72
  Rebeccah 10
  Robert 10
WHELDON
  John 4, 39
WHETMORE
  Izratiab 122
WHIPTEN
  Anne 56, 76
WHITE
  -- Capt. 27
  -- Mr. 80, 93
  & Taylor 46, 72
  Edward 39
  James 105
  John 50, 71, 81, 101
  Peter 125
  William 19, 59
WHITEFIELD
  -- Rev. 111

WHITES
 Henry 9
WHITMAN
 -- Mr. 56
WHITRET
 William 15
WHITSIDE
 John 76
WHITTON
 Thomas 114
WIER
 Hugh 66
WILCOTSON
 Dennis 67
WILDEERE
 Thomas 100
WILDER
 -- Mrs. 108
 Josiah 108
WILDMAN
 -- Capt. 55
 Joseph 55
WILEMAN
 Henry 93, 94
WILCOX/WILLCOX/WILLCOCKS
 George 17
 Hugh 3
 Thomas 36
WILD
 Henry 19
WILKERSON
 Anthony 37
WILKINSON
 Anthony 35
WILLER
 Peter Michael 88
WILLIAMS/WILLIAM
 Bridget 40
 Charles 113, 117
 Cornelius 1
 Ennion 26, 62
 Francis 130
 George 37
 John 3, 6, 10, 66,
  83, 86, 112
 Jonathan 22
 Joseph 40, 105
 Richard 90
 Thomas 23, 42, 97, 118
 William 5, 35

WILLIAMSON
 Timothy 28
WILLICOMB
 William 94
WILLINGS
 -- Mr. 111
 David 47
WILLIS
 Daniel 120
 William 68
WILLOCK
 Alexander 123
 Hannah 123
WILLS
 Robert 4
WILSON/WILLSON
 -- Mr. 40
 Edward 28
 Elizabeth (alias of Eliza-
  beth Cyphers) 32
 James 9, 44, 50, 112
 John 13, 28, 32, 103
 Lingan 64
 Richard 59, 79
 Samuel 39
 Thomas 36, 41, 86
 William 2, 41
WILTSHIRE
 Thomas 71
WINGATE
 Henry 102
WINSLOW
 Josiah 20
WINTER
 Robert 37, 64, 109
 Walter 37
WINTERRERRY
 John 46
WINTHROP
 -- Gov. 61
 Elizabeth 51
 John 51
WIRTH
 Johannes 60
WISE
 Jeremiah 90
WISSEMEMET
 -- Capt. 22
WITTAKER/WHITACER
 Charles 101
 Thomas 36

WITTISIN
  William 56
WOLFRYS
  Edeth 108
WOOD
  Abigail 59
  Catherine 30
  James 29
  John 18, 54, 97
  Joseph 4, 30
  Matthew 119
  Rebecca 119
  S. 59
  Samuel 66
  Sarah (alias of Mary
    Rawlinson) 39
WOODDROP
  Alexander 56, 74, 106,
    122
WOODSEN
  Samuel 99
WOODWARD
  Amos 52
  John 113
  Mary 52
  Thomas 71, 95
WOOLINS
  Joseph 114
WOOLSTON
  John 117
  Jonathan 117
  Samuel 117
WOOTEN
  Richard 12
WORLEY
  Henry 34
WORMLEY/WORMLY
  Eleanor 116
  Henry 116, 121
WORRELL/WORRAL/WOORALL
  John 30
  Peter 113
  Susannah 68
WORTHINGTON
  James 70
  Samuel 38, 41
WOTTSON
  Mary 52
WREN
  Peter 51

WRIGHT
  Edward 121
  Jacob 57
  Jonathan 48
  Richard 29
  Samuel 37
  Thomas 34
  William 76
WYATT
  Edward 107
WYNKOOP
  Henry 92

          Y
YARD
  Joseph 77, 83
  William 11
YATES
  Jasper 16
YAWES
  Henry 75
YEARDLEY
  Thomas 93
YEATMAN
  Thomas 37
YEILDS
  -- Mr. 22
YOAKLEY
  John 71
YOOL
  Mary 91
YORK
  James 84
  John 78
  Thomas 118
YOUNG
  Henry 88
  John 81
  William 56, 111

          Z
ZACHARY
  Lloyd 50, 106
ZANE
  Jonathan 110
ZIN
  Herman 60

NO SURNAME
[Indians, Slaves, etc.]

Abraham 102
Amaro 9

Beck 93
Bedford [see Ducko]
Bristol 84

Caesar/Cesar 6, 20, 96
    113, 115
Charles 64, 88
Claus 115
Cloe 12
Corsey 44
Cubba 114

Daniel 86
David 69
Derenah 73
Dick 11, 38
Ducko [alias of Bedford] 4

Ebenezer 97
Edinburgh 98
Ephraim 20

Flora 95
Franck 17

George 76

Hannah 104
Harry 18, 102
Hazard 44, 64
Hercules [see Occoris] 112

Jack 10, 15, 24, 29, 47,
    98, 105
James 32, 47, 86
Jenny 46, 47, 60
John 109
Johney 1

Kent 12

Lawrence 9
Limos 36

Marmaduke 99
Marra 25
Mingo 121
Mulatto Jem [see James
    Earl and Yelloe Jim] 100

Nan 16
Ninnicraft 11

Occoris [see Hercules] 112
Oppekhersa 50

Peter 25, 35, 36, 45
Philip 33
Pompey 6, 48
Prince 113

Quam 9, 13

Rachel 24
Robin 16, 44

Scipio 18
Sibba 127
Susan 88

Thomas 116
Timothy 116
Tobey/Toby 1, 51
Tom 12, 13, 22, 106

Wan 73
Wequalla 33
Will 26, 32, 35, 64, 98
William [English King], 68
Win'sor 102

Yelloe Jim [see James Earl and
    Mulatto Jem] 92

www.ingramcontent.com/pod-product-compliance
Lightning Source LLC
Chambersburg PA
CBHW070427270326
41926CB00014B/2975